FIDELER SOCIAL STUDIES

Families

Family life: sharing, caring, and working together
A Chartbook of discussion pictures

Families Around the World

How families live in communities around the world.

Our Needs

The needs of people in families and in communities

Our Earth

Our Earth, its geography, its people and communities.

Great Americans and Great Ideas

Biographies of thirteen great Americans.
The great ideas that built our nation.

The United States

The people, geography, and history of the United States. The Northeast, The South, Midwest and Great Plains, The West, Pictorial Story of Our Country. Depth Studies.

American Neighbors

The people, geography, and history of Canada, Mexico, Caribbean Lands, and South America. Depth Studies.

World Cultures

The people, geography, and history of ten world regions. British Isles, Germany, France, Soviet Union, China, Japan, India, Southeast Asia, Africa, South America. Depth Studies.

Inquiring About Freedom

United States history. Depth Studies of the "freedom" concepts that built our nation.

Contributors to The Northeast

BENJAMIN CHINITZ
  Deputy Assistant Secretary
    for Economic Development
  U.S. Department of Commerce
  Washington, D.C.

WALTER E. HAVIGHURST
  Professor Emeritus
  Miami University
  Oxford, Ohio

VINCENT H. MALMSTRÖM
  Professor of Geography
  Dartmouth University
  Hanover, New Hampshire

G. ETZEL PEARCY
  Chairman, Department
    of Geography
  California State College
  Los Angeles, California

CHERYL BALAVITCH
BETTY-JO BUELL
LYNNE A. DEUR
MARGARET S. DeWITT
MARY A. DOWNEY

EVELYN M. DOWNING
RAYMOND E. FIDELER
SUSAN R. GROOVER
MARY MITUS
CAROL S. PRESCOTT

BEV J. ROCHE
MARY JANE SACK
VIRGINIA A. SKALSKY
BARBARA M. SMITH
MARION H. SMITH

JUDY A. TAYLOR
JOANNA VAN ZOEST
AUDREY WITHAM
LISA WRIGHT

THE NORTHEAST

Jerry E. Jennings, Editor

Jerry E. Jennings is an author and editor of textbooks for young people. A graduate of Michigan State University, Mr. Jennings continued his education at Columbia University in New York. Through extensive travel and study, he has gained a comprehensive knowledge of our country and its people. Mr. Jennings has a deep interest in young people and a desire to share with them important concepts of American life and culture in terms they can readily understand.

Earlier Edition Copyright The Fideler Company 1977.

LIBRARY OF CONGRESS CATALOG CARD NUMBER: 78-54254
ISBN: 0-88296-057-1

THE FIDELER COMPANY   GRAND RAPIDS, MICHIGAN • TORONTO, CANADA

CONTENTS

Maps, Charts, and Special Features

THE NORTHEAST

Part 1

Land and Climate

One group of states in our country is known as the Northeast. Do you know exactly where the Northeast is located? What do you know about the land and climate of the states in the Northeast? Do you know the answers to the following questions?

- How many states are in the Northeast? What are their names?
- Parts of three of our country's main land regions lie in the Northeast. What are these regions? (See map on page 14.)
- The growing season differs from one place to another in the Northeast. (See map on page 32.) What facts help to explain why this is so?

As you read the chapters in Part 1, you will discover answers to these and many other questions. The pictures and maps provide additional information that will be helpful.

Skiers in the Green Mountains. Winters are cold and snowy in many parts of the Northeast. What facts help explain why this is so?

1 A Global View

Explore the Universe

1. What is a star? About how many stars do you think there are in the universe?
2. What is a galaxy? What is the solar system?
3. What is the name of the galaxy in which the solar system is located?
4. What are two differences between a star and a planet?
5. What main planets does the solar system include?

The universe

Scattered through the vast, nearly empty space of the universe are billions of stars. These are huge, whirling balls of burning gases. Some of them are many times larger than our sun, which is also a star. But when we look at the stars in the night sky they appear to be much smaller than the sun. This is because they are such a long distance away.

There are so many stars in space that no one could ever count them all. The stars are divided into huge groups called galaxies. Our sun is in a galaxy called the Milky Way. It contains about 100 billion stars. Scientists believe there are billions of galaxies in the universe.

Our solar system

Not all of the lights that we can see in the night sky are stars. A few are balls of fairly solid material, like our earth. These are called planets. They do not give off any light of their own, as the stars do. Instead, they reflect the light of the sun.

The earth on which we live is one of nine main planets that travel around the sun. These planets differ greatly in size. Some planets are much larger than the earth, and some are smaller. The planets also differ in their distance from the sun. Several of the planets have one or more moons. There are also many smaller planets, called asteroids. Together, our sun and its family of planets and smaller bodies are called the solar system. (See the chart above.)

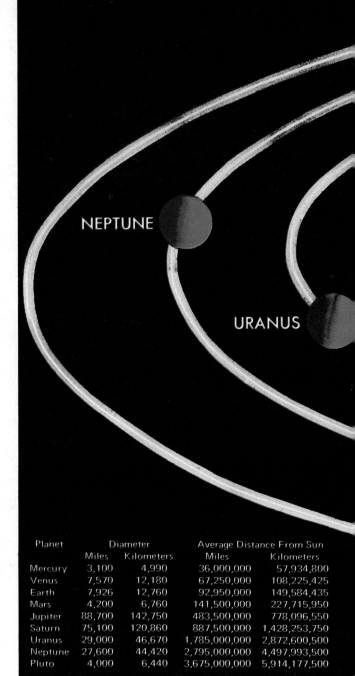

Planet	Diameter		Average Distance From Sun	
	Miles	Kilometers	Miles	Kilometers
Mercury	3,100	4,990	36,000,000	57,934,800
Venus	7,570	12,180	67,250,000	108,225,425
Earth	7,926	12,760	92,950,000	149,584,435
Mars	4,200	6,760	141,500,000	227,715,950
Jupiter	88,700	142,750	483,500,000	778,096,550
Saturn	75,100	120,860	887,500,000	1,428,253,750
Uranus	29,000	46,670	1,785,000,000	2,872,600,500
Neptune	27,600	44,420	2,795,000,000	4,497,993,500
Pluto	4,000	6,440	3,675,000,000	5,914,177,500

The solar system includes nine main planets. It also includes thousands of small planets, called asteroids. Which two planets are our nearest neighbors? Which planet is farthest from the sun?

The earth

The surface of our own planet, the earth, is made up partly of water and partly of land. The largest bodies of water are called oceans. They cover about three fourths of the earth's surface. The largest bodies of land are called continents.

North America

The land area of the earth is divided into about 162 independent countries. There are also a number of territories that are not independent. Some countries, such as the United States and Canada, are very large. Others are very small. On maps, boundary lines may be

A **global view.** This picture of a globe shows the continents of North America and South America. These continents are bordered by two large bodies of water, the Atlantic and Pacific oceans. The dotted line in eastern North America outlines the group of states that make up the Northeast.

drawn to show where different countries are located. These lines are imaginary, however. If you were to fly over the earth in a spacecraft, you would not see any boundary lines. You would not be able to tell where one country ends and another begins.

Most of our country, the United States, is located on the continent of North America. The map on the opposite page shows that the countries of Canada and Mexico are our closest neighbors on this continent.

The United States

Our country is made up of fifty states. Two of these, Alaska and Hawaii, are separated from the others.

Alaska, like most of our country, is on the North American continent. Hawaii, however, is an island state in the Pacific Ocean. The part of our country that is made up of the other forty-eight states is called the conterminous* United States. (See map below.)

The Northeast

The Northeast is a group of twelve states in the northeastern part of the conterminous United States. It also includes a small area called the District of Columbia, which is the home of our national government.

The states of the Northeast may be divided into two groups, New England and the Middle Atlantic states. New England is made up of Maine, New Hampshire, Vermont, Massachusetts, Connecticut, and Rhode Island. The Middle Atlantic states are New York, Pennsylvania, New Jersey, Delaware, Maryland, and West Virginia.

An important region

Although the Northeast covers less than one tenth of the area of the United States, it has about one fourth of our country's population. More than 56 million people make their homes in the Northeast. New York, the largest city in the United States, lies in this region. Several other great cities are also in the Northeast. Among them is our nation's capital city, Washington, D.C.

*See Glossary

The United States

This map shows the location of the fifty states that make up our country. Two of these, Alaska and Hawaii, are separated from the others. Alaska is in the far northern part of North America. Hawaii is an island state in the Pacific Ocean. The other forty-eight states form the part of our country known as the conterminous* United States.

UNITED STATES

0   100   200   300 Miles
0 100 200 300 Kilometers

⊗ National Capitals ★ State Capitals ● Other Cities

Shading from green through yellow, brown, and red
indicates increase in altitude. Figures show approximate altitude for corresponding color.

10,000 ft. (3,048 m.)

5,000 ft. (1,524 m.)

2,000 ft. (610 m.)

1,000 ft. (305 m.)

500 ft. (152 m.)

COPYRIGHT BY RAND McNALLY & CO. MADE IN U.S.A.

THE NORTHEAST

The Northeast was one of the first parts of our country to be settled by people from Europe. There were busy cities here when most of America was still a wilderness. Many great events in our nation's history took place in the Northeast. Over the years, the Northeast continued to grow in population and wealth.

Today the Northeast is a great manufacturing and trading region. There are thousands of factories here, producing many different goods. The Northeast provides other regions of our country with items they need. In return, it buys many things that other regions have to sell.

There are other reasons, too, why the Northeast is an important part of the United States. Many large companies have their main offices here. In the Northeast there are also some of our

country's largest banks. Many of the television programs watched by people throughout the United States are broadcast from studios in the Northeast. Here, too, are companies that publish most of our country's books and magazines. The cities of the Northeast are noted for their fine museums, libraries, theaters, and concert halls. Some of our country's best-known colleges and universities are in the Northeast. This region is also the home of the United Nations.*

In the following chapters of this book, you will learn about the land and the climate of the Northeast. You will also learn about the people of this region and the ways in which they earn their living. In addition, you will come to understand some of the problems and opportunities facing the people of the Northeast today.

Cooperation

See Great Ideas

Penn Center, in downtown Philadelphia. In this busy center, there are hotels, business offices, department stores, restaurants, and theaters. Philadelphia is one of several large cities in the Northeast. Do you think the great idea of cooperation is important to people who live in large cities? Why? Why not? What are some of the ways people who live in large cities cooperate with one another? Do you think people who live in smaller cities and towns must also cooperate with one another? Give reasons for your answers.

Learn To Read Maps
Maps will help you gain much information during your study of the Northeast. To use maps well, there are certain things you must know. Study "Learning Map Skills" in the Skills Manual. Then answer the following questions.
1. What is the "scale" of a map?
2. What does a map legend, or key, show?
3. What do the terms longitude and latitude mean?
4. What do the terms parallel and meridian mean?
5. What is a topographic map?

Boothbay Harbor, on the coast of Maine. Hundreds of bays and inlets indent the lowlands along the Atlantic coast of New England. Some of them are natural harbors. In what ways have harbors and other physical features helped to determine where the cities in the Northeast grew up?

2 Land

A Problem To Solve

Mountains and rolling hills make up much of the Northeast. Very little of this part of our country is low and level. How do the land features of the Northeast affect the lives of the people? In forming hypotheses* to solve this problem, you will need to think about how the land features of the Northeast affect the following:

a. where the cities grew up

b. industry

c. farming

Information in Chapters 5, 8, and 10 will also be helpful in solving this problem.

See Skills Manual, "Thinking and Solving Problems"

If you were to take a trip through the Northeast, you would notice that the land is very different from place to place. In some areas there are forest-covered mountains. In others there are plateaus and rolling hills. Only a small part of the Northeast is low and level. The lowlands are very important, however, since many of the people in the Northeast live here. To find out more about the Northeast we will take a trip by helicopter over this important part of our country.

*See Glossary

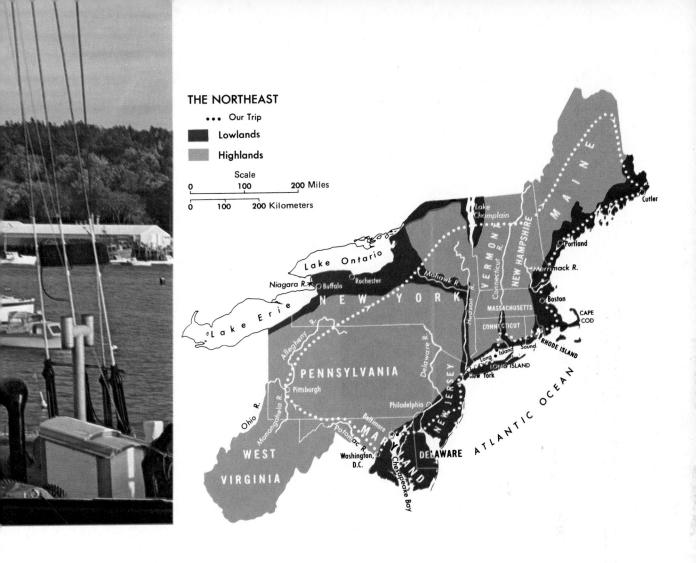

THE NORTHEAST

... Our Trip

■ Lowlands

▨ Highlands

The Lowlands

Our trip will first take us over lowlands along the Atlantic coast of the Northeast. We will also learn about the Northeast's other lowland areas. Some of these lowlands lie along rivers that cut far inland through highland areas. Others lie along Lake Ontario, Lake Erie, and Lake Champlain.

Lowlands of New England

The sun is rising as we board our helicopter at Cutler, a small fishing village in eastern Maine. (See map above.)

As our helicopter rises high in the air, we see the blue green waters of the Atlantic Ocean.

Our trip will take us southward. We will fly over the coastal lowlands of Maine, New Hampshire, Massachusetts, Rhode Island, and Connecticut. Most of the people in New England live on these coastal lowlands.

The coast of Maine

As we fly southwest along the coast of Maine, we notice hundreds of little bays and inlets. In sheltered inlets, we can see small fishing villages. Some

LAND REGIONS

COASTAL PLAIN

APPALACHIAN HIGHLANDS
1   The Piedmont Plateau
2   Blue Ridge
3   Appalachian Ridges and Valleys
4   Appalachian Plateau
5   New England Lowlands
6   New England Highlands
7   Adirondack Mountains
8   St. Lawrence Valley

INTERIOR PLAINS

INTERIOR HIGHLANDS
9   Ozark Plateau
10 Arkansas Valley
11 Ouachita Mountains

SUPERIOR UPLAND

////// The Northeast

fishers wave to us from their boats that are heading out to sea. Our guide tells us that these people earn their living by catching lobster.

Looking inland from the coast, we notice that large forests of evergreen trees cover much of the land. From time to time we see neat white farmhouses surrounded by green pastures and fields of crops. As we fly farther along the coast, we see more towns and villages. Soon a large seaport comes into view. This is Portland. Although it is the largest city in Maine, fewer than sixty thousand people live here.

Massachusetts

Now we are flying over northeastern Massachusetts. Below us is the winding Merrimack River. Along its banks are the manufacturing cities of Lowell, Lawrence, and Haverhill. Our guide tells us that the Merrimack helped these cities grow. In the 1800's, waterpower was used to run factory machinery. Textile* mills and other factories were built near falls in the river. Today, waterpower is used by hydroelectric* plants along the banks of the Merrimack to produce electricity for factories and homes.

Farther south, we come to the city of Boston, the capital of Massachusetts. Along the harbor of the city we see docks and warehouses. In the water below us, we notice ocean liners, freighters, and fishing vessels. Inland from the harbor, the city seems to stretch out as far as we can see. Our guide tells us that this is not just one city, but about seventy-five separate cities and towns. Boston and its neighboring communities are so close together that they appear to be one great city. Together they are called Greater Boston. About three million people live here.

Flying southeast from Boston, we see Cape Cod, a peninsula that reaches far out into the Atlantic Ocean. (See map on page 13.) Many visitors come to Cape Cod each year to spend their summer vacations.

Rhode Island

Our helicopter turns westward toward the tiny state of Rhode Island. Soon we pass over Narragansett Bay. This narrow inlet almost divides the state into two parts. Rhode Island is the smallest state in our country.

Connecticut

West of Rhode Island, we see the sandy beaches and gently rolling hills of Connecticut's coastal lowland. We turn northwest and fly to the central

Hartford, the capital of Connecticut, is located along the banks of the Connecticut River. The valley of this river contains some of the most fertile farmland in the entire Northeast.

part of the state. Soon we are over the Connecticut River. This is the longest river in New England. It begins far to the north, in the mountains of New Hampshire.

The valley of the Connecticut River has some of the best farmland in the Northeast. Farmers here grow fruits, vegetables, and tobacco.* They also raise poultry and dairy cattle.

Middle Atlantic Lowlands

Now we turn southward and fly back to the coast of Connecticut. Our guide tells us that we will next visit the Middle Atlantic lowlands. These important lowlands stretch along the Atlantic coast between Connecticut and Virginia. They are part of a vast region called the Coastal Plain. The land here is level or gently rolling, and the soil is generally sandy. Only a small part of the Northeast lies in the Coastal Plain. (See map on page 14.)

New York

Ahead of us is Long Island Sound. This is an arm of the Atlantic Ocean. (See map on page 13.) After crossing the sound, we fly westward over Long Island. This island is in New York State. Our guide tells us that part of the great city of New York is on the western end of Long Island. In a short while, our helicopter lands at New York's busy La Guardia Airport to get more fuel.

Soon we are ready to go on with our flight. As our helicopter rises, we have a beautiful view of New York City. Tall buildings reach high into the sky. In the harbor are huge ocean liners, tugboats, freighters, and ferryboats. More ships load and unload cargo at New

York than at any other seaport in the United States.

New Jersey

As we fly southward over the lowlands of New Jersey, we notice long, sandy beaches along the coast. People are swimming in the ocean below us. We also see many large hotels along the beach. New Jersey is famous for its seashore resorts.

When our helicopter turns inland over New Jersey, we begin to see fields

A ship in New York Harbor. New York is our country's greatest trading city. More ships load and unload cargo here than at any other seaport in the United States. New York City lies on the Atlantic coast at the mouth of the Hudson River. In which lowland region is New York located?

of green beans, tomatoes, and other vegetables. Vegetables raised here are shipped to nearby cities, where they are sold to supermarkets and restaurants. Raising vegetables for sale is called truck farming. This type of farming is usually very profitable in the Northeast. There are millions of people in the cities of this region to buy and eat the vegetables raised here.

In the distance we can see the buildings of several cities. Our guide tells us that these are the cities of Trenton and Camden in New Jersey and Philadelphia in Pennsylvania. All of these cities are along the Delaware River.

Delaware and Maryland

Soon we leave New Jersey and cross Delaware Bay. Now we are flying over a large peninsula that stretches far southward into the Atlantic Ocean. Most of Delaware and part of Maryland are located on this peninsula. The land here is very low and level. We see few large towns, but there are a great number of farms. Many are truck farms, and there are also poultry farms. Farmers in Delaware and Maryland raise millions of chickens each year to ship to the great cities of the Northeast.

Chesapeake Bay

Now we are flying over Chesapeake Bay. (See map on page 13.) The water below us is crowded with fishing boats and ocean freighters. To our right, we see tall buildings and the smoke from many factories. Our guide tells us that this is the great port city of Baltimore, Maryland. We are approaching our nation's capital, Washington, D.C., where we will spend the night before continuing our trip.

Other Lowlands

In our trip along the Atlantic coast, we could not see all the lowland areas of the Northeast. There are some important lowlands that lie far inland.

The Erie-Ontario Lowland

The Erie-Ontario Lowland is a broad fertile plain in the western part of New York and the northwestern part of Pennsylvania. This lowland lies along Lake Ontario and Lake Erie. (See map on page 13.)

If you could visit this part of the Northeast, you would see people working in vineyards and orchards and on dairy farms. In large cities like Buffalo and Rochester, you would see many factories and mills.

One of the most interesting sights in the Erie-Ontario Lowland is beautiful Niagara Falls. These falls are located on the Niagara River, which forms part of the border between the United States and Canada. The Niagara River flows northward from Lake Erie to Lake Ontario. About halfway between these two lakes, the river plunges over a steep cliff, forming Niagara Falls. Each year, thousands of tourists come to see these famous falls. Waterpower from the falls is used to produce electricity for factories and homes in both the United States and Canada.

Niagara Falls, on the border between the United States and Canada. These falls are an important natural resource to people who live in the nearby area. Can you explain why this is so?

Hudson-Mohawk Lowland

East of the plain along Lake Erie and Lake Ontario is another important lowland area. Here, the valleys of the Hudson and Mohawk rivers form a natural pathway through the highlands of New York. Large boats carry goods up the Hudson River from New York City as far north as Albany. From a point near here the goods are transported westward on the New York State Barge Canal, which extends through the Mohawk Valley and the Erie-Ontario Lowland to Buffalo, on Lake Erie. Good roads and railroads in the Hudson-Mohawk Lowland also help to make this part of the Northeast an important trade route.

St. Lawrence Valley

In northern New York and Vermont is another lowland area, which extends along the St. Lawrence River and Lake Champlain. This is the St. Lawrence Valley. (See map on page 14.) Most of the land in this section is flat or gently rolling. Dairy farms here supply milk to people in New York and other large cities. Fruit growing is also important in this area.

The Highlands

More than three fourths of the Northeast lies in a vast region called the Appalachian Highlands. (See map on page 14.) These highlands extend for more than 1,600 miles (2,574 km.)† from central Alabama northeastward into Canada. In this region are mountain ranges, high ridges, and deep valleys. Plateaus and hilly land also make up a large part of the Appalachian Highlands. During the remainder of our trip, we will be flying over these highlands.

Piedmont Plateau

Our helicopter rises over Washington, D.C., and we follow the winding Potomac River northwestward. The land below is gently rolling. We are flying over a plateau that slopes gradually upward from the Coastal Plain to the mountainous land that lies to the west. This part of the Appalachian Highlands is called the Piedmont Plateau. (See map on page 14.) The word piedmont means "foot of the mountain."

Fall Line

Many fast-flowing rivers cross the Piedmont on their way to the Atlantic Ocean. As these rivers drop from the plateau onto the Coastal Plain, they form swift rapids and waterfalls. For this reason, the dividing line between the Piedmont and the Coastal Plain is called the Fall Line.

Some of the Northeast's largest cities lie along the Fall Line. In the early days of our country, settlers traveling upstream by boat were stopped at the Fall Line by the falls and rapids. Here they had to unload their goods, and many of them settled nearby. Water-

† km. means kilometer

power from the falls was used to run machines in small mills and factories. Gradually, many of the settlements along the Fall Line grew into important cities.

Blue Ridge

Soon we leave the Piedmont Plateau and fly over a broad, forest-covered ridge. This is part of the Blue Ridge, a chain of mountain ranges that extends from Pennsylvania southwestward into Georgia. It is called the Blue Ridge because its slopes often look blue from a distance.

Appalachian Ridges and Valleys

Beyond the Blue Ridge, we come to a broad valley. We learn that this is the easternmost part of the Appalachian Ridges and Valleys section of the Appalachian Highlands. The valley below us is part of a long chain of valleys, called the Great Valley. On the valley floor, we see herds of dairy cattle grazing in green meadows.

Northwestward from the Great Valley, we cross a series of heavily wooded ridges separated by narrow valleys. Occasionally we fly over a small town, but we have not seen a large city since leaving Washington. One reason why this area has not been heavily settled is lack of transportation. It has been difficult to build roads and railroads through this mountainous area.

Appalachian Plateau

Our guide tells us that we have crossed into southern Pennsylvania and are now flying over the Appalachian

The Appalachian Plateau section of the Northeast is an area of rugged hills and low mountains. Long ago, the surface of this plateau was smooth and unbroken. What caused changes in the land?

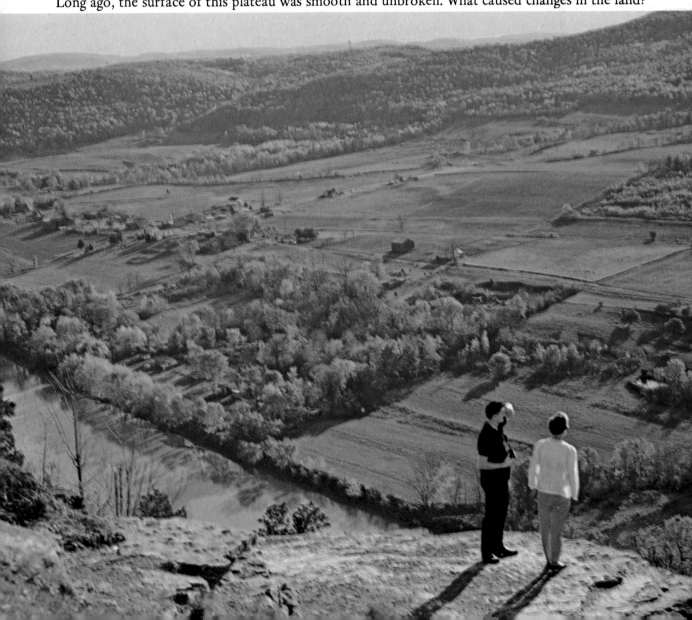

Plateau. In the Northeast, this section of the Appalachian Highlands extends over large areas of Pennsylvania, New York, and West Virginia. (See map on page 14.)

The land below us is hilly and rugged. Usually we think of a plateau as an area of high, flat land. We learn that at one time the surface of the Appalachian Plateau was smooth and unbroken. Through the centuries, however, rivers and streams have cut thousands of valleys into the plateau, leaving rugged hills and mountains. We see few farms in this area, but in some of the valleys below us there are small mining communities. The hills of the Appalachian Plateau contain large deposits of bituminous* coal. West Virginia and Pennsylvania rank among the leading coal-producing states in the nation.

Ahead of us we see the tall buildings of a large city. This is Pittsburgh, one of the greatest steelmaking cities in the world. It is situated at the point where the Allegheny and Monongahela rivers meet to form the Ohio River. (See map on page 13.) Tall furnaces of steel mills rise near the riverbanks. Towboats are pushing barges loaded with coal and other raw materials needed to make steel. Nearby raw materials and cheap transportation have helped Pittsburgh become a great manufacturing city.

Adirondack Mountains

From Pittsburgh, our trip takes us far northeastward to the Adirondack Mountains of New York. (Compare maps on pages 13 and 14.) These are the oldest mountains in the Appalachian Highlands.

As we fly over the Adirondacks, we notice that the mountain peaks are not

very high or rugged. Through countless centuries, the forces of nature have worn down the slopes and rounded the peaks of these mountains. Many thousands of years ago, the land here was covered with huge masses of ice called glaciers.* As the glaciers moved slowly

A river in the Adirondack Mountains. The Adirondacks lie in the northern part of New York State. They are the oldest mountains in the Appalachian Highlands region. Every year many people visit the Adirondacks to hunt and fish, and enjoy the beautiful scenery.

over the land, they smoothed the mountain peaks, carved out hollows, and deposited stones and gravel.

In the forested valleys below us, hundreds of lakes glisten like jewels. Our guide points out hotels and hunting lodges along many of the lakes. The beautiful scenery and the wildlife of the Adirondacks attract thousands of tourists each year.

Highlands of New England

To the east of the Adirondack Mountains are the highlands of New England.

These highlands, like the Adirondacks, are very old. They, too, were covered by glaciers thousands of years ago. As the glaciers moved down the mountains and valleys, they scraped away the soil in many places. When the glaciers melted, they left large amounts of stones and gravel behind. As a result, much of the soil in New England is thin and stony. It is difficult to raise crops in this area.

Green Mountains

We begin our trip over the highlands of New England by flying eastward across Lake Champlain. Soon we are over the gently rounded Green Mountains of Vermont. The Green Moun-

A village in the Green Mountains of Vermont. These mountains are popular with vacationers both in summer and in winter. Why do you suppose they are called the Green Mountains?

tains owe their name to the forests of evergreen trees that cover their slopes. We notice there are many resort hotels here, as in the Adirondacks. Tourists come to the cool mountains during the summer months to escape the heat of the cities. Many vacationers also come during the winter to ski and enjoy other sports.

White Mountains

Now we are flying over the White Mountains of New Hampshire. These mountains seem to rise higher than any others we have seen on our trip. Our guide tells us that one of these peaks, Mt. Washington, rises to nearly 6,300 feet (1,920 m.)† above sea level. This is the highest point in the Northeast.

Soon we cross the border between New Hampshire and Maine and fly northeastward. As far as we can see there are forested mountains and hills. Forests cover more than four fifths of the land in Maine. Very seldom do we see any farmland or a town.

Northeastern Maine

When our helicopter reaches north-eastern Maine, we see many farms below us. Our guide tells us that this is Aroostook County. It has the only large area of fertile land in Maine. This county is famous for its fine potatoes.

Now our trip is almost over. Our flight over the Northeast has helped us to understand how land features affect the ways in which people live and work.

† m. means meter

Imagine You Are a Geographer

Imagine you are a geographer who has been asked to write a magazine article about a trip through the Northeast. Choose one of the following trips, or plan your own.
1. an automobile trip from New York City to the Adirondack Mountains
2. a boat trip on the New York State Barge Canal from Lake Champlain to Lake Erie
3. a helicopter trip from Philadelphia to Pittsburgh, Pennsylvania

You will need to do research about land and water features along your route. Illustrate your article with a map showing the route and the names of places to visit.

3 Climate

A Problem To Solve

In the Northeast, temperatures differ considerably from place to place. Why is this true? In order to solve this problem, you will need to find out what the climate is like in different parts of the Northeast. Then you will need to make a number of "educated guesses," or hypotheses, that you think explain these differences. In forming your hypotheses, you may find it helpful to consider each of the following questions.

a. How are temperatures in different places affected by distance from the equator?

b. How does altitude affect temperature?

c. How are temperatures in different places affected by distance from large bodies of water?

See Skills Manual, "Thinking and Solving Problems"

In the Northeast, each season brings great changes in the weather. Summer days in most parts of this region are often hot and damp. Winter days are usually cold. In some places, snow covers the ground for weeks at a time. During the spring and autumn months, the weather is not often very hot or very cold.

The weather in the Northeast differs not only from season to season but also from place to place. In the northern part of this region, temperatures are usually different from those in the southern part. The weather in the highlands is not the same as that in the lowlands. There are also differences between the weather along the seacoast and the weather farther inland.

To learn more about the climate of the Northeast, let us imagine that we are spending a year in this part of our country. We will begin our visit in the winter.

Winter

A visit to the White Mountains

We are visiting a ski resort in the White Mountains of New Hampshire. The temperature on this January afternoon is 20° F. (-7° C.).[†] The mountains and the valleys are covered with a blanket of fresh, white snow. In many places, strong winds have piled the snow into deep drifts. We notice that a pond nearby is covered with ice. All around us, skiers dressed in bright winter clothing are gliding down the snowy mountains.

† F. means Fahrenheit scale
C. means Celsius scale

Winter in New York City. In parts of the Northeast, heavy snowfall sometimes makes it hard for people to travel from place to place. They must wait while snowplows clear the streets and highways. What are some other ways in which snowfall affects the lives of people in the Northeast?

Shortly after four o'clock, the sun sets behind a mountain peak to the west. Here in New Hampshire, January days are short. The time between sunrise and sunset is less than ten hours long. As the sky grows darker, the evening air becomes very cold. Tonight the temperature will probably go down to 0° F. (-18° C.)

Why winters are cold and snowy

One reason winters are so cold in the Northeast is that this region lies in the northern part of the United States.

The weather in the northern part of our country is generally cooler than the weather in the southern part. (See the feature on pages 30 and 31.)

There is also another reason why the Northeast has such cold winters. During the winter months, the winds that pass over this region are often from the northwest. These winds, which come from northern Canada, are very cold and dry. They help to bring bitterly cold weather to the Northeast.

Not all of the winds that blow across the Northeast during the winter come from Canada. Often a large amount of warm, moist air moves northward from the Gulf of Mexico. When this air meets the cold air from the north, it rises and becomes cooler. As it becomes cooler, it drops some of its moisture in the form of snow. This helps to explain why many areas in the Northeast receive heavy snowfall.

How winter affects the people

There are many ways in which cold, snowy winters affect the lives of people in the Northeast. The houses in this region are well built to keep out the cold. They are usually heated by furnaces. People in the Northeast need to wear warm clothing in the winter. Although a snowy land is a beautiful sight, snowstorms can cause much trouble. After a storm, people must shovel the snow off their walks and driveways. Cities must use snowplows to clear the streets. Cars often become stuck in snowdrifts, and icy roads make driving dangerous. Buses and trains sometimes cannot run on time because of heavy snow. Airport runways are sometimes blocked by drifts or covered with ice so that planes cannot take off or land.

Winters in the highlands

Winters are cold and snowy in most of the highlands of the Northeast. Temperatures often stay below freezing for weeks at a time, and snowstorms are frequent. In some of the mountains of the Northeast, more than 144 inches (366 cm.)[†] may fall during the winter. Many people go to the mountains in winter to enjoy skiing and other winter sports.

[†] cm. means centimeter

Winters in the lowlands

In the lowlands along the Atlantic coast, winter weather is not as cold as it is in the highlands. Large bodies of water lose their heat more slowly than land does. For this reason, the Atlantic Ocean is warmer during the winter than the land nearby. Breezes from the ocean bring mild weather to the lowlands along the coast. In the lowlands of Maryland and Delaware, winters are so mild that snow does not often stay on the ground for more than a day or two at a time.

On the plain along Lake Erie and Lake Ontario, winters are a little milder than they are in the highlands. Winds from the north and west are warmed as they blow across the Great Lakes. They help to keep very cold weather from coming to the eastern and southern shores of the lakes. As these winds pass over the lakes, they take up much moisture. Some of this moisture later returns to the earth in the form of snow. Buffalo and other cities in western New York often receive large amounts of snow in the winter.

Spring

It is April, and we are visiting the city of Washington, D.C. (See map on page 13.) The air is warm, and a soft breeze is blowing. The cherry trees are in bloom. The gardens and parks that we see as we tour the city are fresh and green.

In the countryside around Washington, we see farmers plowing their fields. They are turning over the soil so it will be ready for spring planting. The weather should be warm enough from

In Washington, D.C., cherry trees blossom in April. Here, as in some other lowland areas of the Northeast, spring comes early. How does an early spring help farmers in these areas?

THE SEASONS

The year is divided into four natural periods, or seasons. We call them summer, autumn, winter, and spring. Each season is marked by changes in the length of day and night and by changes in temperature.

The seasons are caused by the tilt of the earth's axis and the revolution of the earth around the sun. It takes one year for the earth to revolve around the sun. On this trip, the earth remains tilted at the same angle to the path along which it travels. The chart below shows how this causes the Northern Hemisphere to be tilted toward the sun on June 21 and away from the sun on December 22. On March 21 and September 22, the Northern Hemisphere is tilted neither toward the sun nor away from it.

The chart on the left shows that on June 21 the sun shines directly on the Tropic of Cancer.* This is the northernmost point ever reached by the sun's direct rays. In the Northern Hemisphere, June 21 is the first day of summer and the longest day of the year.

The chart on the right shows that on December 22 the sun shines directly on the Tropic of Capricorn.* This is the southernmost point ever reached by the sun's direct

A large area around the
North Pole is lighted.

The axis of the earth
is tilted toward the sun.

North Pole

Arctic Circle

Tropic of Cancer

Equator

Tropic of Capricorn

DIRECT RAYS

OF THE SUN

South Pole

A large area around the
South Pole is in darkness.

SUMMER IN THE NORTHERN HEMISPHERE

The chart above shows how the earth is lighted by the sun at noon on June 21, the first day of summer in the Northern Hemisphere.

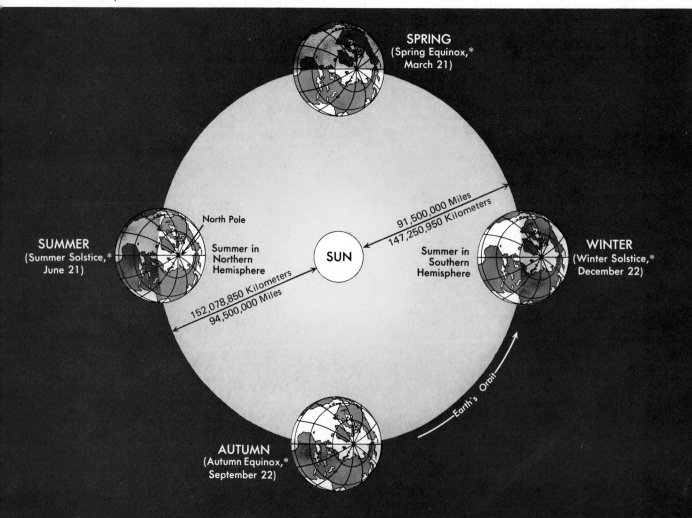

SPRING
(Spring Equinox,*
March 21)

SUMMER
(Summer Solstice,*
June 21)

North Pole

Summer in
Northern
Hemisphere

SUN

91,500,000 Miles
147,250,950 Kilometers

Summer in
Southern
Hemisphere

WINTER
(Winter Solstice,*
December 22)

152,078,850 Kilometers
94,500,000 Miles

Earth's Orbit

AUTUMN
(Autumn Equinox,*
September 22)

OF THE YEAR

rays. In the Northern Hemisphere, December 22 is the first day of winter and the shortest day of the year.

When one hemisphere is tilted toward the sun, the other is tilted away from the sun. For this reason, the seasons in the Southern Hemisphere are just the opposite of those in the Northern Hemisphere. Summer in the Southern Hemisphere begins on December 22, and winter begins on June 21.

Temperatures are affected by the slant of the sun's rays as they strike the surface of the earth. Study the chart below, and the picture of Washington, D.C., to help you understand why this is true.

Near the equator, the sun is almost directly overhead throughout the year. For this reason, the weather near the equator is always hot, except in the mountains. In areas farther away from the equator, the sun's rays are more slanted. Therefore, the weather is usually cooler.

The southern part of the United States is nearer the equator than the northern part. This helps to explain why the weather is generally warmer in the southern part of our country than it is in the northern part.

*See Glossary

WINTER IN THE NORTHERN HEMISPHERE

The chart above shows how the earth is lighted by the sun at noon on December 22, the first day of winter in the Northern Hemisphere.

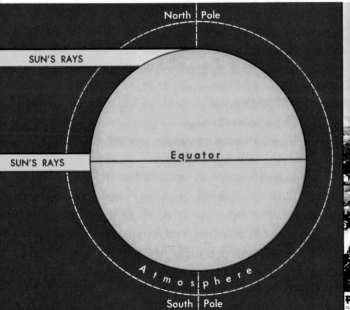

The chart above shows that when the sun's rays strike the earth at a slant, they must travel through more atmosphere, or air, than when they strike it directly. This affects temperatures because the air soaks up heat from the sun's rays. The more air the rays must pass through, the less heat they hold to warm the earth. This is one reason why temperatures are higher if the sun is directly overhead than they are if the sun is low in the sky.

This picture also helps to explain how changes in temperature are caused by the different angles at which the sun's rays strike the earth. During the summer, the noon sun is high in the sky. The rays of the sun are concentrated into small areas. For this reason, they give large amounts of heat. During the winter, the noon sun is lower in the sky. The slanting rays of the sun are spread over much wider areas, so they give less heat.

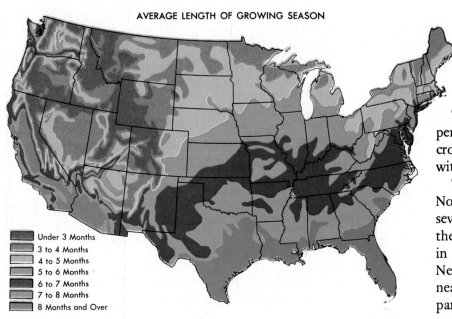

AVERAGE LENGTH OF GROWING SEASON

Under 3 Months
3 to 4 Months
4 to 5 Months
5 to 6 Months
6 to 7 Months
7 to 8 Months
8 Months and Over

The growing season is the period of time during which crops can be grown outdoors without being killed by frost.

The growing season in the Northeast lasts from three to seven months. It is shortest in the Adirondack Mountains and in the highlands of northern New England. It is longest near the coast in the southern part of the Northeast.

now on so that tender young plants will not be killed by frost.

What is the growing season?

In this part of the Northeast, the last hard frost comes in early April. The first hard frost of autumn usually comes some time in October. Therefore, crops can be grown outdoors for six months of the year without danger of being killed by frost. This frost-free period is known as the growing season.

The growing season
along the Atlantic coast

The map above shows the length of the growing season in different parts of the Northeast. You can see that the growing season is quite long in the lowlands along the Atlantic coast. In some places, farmers can grow crops outdoors for nearly seven months.

The long growing season along the Atlantic coast is helpful to farmers. There are many truck farms on Long Island, and in New Jersey, Delaware,

and Maryland. Vegetables are grown on these farms and sold to people in the large cities of the Northeast. Because the farmers can plant their crops early in the spring, they can get their vegetables to market sooner than farmers in other parts of the Northeast.

The growing season
in the Erie-Ontario Lowland

The growing season in the Erie-Ontario Lowland is also fairly long. The climate here is very good for growing fruit. In the spring, the Great Lakes do not become warm as quickly as the land nearby. Winds from the north and west are cooled as they blow across the lakes. The cool winds keep fruit trees and grapevines from budding while there is danger of frost. In the fall, the Great Lakes are warmer than the land. Warm winds from the lakes help to protect ripening fruit from early frosts. Large amounts of apples, peaches, grapes, and other fruit are grown in the Erie-Ontario Lowland.

The growing season in the highlands

At the same time that flowers are blooming in the lowlands, snow still covers many hills and mountains in the Northeast. The growing season in the highlands is generally shorter than the growing season in the lowlands.

The growing season is quite short in the Adirondack Mountains and the highlands of northern New England. In some places, farmers cannot plant their crops until late May. The first killing frost may come in September. Therefore, farmers here cannot raise crops that need a long growing season. They must grow crops such as hay and potatoes, which do not take long to ripen.

Summer

We are strolling along Fifth Avenue in New York City on a hot day in July. The sun is shining brightly, and the temperature is 90° F. (32° C.). Because the air is very humid,* we feel even warmer than we would if it were dry. We wish that we could drive to one of the beaches on Long Island for a cooling swim in the Atlantic Ocean.

In the middle of the afternoon, large, dark clouds called thunderheads appear in the west. The air is very still. Suddenly we hear a loud crash of thunder, and rain begins to fall in large drops. We stand in a doorway to get out of

*See Glossary

A hot summer day in New York City. Water from a fire hydrant helps these children cool off on a hot summer day. Why are summers hot and humid in most parts of the Northeast?

the rain. Within an hour, the storm is over. Now the air feels cooler.

Why summers are hot and humid

There are many hot, humid days like this in most parts of the Northeast in the summer. The feature on pages 30 and 31 helps to explain why. During the summer months, the northern part of the earth is tilted toward the sun. Therefore, lands in the Northern Hemisphere receive large amounts of warm sunshine.

There is also another reason why summers are so warm in the Northeast. During the summer, many of the winds that blow across this region come from the Gulf of Mexico. (See map on page 7.) These winds are very warm and moist. They bring hot, humid weather to many parts of the Northeast.

The winds from the Gulf of Mexico also bring frequent rains to the Northeast during the summer. As the moist air passes over the hot land, it rises and cools quickly, losing some of its moisture in the form of rain. There is often thunder and lightning with this kind of rainfall.

Summers in large cities

Hot, humid weather can be very unpleasant for people in large cities, where the buildings and pavements reflect the sun's heat. Sometimes a "heat wave" may last for weeks. It is hard to work when the weather is hot and humid. It is hard to sleep. On hot days, city dwellers go to parks or sit on porches and balconies. On weekends, many people go to the seacoast or to the mountains to escape the heat.

Using Natural Resources

See Great Ideas

The map below shows average annual rainfall in different parts of the United States. The term "rainfall" includes the amount of water that falls as rain, snow, and sleet. Rainfall is an important natural resource in the Northeast, as it is in other parts of our country. Almost all parts of the Northeast receive enough rainfall for growing most kinds of crops. What other natural resources do people need for growing crops?

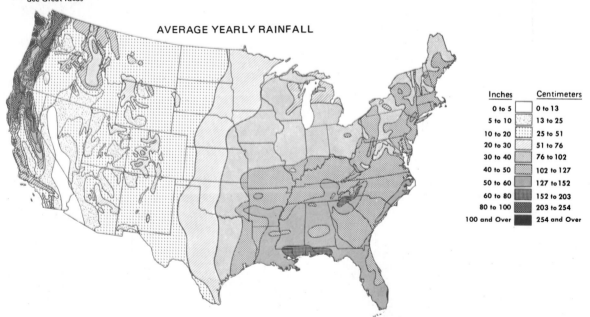

AVERAGE YEARLY RAINFALL

Inches	Centimeters
0 to 5	0 to 13
5 to 10	13 to 25
10 to 20	25 to 51
20 to 30	51 to 76
30 to 40	76 to 102
40 to 50	102 to 127
50 to 60	127 to 152
60 to 80	152 to 203
80 to 100	203 to 254
100 and Over	254 and Over

A beach on the Atlantic coast of Delaware. In the summer, some city people go to the seacoast to escape the hot, humid weather. Other people visit mountainous areas where it is cooler than it is in the lowlands. What facts help explain why it is cooler in the mountains?

Summers in the highlands

From New York City we take a trip to the Adirondack Mountains. We find that the summer weather here is cooler and more pleasant than it is in the lowlands. Summers are also pleasant in other mountainous areas in the Northeast. Many people come to these areas during the summer to enjoy the cool mountain air.

Mountainous parts of the Northeast are generally cooler than nearby lowlands because they are so much higher above the level of the sea. The higher you go above sea level, the cooler the air becomes. As you may have learned in your science class, the earth gives off heat that it has received from the sun. At low elevations, much of this heat is taken up by the moisture and

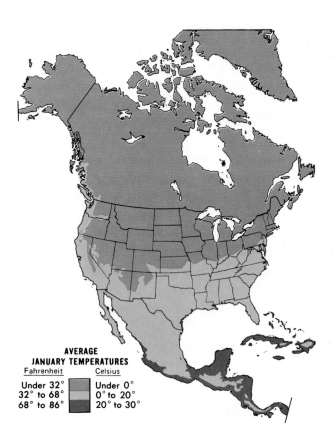

**AVERAGE
JANUARY TEMPERATURES**

Fahrenheit	Celsius
Under 32°	Under 0°
32° to 68°	0° to 20°
68° to 86°	20° to 30°

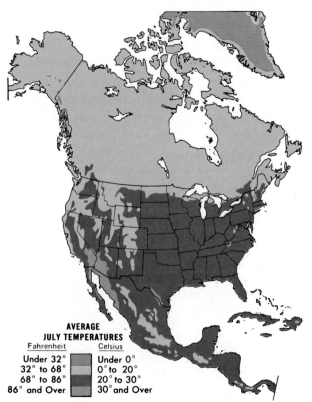

**AVERAGE
JULY TEMPERATURES**

Fahrenheit	Celsius
Under 32°	Under 0°
32° to 68°	0° to 20°
68° to 86°	20° to 30°
86° and Over	30° and Over

dust in the air. At high elevations, however, the air is much cleaner and drier. Therefore, it cannot take up as much heat. As a result, the temperature is usually cooler at high elevations.

Summers along the Atlantic coast

Another place where summers are mild is the Atlantic coast of New England. Cool breezes from the ocean keep the temperature from becoming very hot. This is one reason why many people spend their vacations on Cape Cod or along the coast of Maine.

Autumn

Now it is October, and we are hiking through the Berkshire Hills in western Massachusetts. We are wearing light

Autumn in the highlands of Vermont. In the Northeast, autumn is a season of many colors. It brings cool, pleasant weather and shorter days to this part of our country.

jackets, because the temperature here is about 50° F. (10° C.). The air here is so cool and fresh that it makes us feel very healthy. Wherever we go in the Northeast during the autumn, we are likely to find cool, pleasant weather.

The oaks, maples, and birches that cover the hills around us are clothed in red and gold. Although the sky above is blue and without clouds, the air seems smoky. Farmers are busy harvesting the last of their crops. Tomorrow morning, the ground will probably have a white coating of frost.

The days are growing shorter. Each day the sun is a little lower in the sky. Winter will soon be here.

Explore the Climate of the Northeast
1. What facts help to explain why many areas in the Northeast receive heavy snowfall?
2. How does the long growing season along the Atlantic coast help farmers here?
3. Why is the climate along Lake Ontario and Lake Erie good for growing fruit?

Climate Where You Live
What is the climate like where you live? How does it affect your everyday life? Think carefully about these two questions. Then, draw or paint several pictures that show how the weather affects your life during each season of the year. You may wish to write labels for your pictures. Share the pictures with your class.

Part 2

People

The people of the Northeast are very much like people in other parts of our country. They share the same basic human needs and the same important beliefs about how our country should be governed. As you learn about the people of this region, you may wish to discover answers to the following questions:

- Who lives in the Northeast?
- Why is the Northeast thickly populated?
- What are some of the ways in which the people of the Northeast meet their basic needs? (See "Needs of People" at the back of this book. Part 3 also has information that will help you answer this question.)
- What is the "super city?"
- What are some of the rights that people of the Northeast share as citizens of our country?
- What are some of the responsibilities the people of this region have as citizens of our country?

People at a street fair in New York City. People of many different national* origins, races, and religions live in the great cities of the Northeast.
*See Glossary

4 People

Population of the Northeast

The Northeast is the most thickly populated part of our country. More than 56 million people live in the Northeast. This is about one fourth of the entire population of the United States. However, the Northeast covers less than one tenth of the total land area of our country.

Where do the people live?

About four fifths of the people who make their homes in the Northeast live in large cities or other thickly populated areas. Others live on farms or in small towns and villages.

Most of the Northeast's towns and cities have grown up in the lowland areas along the Atlantic Ocean and the Great Lakes, or in river valleys. Many early colonists settled near the fine natural harbors along the coast. Others settled along rivers, which provided good water transportation routes. As people moved westward, they settled mainly on plains or in river valleys. In

Shoppers at a sidewalk market in New York City. Millions of people live and work in the Northeast. This region is the most thickly populated part of our country. What are some of the reasons why so many people have made their homes in the Northeast?

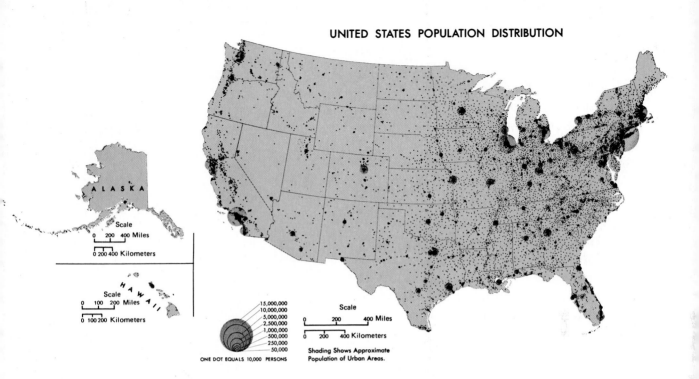

Scale
0 200 400 Miles
0 200 400 Kilometers

ALASKA

Scale
0 100 200 Miles
0 100 200 Kilometers

15,000,000
10,000,000
5,000,000
2,500,000
1,000,000
500,000
250,000
50,000

ONE DOT EQUALS 10,000 PERSONS

Scale
0   200   400 Miles
0   200   400 Kilometers

Shading Shows Approximate
Population of Urban Areas.

these areas, they generally found the land and climate well suited to farming. Also, it was easier to build roads and railroads through plains and valleys than through the highlands. Few people settled in the mountainous parts of the Northeast, such as the Adirondacks in New York or the highlands of Maine. Today, these areas are still thinly populated. (Compare map on page 14 with map above.)

Three main areas with many people

The most thickly populated part of the Northeast begins in southern New Hampshire and extends south along the Atlantic coast. This area is known as Megalopolis, or the "super city." (See Chapter 5.) Megalopolis includes the great Atlantic port cities of Boston, New York, Philadelphia, and Baltimore, as well as Washington, D.C. It also includes the many smaller cities, towns, and suburban communities between these larger cities.

Another thickly populated part of the Northeast is in western Pennsylvania, along the Ohio River and its branches. Large supplies of coal have helped this to become one of our country's leading industrial areas. More steel is made here than in any other part of the Northeast. Pittsburgh is the largest city in western Pennsylvania, and one of the oldest.

Still another thickly populated area extends from east to west across central New York. It lies along the route of the Erie Canal. This area includes the cities of Albany, Utica, Syracuse, Rochester, and Buffalo.

People from many lands

Most people in the Northeast are American-born citizens, just as most people are in other regions of the United States. In our country, however, almost all American-born citizens are descended from immigrants who have come here during the last four hundred years. Indians, Eskimos, and Hawaiians are the only exceptions. In the Northeast, by far the largest number of American-born citizens are of European descent. Their ancestors came to America from many different countries in Europe. The blacks in the Northeast are descended from people who lived in Africa.

Immigration in early times

People from several different European countries came to America during colonial times. Most of the colonists in the Northeast came from England. Others came from Scotland and Ireland. There were Dutch settlers in New York and New Jersey, Germans in Pennsylvania, and Swedes in Delaware. French Huguenots* also settled in the Northeast, mainly in New York. In addition to the settlers who came from Europe, there were also many black people who were brought from Africa to work as slaves.

The years 1820 to 1900

After the Revolutionary War* few settlers came to the United States.

About 1820, however, immigration to America began to increase rapidly. By this time, the United States was a successful democracy. It was a land of freedom and opportunity. Many Americans were moving from the east into the vast lands that had been opened up for settlement in the west. This left a shortage of workers in the factories that were growing up in the Northeast.

At this same time, many people in Europe were becoming unhappy and restless. One reason for this was that thousands of workers could not find

*See Glossary

Migration

A Problem To Solve

The picture at left shows immigrants arriving in the Northeast. Ever since the United States became a nation, people from many different lands have come to the Northeast to live. <u>Why have so many immigrants made their homes in the Northeast?</u> In forming hypotheses* to solve this problem, you may wish to think about each of the following questions.

a. What facts about religious and political freedom in the United States help to solve this problem?

b. What facts about job opportunities in the Northeast help solve it?

c. How has the location of the Northeast affected the number of immigrants who have come to this region?

See Skills Manual, "Thinking and Solving Problems"

jobs. Everywhere in Europe, the population was getting larger. There was no new land for farming, and the cities could not provide jobs for all the people who needed work. In addition, many Europeans were dissatisfied with the governments under which they lived. Democracy and religious freedom were unknown in most of the countries in Europe. Also, crop failures made it difficult for some people in Europe to obtain enough food.

Between 1840 and 1860, more than one and one-half million people left their homes in Ireland and came to America. Many left Ireland because crop failures were causing great hardship and suffering.

A steady stream of German immigrants came to America during the second half of the nineteenth century. Many of these people came because they were unhappy with their government at home. Crop failures also caused people from Germany to come to the United States. Some of these Germans had saved enough money to buy farmland. They generally moved farther

west, where more land was available. Many settled in the towns and cities of the Northeast, however.

In addition to the large number of immigrants from Ireland and Germany, people came to America from many other parts of the world. They came from England as they always had. They also came from Sweden, Norway, Finland, and the Netherlands. After the Civil War, many French Canadians also came to the United States. Most of them settled in New England.

Altogether, about twenty million immigrants came to America between 1820 and 1900. Most of these people entered our country through the great port cities of the Northeast. Large numbers of these immigrants found jobs in the cities where they landed. Some moved on to other parts of the Northeast or to other regions of our country.

The twentieth century

During the first ten years of the twentieth century, almost nine million immigrants came to the United States. By that time immigration from the countries of northern and western Europe was decreasing. More people were coming from southern and eastern Europe. Each year, thousands of Italians, Poles, Greeks, Russians, Jews, and

Freedom

See Great Ideas

The Statue of Liberty, in New York Harbor, reminds people of freedom. Millions of people have come to America from other lands in search of freedom. What different kinds of freedom were these people looking for? What kinds of freedom do people enjoy in the United States?

Puerto Ricans taking part in a parade in New York City. Many Spanish-speaking people of Puerto Rican descent make their homes in the cities of the Northeast.

Czechs came to America. Most of these immigrants became industrial workers in the great cities of the Northeast and the Midwest. Some found jobs in the coal mines of West Virginia and western Pennsylvania.

Other newcomers

Although immigration from Europe declined after 1910, the great industrial cities of the Northeast continued to grow. Many farm workers left rural areas to take factory jobs in the cities. Among these people were large numbers of blacks from the South. In the past, most of them had made their living by farming small plots of land, or by working at other jobs that paid them very little money. They came to New York and other cities of the Northeast hoping to find work in industry.

In the late 1930's, Spanish-speaking Americans from the island of Puerto Rico* began to move into the cities of the Northeast. At that time, many of the people in Puerto Rico were very poor. Large numbers of Puerto Ricans came to the Northeast to look for better-paying jobs. Today there are more than 800,000 people of Puerto Rican descent living in New York City.

The Northeast today

As you have seen, people have been moving to the Northeast for hundreds of years. Today, people of many different races and national origins live here. About nine tenths of the people are white. Nearly all of the others are black. Most of the rest are of Asian descent. They are mainly Chinese, Japanese, or Filipino.* A small number of Native Americans (Indians) also live in the Northeast.

Christianity is the leading religion in the Northeast, just as it is in other parts of our country. Roman Catholics make up the largest single religious group.

Education

See Great Ideas

A drugstore owner in the Northeast. This picture shows a successful pharmacist at work in his drugstore. He earns his living partly by preparing medicines for customers according to their doctors' instructions. How do you suppose this man learned the skills needed to prepare medicines? Do you think this man could be successful in his job without the great idea of education? Give reasons for your answer.

The Eastern Orthodox* churches also have many members. Some of the main Protestant groups in the Northeast are the Methodists, the Presbyterians, and the Baptists.

Another large religious group in the Northeast is made up of Jews. There are hundreds of Jewish congregations in this region, especially in New York and other large cities. In addition, people of other faiths such as Islam* and Buddhism* live in the Northeast.

Americans all

Life in the Northeast, as in all of America, is more interesting because of the many races, religions, and nationalities that are represented among the people. Each group, in its own way, has had an influence on the American way of life.

People of almost every different group in the Northeast have made important contributions to American life. For example, Andrew Carnegie, an immigrant from Scotland, helped to develop America's steel industry. Gian-Carlo Menotti, who came to the Northeast from Italy, is a world-famous composer of music. Senator Edward Brooke and Representative Shirley Chisholm are black Americans. The German-born scientist Albert Einstein was a Jew. John F. Kennedy, whose great-grandparents came from Ireland, was our first Roman Catholic president.

The people of the Northeast, through their labor, their skills, and their talents, have all helped to make the United States the strong country it is today. Whatever their race, religion, or national origin, the people of the Northeast have one very important thing in common. They are all Americans.

The famous scientist Albert Einstein was a German-born Jew who lived in New Jersey. People of almost every group in the Northeast have made important contributions to America.

Famous People

People of many different races and nationalities have influenced life in our country. Eight of these people are listed below. Make a chart for your classroom that shows the national origin of each person and how he or she has influenced American life. As you do your research, you may find other names to add to your chart.

John James Audubon	Lin Yutang
Marian Anderson	Maria Tallchief
Arturo Toscanini	Knute Rockne
Wernher von Braun	Igor Stravinsky

For help in finding information, see "Learning Social Studies Skills" in the Skills Manual.

Boston, Massachusetts, is part of a long chain of cities, towns, and suburbs. This chain extends along the Atlantic coast of our country from southern New Hampshire into northern Virginia. This densely populated part of the Northeast is known as Megalopolis, or the "super city."

5 Cities

A Problem To Solve

Why have so many great cities grown up in the Northeast? In forming your hypotheses,* think about the following:

1. location of early settlements in this region
2. location of industry
3. transportation routes
4. immigration to our country

This chapter, as well as other chapters in this book, contain much useful information for solving this problem.

See Skills Manual, "Thinking and Solving Problems"

A region of great cities

If you were to go by train from Washington, D.C., to Boston, Massachusetts, you would travel through an almost unbroken line of cities, towns, and suburbs.* You would see open countryside and farmland from time to time. But, you would sometimes find it difficult to tell where one city ends and another begins.

*See Glossary

Pittsburgh is the only one of these areas that is not located in New York State. More than two million people live in or near Pittsburgh, Pennsylvania. The Buffalo metropolitan area has a population of more than one million. Other large metropolitan areas in western or central New York are Rochester and Syracuse. Also, Albany and its neighboring cities of Schenectady and Troy make up a large metropolitan area.

The Northeast has not always been a region of great cities. Three hundred years ago, very few people lived here. Only along the coast and in some of the river valleys were there small towns and settlements. Today, about four out of every five people in this region live in or near cities or towns. Let us learn how the Northeast became a region of great cities.

How Cities Grew

Cities do not grow up in a certain place by accident. There are always reasons for their growth. To understand why the Northeast has become a region of great cities, we need to know about the history of some of these cities.

The entire area along the Atlantic coast from southern New Hampshire into northern Virginia appears to be a single huge city. For this reason, this area has been called Megalopolis, or the "super city." (See map on page 50.) Several of the largest metropolitan* areas in the Northeast form part of the super city. In addition to these great metropolitan areas, there are many smaller urban* areas in the super city.

There are also large metropolitan areas in other parts of the Northeast.

Early settlements along the coast

Many of the Europeans who came to the Northeast in early colonial days settled along bays and inlets on the Atlantic coast. Some of these settlers turned to the sea for their living. They became shipbuilders, sailors, and fishers. Many of the early settlements along the coast became seaports. Some ships sailed from these ports to the nearby fishing grounds in the Atlantic Ocean. Others made long trips to trade with other parts of the world. This trade helped the seacoast towns to grow. Even before the Revolutionary War,* seaports such as New York, Boston, and Philadelphia had become important cities.

Early settlements in the river valleys

Some early settlements were made in the river valleys of the Northeast. Since there were no roads through the forests, the early settlers usually traveled by river. They found some places along the rivers favorable for starting settlements. Other settlements started as fur-trading posts. One of these is Albany, New York, on the west bank of the Hudson River. Pittsburgh, in western Pennsylvania, also started as a fur-trading post.

Early industrial cities

Many of the first settlements in the Northeast became important manufacturing cities. Textile* mills and other

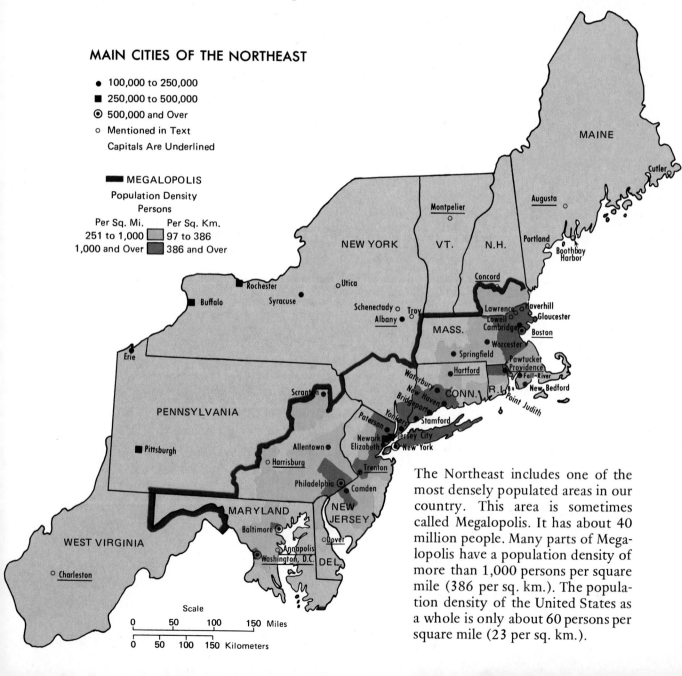

MAIN CITIES OF THE NORTHEAST

- ● 100,000 to 250,000
- ■ 250,000 to 500,000
- ◉ 500,000 and Over
- ○ Mentioned in Text

Capitals Are Underlined

▬ MEGALOPOLIS

Population Density
Persons

Per Sq. Mi.	Per Sq. Km.
251 to 1,000	97 to 386
1,000 and Over	386 and Over

The Northeast includes one of the most densely populated areas in our country. This area is sometimes called Megalopolis. It has about 40 million people. Many parts of Megalopolis have a population density of more than 1,000 persons per square mile (386 per sq. km.). The population density of the United States as a whole is only about 60 persons per square mile (23 per sq. km.).

Scale
0   50   100   150 Miles
0 50 100 150 Kilometers

factories were built in this region in the early 1800's. Many of these factories were started in port cities. Here, there were store owners and ship owners who had money to help build factories. Also, most of the people lived near the coast. The large population here provided workers for factories and customers for manufactured goods.

Some industrial cities grew up around factories located near waterfalls. The force of falling water was used to run machines in certain types of factories, such as gristmills* and textile mills. Among the New England cities that grew up near waterfalls were Lowell, in Massachusetts, and Pawtucket, in Rhode Island.

Good transportation routes

Good transportation routes helped some cities in the Northeast grow. From the Atlantic coast, several river valleys lead through the Appalachian Mountains. The most important of these is the Hudson-Mohawk Lowland in New York State. Others are in Pennsylvania and Maryland. In the 1800's, roads, canals, and railroads were built through these lowland areas. These transportation routes led westward from three of the region's largest cities —New York, Philadelphia, and Baltimore.

Many people from the Northeast moved westward along these routes. They began to farm, and settlements grew up in the lands beyond the mountains. A lively trade began between the manufacturing cities near the coast and the inland farming settlements. This trade helped the coastal cities to grow. It also helped settlements along the transportation routes to grow rapidly. For example, the small settlements of Buffalo, Rochester, and Syracuse became important cities after the Erie Canal* was finished in 1825.

Newcomers help the cities grow

About the middle of the 1800's, the cities of the Northeast began to grow very rapidly. Between 1840 and 1870, Philadelphia and Boston more than tripled in population. New York grew even more rapidly. By 1900, it was the world's second largest city. Only London, England, was larger.

There were several reasons for this rapid growth of the cities. One reason was the great increase in the number of immigrants coming to the United States. (See pages 43-44.) Many of these immigrants settled in the cities of the Northeast, where they could find jobs.

EIGHT METROPOLITAN AREAS		
Metropolitan Area	Population of Entire Area	Population of Central City
New York City	9,526,800	7,509,300
Philadelphia	4,822,400	1,804,100
Boston	2,890,000	621,300
Washington, D.C.	3,035,900	713,900
Nassau-Suffolk	2,675,300	
Pittsburgh	2,306,300	448,900
Baltimore	2,152,400	826,400
Newark	1,988,300	352,600

The eight largest metropolitan* areas in the Northeast are listed above. Their populations are given in the middle column. For seven of these areas, the population of the central city is also given. The counties of Nassau and Suffolk are on Long Island, near New York City. They form a separate metropolitan area, even though this area has no central city.

*See Glossary

During the last half of the 1800's, many people from farming areas in the Northeast also moved to the cities. New kinds of farm machinery and better ways of farming had come into use. As a result, farmers were producing larger harvests than ever before. Since fewer farmers were needed to supply our country with food, many people decided to leave their farms. They moved to cities to work in the rapidly growing businesses and industries. After 1900, the cities grew still more in population. (See pages 44-45.)

Great Cities Today

People are still coming to the great cities of the Northeast. However, most of the central cities have smaller populations today than they did fifteen years ago. This is because many people have left the crowded cities and moved to the suburbs. Unlike the central cities, most of the metropolitan areas are still growing in population.

From cities to suburbs

Many people have moved to the suburbs because the central cities have become so crowded. In the suburbs, the streets are not usually so busy with traffic. Also, there is more open land where people can build houses. People can have larger lawns and more room for their children to play.

Many people have also moved to the suburbs to be near the places where they work. As the cities became more and more crowded, they had less open land where large factories could be built. Many new factories were then built in less crowded areas, outside the cities. The suburbs grew as people moved from the cities to be near the factories where they worked.

New York City

A visit to New York

We are flying northward along the coast of New Jersey. Soon we see the tall buildings of a great city. This is New York. Below us, we see a wide harbor. Miles of docks line the water-

front. In the harbor we see many different kinds of ships. Most of the city is located on islands. As far as we can see, the land is covered with tall buildings, factories, and homes.

New York is located in the southeastern part of New York State, at the mouth of the Hudson River. Across the Hudson from New York City is the state of New Jersey. Here are several densely populated cities. They are part of the New York metropolitan area.

Our country's largest city

New York, with a population of about seven and one-half million, is the largest city in the United States. In addition to the people who live in the central city, millions of others live in cities and suburbs close to New York.

New York City is in the southeastern part of New York State, at the mouth of the Hudson River. It is the largest city in our country. About how many people live in the New York metropolitan area?

About nine and one-half million people live in the New York metropolitan area.

An important gateway for trade

New York is our country's leading seaport. Each year, thousands of ships enter and leave New York Harbor. These ships carry many different kinds of raw materials and manufactured goods. Much of the freight entering New York is shipped to other cities throughout the country. Goods produced in the Northeast and other regions of the nation are shipped to all parts of the world through the port of New York. In addition, most of the freight that is shipped by air between the United States and other countries passes through New York's John F. Kennedy International Airport.

More wholesale* and retail* trade is carried on in New York than in any other city in our nation. Wholesale companies in this city sell goods to people throughout the United States and in many other parts of the world. Hundreds of thousands of New Yorkers earn their living from wholesale trade. Retail stores in New York also employ large numbers of people. These stores sell food, clothing, furniture, and hundreds of other goods needed by people in the city. New York has some of the country's largest department stores. Along Fifth Avenue in Manhattan* are many fine clothing stores and other shops. People from hundreds of miles away come to shop in stores in New York City.

Our country's banking capital

Some of our nation's largest banks and insurance companies are located in New York City. They provide money

Meeting Needs

See Needs of People

Apartment buildings in New York City. People who live in this city share the same needs that all other people do. Do you think it is easier for people in a large city like New York to meet their needs than it is for people who live on farms? Explain.

New York City is made up of five sections called boroughs. These are Manhattan, Brooklyn, Queens, the Bronx, and Staten Island. (See map at right.) A visitor to New York can see the Statue of Liberty in New York Bay. Nearby is Ellis Island, where millions of immigrants first landed in our country. Central Park, in Manhattan, is also a popular place to visit. North of Central Park is Harlem, one of the best-known black communities in the United States. Many New Yorkers go to the beaches on Coney Island during the summer.

NEW YORK CITY

① Statue of Liberty
② Ellis Island
③ John F. Kennedy International Airport
④ Central Park
⑤ Harlem
⑥ La Guardia Airport
⑦ Coney Island

New York City
Parks
Airports
— Bridges
= Tunnels

for businesses throughout the United States as well as in many countries around the world. Many of the banks and insurance companies are located on or near Wall Street in Manhattan.

A leading industrial city

Most people who visit New York do not think of it as a great manufacturing city. They see few tall smokestacks or huge factories, like those in other industrial cities. Yet New York earns more money from manufacturing than any other American city except Chicago. Because of the high cost of land in this city, manufacturers here specialize in industries that do not need a large amount of factory space. Among New York's most important industries are printing and publishing and the manufacture of clothing.

Boston

The largest city in the northern part of Megalopolis is Boston. (See map on page 50.) Boston is located on the Atlantic coast where the Charles River empties into Massachusetts Bay. Many fine harbors along the bay help make Boston an important port city.

Boston is the capital of Massachusetts, and the state's largest city. About three million people live in the Boston metropolitan area.

Industry

There are more than 5,000 factories in the Boston metropolitan area. They produce machinery, medical instruments, and many other products. Printing and publishing are also important.

Education and the arts

Since colonial times, Boston has been a leading center of education. Our country's oldest public school, the Boston Latin School, was started here by settlers in 1635. Today, more than forty colleges and universities are in the Boston area. One of these is Harvard, the oldest college in the United States. Harvard is in the city of Cambridge, across the Charles River from Boston. It was founded in 1636 and has become one of our country's leading universities.

Boston has many fine museums and concert halls. Many people enjoy looking at paintings and other works of art in the Museum of Fine Arts. Other people enjoy listening to concerts by the Boston Symphony Orchestra.

Historic Boston

Many people come to Boston every year to walk the Freedom Trail. This trail is a walkway through part of the city. It guides visitors to many old buildings where important events in our country's history took place. They see the Old State House,* which was built in 1713. They also see Paul Revere's House and the place where Benjamin Franklin was born.

Philadelphia

Philadelphia was founded in 1682. It grew from a small settlement to become the largest city in the state of Pennsylvania. Philadelphia is now the fourth largest city in the United States. About five million people live in the Philadelphia metropolitan area.

An important inland port

Although Philadelphia is about 100 miles (161 km.)† from the Atlantic Ocean, it is one of our country's most important ports. It is in the southeastern part of the state. (See map on page 50.) Philadelphia lies along the Delaware River, which flows to the Atlantic Ocean. Dock workers at the port of Philadelphia load and unload more than 5,000 ships every year.

Industry

Philadelphia is the third largest clothing and manufacturing city in our country. Oil refining and shipbuilding are two other major industries in the Philadelphia area. Some of Philadelphia's plants process* farm products that are raised nearby. Other industries produce chemicals and machinery.

An historic city

If you were to visit Philadelphia, you might be reminded of many events in our country's history. Thousands of tourists visit the city each day to see Independence Hall, where the Declaration of Independence and the Constitution were signed. The Liberty Bell, a well-loved symbol of American freedom, can be seen in Independence Hall.

Baltimore

Baltimore is Maryland's largest city. More than two million people live in the Baltimore metropolitan area. Parts of this city have not changed for a hundred years. There are old streets that are lined with narrow, brick buildings, called row houses. In other parts of Baltimore are skyscrapers and modern apartment buildings.

A major seaport

Baltimore lies along a wide harbor where the Patapsco River empties into Chesapeake Bay. (See map on page 13.) This fine harbor and miles of docks help make Baltimore one of the leading port cities in our country. Ships from other parts of the United States and around the world carry goods to and from this port city every day.

Industry

Baltimore's leading industry is the metals industry. The Bethlehem Steel plant near this city is one of the largest steel producers in the world. Copper is

† km. means kilometer

also produced in the Baltimore area. Other main industries here produce chemicals and electronic* equipment.

Pittsburgh

Pittsburgh is one of the few major cities in the Northeast that are not part of Megalopolis. (See map on page 50.) It is located in the southwestern part of Pennsylvania. Pittsburgh is the second largest city in the state. More than two million people live in the Pittsburgh metropolitan area.

The Golden Triangle

Downtown Pittsburgh is beautiful and modern. This area, located between the Allegheny and Monongahela rivers, is called the Golden Triangle. New skyscrapers and large, green parks have taken the place of some of the old buildings that used to be here.

Industry

Pittsburgh is one of the great iron and steel centers of the world. At night, flames from the huge steelmaking furnaces are seen for many miles. Large amounts of coal from nearby mines are used in making the iron and steel.

Pittsburgh also ranks high in the production of bottles and window glass. The Pittsburgh area's 2,500 manufacturing plants also make chemicals, metal products, and machinery. Food processing is another leading industry.

Pittsburgh is the second largest city in Pennsylvania. It began in the 1700's as a trading post. This city is at the point where the Allegheny and Monongahela rivers join to form the Ohio River.

Washington, D.C.

Washington, D.C., is our country's capital. It is also one of our most beautiful cities. It lies in the eastern part of our country, between Maryland and Virginia. (See map on the opposite page.) Washington is the only city or town in our country that is not part of a state. It covers the entire area of the District of Columbia. This area is a piece of land set apart as the home of our federal government. More than three million people live in the Washington metropolitan area. This area spreads into Maryland and Virginia.

Earning a living

More than one fourth of the people in the Washington metropolitan area have government jobs. Many others earn their living by working in hotels and restaurants. They serve the millions of people who visit Washington every year. Stores and shops also provide many jobs.

The White House, in Washington, D.C. Washington is our country's capital. The president of our country lives and works in the White House. Thousands of Americans visit the White House each year.

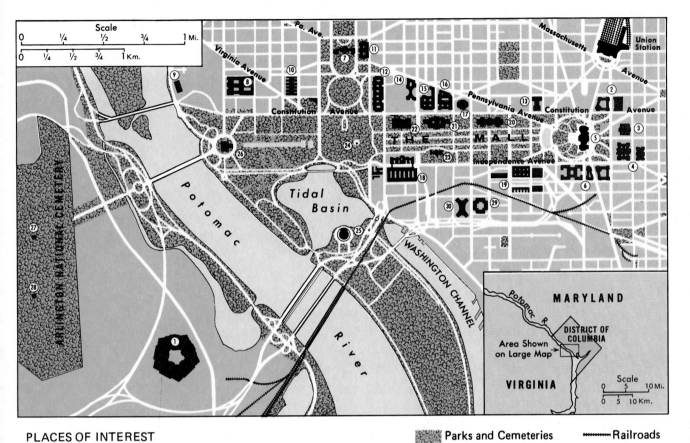

PLACES OF INTEREST

1. The Pentagon
2. Senate Office Buildings
3. Supreme Court
4. Library of Congress
5. Capitol
6. House of Representatives Office Buildings
7. White House
8. Department of State
9. John F. Kennedy Center for the Performing Arts
10. Department of the Interior
11. Department of the Treasury
12. Department of Commerce
13. Department of Labor
14. United States Postal Service
15. Internal Revenue Service
16. Department of Justice
17. National Archives
18. Department of Agriculture
19. Department of Health, Education, and Welfare
20. National Gallery of Art
21. National Museum of Natural History
22. National Museum of History and Technology
23. Smithsonian Building (Administration Offices)
24. Washington Monument
25. Jefferson Memorial
26. Lincoln Memorial
27. Grave of President Kennedy
28. Tomb of the Unknowns
29. Department of Transportation
30. Department of Housing and Urban Development

Early history

In 1783 Congress decided that our country needed a permanent capital. In 1790 they finally agreed that it should be built along the Potomac River. President George Washington chose the place along the river where the city was to be built. He also hired a French engineer to draw up plans for the city. The federal government moved from Philadelphia to Washington, D.C., in 1800.

A Visit to New York City

New York City is an interesting place to visit. Do research in other sources about one or more of the following:

1. the arts of New York City
2. the United Nations
3. the Statue of Liberty
4. the Empire State Building

Take careful notes as you do your research. Then imagine you have visited New York City and prepare a report about one or more of the above subjects. Share the report with your class.

6 Citizenship and Government

Our National Government

In Chapter 5, you discovered that our nation's capital city is in the Northeast. This city is Washington, D.C. The main offices of our national government are located here. Let's take a trip to Washington to find out how the government works.

How our government began

In Washington, we hire a guide to show us around the city. Our guide tells us there are certain things we ought to know before we begin our tour.

She reminds us that our country was founded more than two hundred years ago. At that time, there were thirteen colonies along the Atlantic coast of North America. (See pages 17-18 in "Pictorial Story of Our Country.") These thirteen colonies belonged to the country of Great Britain.

People in the colonies wanted more freedom than the British government would give them. In 1775 a war broke out between the colonies and Great Britain. This became known as the Revolutionary War. It lasted for eight years. When it ended, the colonists had won their freedom from British rule. They formed a new nation called the United States of America.

The government of the new nation was very weak. It could make laws. But it had no way to make sure these laws were carried out. Many Americans felt a stronger government was needed. In 1787, some of our country's leaders met in the city of Philadelphia. They drew up a new plan of government. This was the United States Constitution.

Our government today

The Constitution is the most important set of laws in the United States. It tells how our government is supposed to be run. All other laws that are passed in our country must agree with the Constitution.

Rules and Government

See Great Ideas

President Jimmy Carter speaking to the United States Congress. Congress makes the laws for our country. What two groups make up the Congress? How are the members of each of these two groups chosen? Would you like to be a member of Congress some day? Give reasons for your answer.

Under the Constitution, the United States has a federal form of government. This means that power is divided between the national government in Washington and the governments of the fifty states. (See pages 6-7.) The federal government can do certain things that the states cannot do. For example, it can issue money. It can also carry on wars against other countries. The states can do certain things that the federal government is not supposed to do. One of these is running the schools.

In the United States, all citizens of voting age can take part in running the government. They do this by electing men and women to make and carry out the laws. A country with this kind of government is known as a democracy.

Congress

Now we are ready to begin our tour. Our first stop is the Capitol. (See picture on Table of Contents pages.) The United States Congress meets here. Congress is a group of men and women who are elected by the people. They make laws for our nation.

Our guide says that Congress is made up of two groups. These are the Senate and the House of Representatives. The Senate has one hundred members—two

Our Federal Government

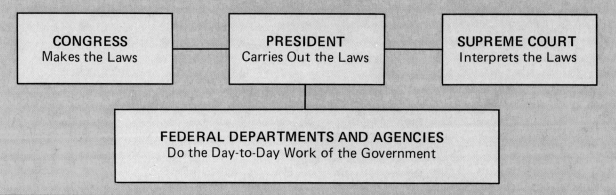

CONGRESS Makes the Laws	PRESIDENT Carries Out the Laws	SUPREME COURT Interprets the Laws

FEDERAL DEPARTMENTS AND AGENCIES
Do the Day-to-Day Work of the Government

from each state in our country. These people are elected for terms of six years. The House of Representatives has 435 members. They are elected for two-year terms. Each state chooses a certain number of representatives according to its population. For example, California—the state with the most people—has forty-three representatives. Wyoming—the state with the fewest people—has only one representative.

Now we enter the Capitol and go into a large room where the Senate is meeting. From our seats in the balcony, we can watch the senators at work. One senator is making a speech. The others are sitting at their desks. They are listening to the speaker or talking quietly among themselves.

Our guide tells us that the speaker is trying to talk the other senators into voting for a bill.* Before a bill can become a law, it must be approved by both the Senate and the House of Representatives. All decisions are made by majority* vote.

The president and vice-president

Leaving the Capitol, we drive along a wide, busy street called Pennsylvania Avenue. (See map on page 59.) Soon we come to a large, beautiful house with lawns and gardens around it. This is the White House. The president of the United States lives and works here.

Our guide says the president is in charge of carrying out the laws Congress has made. A president is elected every four years by the citizens of our country. At the same time, the voters also choose a vice-president. If the president dies, the vice-president becomes the president.

Our guide tells us about the president's duties. For instance, the president is in charge of our dealings with other countries. The president is also the commander of our army, navy, and air force. The president suggests laws for Congress to vote on. Another of the president's duties is taking part in ceremonies, such as welcoming foreign leaders.

Federal departments and agencies

After we leave the White House, we drive past several office buildings. Our guide tells us that these are the offices of some of the people who work for the federal government.

Our guide explains that there are many people who help the president carry out the nation's laws. In fact, nearly three million people work for the federal government. Some of these people live in Washington. A much

*See Glossary

larger number live in cities all over the country.

The people who work for the federal government are grouped into a number of departments and agencies. Each has a different job to do. For example:

. . . The Department of State handles our dealings with other countries.

. . . The Department of Defense helps protect our country from being attacked by our enemies.

. . . The Department of Justice makes sure people obey federal laws.

. . . The Department of the Interior helps to protect our natural resources.

. . . The United States Postal Service delivers our mail.

The people in charge of all the main departments in the government are chosen by the president. Together they make up a group called the Cabinet. Members of the Cabinet meet with the president about once a week to talk about important problems.

The Supreme Court

The last stop on our tour is the Supreme Court Building. (See map on page 59.) The United States Supreme Court is the most important law court in our country. It is made up of nine judges called justices, who are chosen by the president. The justices serve on the court until they die or resign.

A Cabinet meeting. The people in charge of the main departments in our federal government are chosen by the president. Together they make up a group called the Cabinet. Members of the Cabinet meet with the president about once a week to talk about important problems.

The main job of the Supreme Court is to decide whether the people who make and carry out our laws are following the Constitution. Important cases are brought to the Supreme Court from other law courts in the United States. When the Supreme Court makes a decision, all other courts in our country must follow that decision.

Our tour of Washington is over now. But our guide has one more thing to say. She tells us that in a democracy like the United States, the government is not able to do its job well without the help of all of the citizens. "If you want to have a good government," she says, "you must be a good citizen and be willing to do your part."

Your Job as a Citizen

When you are eighteen years old, you will be able to vote. Then you can help choose the men and women who run our government. To vote wisely, you need to learn as much as you can about how our government works. You also need to learn about some of the ideas that make our democracy possible.

A worker in a factory where television tubes are made. People in a democracy share seven important beliefs. For example, they believe that citizens have responsibilities as well as rights. One of these responsibilities is doing useful work. What are some other responsibilities of citizens?

SEVEN IMPORTANT BELIEFS SHARED BY PEOPLE IN A DEMOCRACY

1. Every person is important.

Most Americans believe that every person is important. It does not matter if you are young or old, a man or a woman. You are just as important as every other person. You are important whether your skin is black, white, or some other color. You are important no matter what religion you follow or what country your grandparents came from.

2. People have the right to govern themselves.

Americans believe the citizens of a country have the right to govern themselves. We think every person should be able to have some part in running our government.

3. Decisions should be made by majority* vote.

In the United States, all citizens have a chance to help choose the people who run the government. They do this by voting in elections. The candidate* with the most votes is elected. This is known as majority vote. Most Americans believe the fairest way for people to govern themselves is by majority vote.

4. All citizens should have a chance to get a good education.

Education is very important in a democracy. To have good government, citizens must be able to vote wisely for the people who make and carry out the laws. Most Americans believe that all young people should have a chance for a good education.

5. Laws should be the same for all citizens.

Most Americans believe all citizens should be treated the same by their government. Everyone should be required to obey the same laws. People should never gain or lose any rights because of such things as the color of their skin, or how much money they have.

6. All people have certain rights that no one can take away from them.

Most Americans believe that every person has a number of important rights and freedoms. Among these are freedom of speech and freedom of religion. Also every person has the right to a fair trial in a court of law. We believe that these rights cannot be taken away from any person, even by a majority vote. In a democracy, the government is expected to protect the rights of all citizens.

7. Citizens have responsibilities as well as rights.

For a democracy to work, all citizens must be willing to do their part. In other words, citizens have responsibilities as well as rights. Among these responsibilities are obeying the laws of the community, taking part in the government, and doing useful work.

*See Glossary

Seven important beliefs

The feature above tells about seven important beliefs shared by people in a democracy. These beliefs touch our lives every day—at home, at school, at church, and at work. Wherever we go, we find people who are either following or not following these beliefs in their daily lives.

Study these seven beliefs carefully, and decide whether they are important to you. Do you understand all seven beliefs? Do you agree with them? Are there any that you do not agree with?

RESPONSIBILITIES OF CITIZENS

Obeying the laws

Good citizens obey the laws of their community, state, and country. Even if they think a law is unfair, they will not disobey it. Instead, they will work in a peaceful way to get the law changed.

Treating other people with respect

Good citizens treat other people the same way they would like to be treated. They try to be friendly and polite to everyone. This is because they truly believe that every person is important.

Getting a good education

In the United States, most people have an opportunity for an education. Young people are responsible for making good use of this opportunity. By learning as much as they can, they are preparing to become useful citizens when they grow up.

Doing useful work

Most Americans feel they are responsible for doing useful work. When they become adults they do not expect other people to take care of them. Instead, they expect to work hard and do their job well.

Taking part in the government

In the United States, it is important for every citizen to take part in the government. People who are over eighteen can do this by voting in all elections. Also they can work for candidates* they think would do a good job. Young people have a responsibility to learn as much as they can about their government. This will help prepare them to make wise decisions when they are older.

Cooperating with other people

Many jobs in a community cannot be done well by persons working alone. Instead, there must be cooperation among many people. Citizens of a community have a responsibility to work together. In this way, they can make their community a better place to live.

*See Glossary

If so, which ones? Give reasons for your answer.

Why the seven beliefs are important

Most Americans are loyal to the seven beliefs. They know that if people did not follow these beliefs, it would not be possible to have a democracy like ours.

Suppose people did not think it was important for everyone to have an education. They might not be willing to pay taxes to support free public schools. If people wanted to go to school, they would have to pay a fee. Many families would not have enough money to send their children to school. As a result, many young people would grow up without learning how to read and write. When it came time to vote, they would not have enough knowledge to make wise decisions.

Here is another example. Imagine what might happen if Americans did not believe citizens have responsibilities as well as rights. Every person would feel free to do just as he or she pleased. Some people would break the laws or cheat others whenever they wanted. Soon, no one would be able to trust anyone else. People would be too busy protecting their own lives and property. They would not have time to do any useful work.

Becoming a responsible citizen

You are already a citizen, even though you cannot vote until you are eighteen. As a citizen, you enjoy a number of rights and freedoms. In return for these rights and freedoms, you have certain responsibilities. Some of these are shown in the feature at left.

Problems Facing Our Nation

One of the main duties of each citizen is to think carefully about the problems that face our country. Today there are several important problems that keep many Americans from meeting their basic needs. (See "Needs of People" at the back of this book.) These are known as social problems.

The feature below shows seven social problems facing our country. Let's look more closely at two of these.

The Need for More Jobs

The greatest problem many Americans face is that of earning a living. Some people work at jobs that pay them very little money. Others cannot find jobs at all. Today, about six out of every one hundred workers in the United States do not have jobs. Let's look at some of the reasons why.

Recessions*

Sometimes the United States goes through a time of business troubles known as a recession. When this happens, many stores and factories are not able to make a profit.* Some of them have to lay off many workers. Others may go out of business. As a result, there are not enough jobs for all the people who need them.

Depressed* areas

In some parts of our country, there is always a shortage of jobs. These are

SEVEN SOCIAL PROBLEMS

In our country, a number of serious problems prevent people from meeting their needs. These are called social problems. The government and the people of our country have been working hard to solve these problems. As we make progress toward this goal, more Americans will have happier and more successful lives. Our country's social problems include:

1. **The need for more jobs.** At the present time, about six out of every hundred workers in the United States are unable to find jobs.
2. **The high cost of living.** In recent years, the high cost of goods and services has kept many people from meeting their needs. This continuing rise in prices is called inflation.
3. **The need for better education.** Many people in our country are not getting a good education. They are not gaining the knowledge they need for good citizenship.
4. **Illness and handicaps.** Americans are among the healthiest people in the world. However, millions of people in our country suffer from serious illnesses and handicaps.
5. **Lack of freedom for certain groups.** In the past, some groups of people in our country did not have the same freedoms as other people. Today, our laws give every person the right to fair treatment and equal opportunity. Even so, some Americans still do not have all the rights and freedoms promised by our laws.
6. **Crime.** Over the years, there has been a great increase in the number of major crimes in our country. In many areas, people live in fear for their lives.
7. **Unsuccessful communities.** In many parts of the United States there are unsuccessful communities. Many of the people in these communities are not doing useful work. They are not getting the education they need to get jobs or to be good citizens. The crime rate in these communities is very high.

known as depressed areas. There are several reasons why areas become depressed. In some places, poor farming methods or strip* mining has ruined good farmland. Sometimes mines have been closed because all the valuable minerals have been removed. In other cases, businesses have moved from a community because the owners could no longer make a profit there. Factories have sometimes closed down because people stopped buying the goods they were making.

Discrimination*

Even in communities where there are plenty of jobs, many people cannot find work. Sometimes this is because they are thought to be too old for certain jobs. Other times, it is because they belong to a group of people who are not treated the same as other Americans. For example, women, blacks, or Mexican-Americans are sometimes refused jobs that others might get easily. This kind of unfair treatment is called discrimination.

The control panel of a steelmaking furnace. Many jobs in our country today are done by machines like the one in this picture. These machines need only a few skilled workers to run them. The use of machines that need few people to run them is called automation. Automation has created many new jobs for skilled workers. But fewer jobs are now open to unskilled workers.

Lack of education

There is another important reason why many Americans do not have jobs today. They do not have the education or the skills needed for the jobs they can find.

In the past, many jobs were open to people who did not have much education. Today, most of these jobs are done by machines. The use of machines that need few people to run them is called automation. Automation has created many new jobs for engineers* and other specially trained people. Many skilled workers are needed to build the new machines and keep them running. But fewer jobs are now open to unskilled workers.

Helping people without jobs

Today, a number of things are being done to help people who cannot find jobs. Our government is studying ways to help business grow and to prevent recessions. Sometimes the government lends money to companies that are in trouble. To provide more jobs, a state or a city will sometimes give help to business people who want to build a new factory there.

The federal government has passed laws against job discrimination. So have many of our states. These laws say that anyone who hires workers must treat them all the same. An employer cannot refuse to hire or promote a person because that person belongs to a certain group. For example, an employer cannot discriminate against women or blacks. These laws are helping many people who used to find it hard to get well-paying jobs.

Many companies and community groups have started programs to help people find work. They have also set up job-training centers. There, people can learn the skills they need to hold good jobs in factories or offices. A number of businesses have classes for workers who are losing their jobs because of automation. In these classes, workers learn new skills that they can use both now and in the future.

Our federal government also helps provide job training. For example, it runs a program called the Job Corps. Young men and women who do not have jobs can stay a few months at special Job Corps centers. There they learn valuable skills. They are also given a chance to earn money.

The High Cost of Living

There is another reason why many people find it hard to meet their needs. They have to pay higher prices than they used to for the things they buy. The problem of rising prices is known as inflation. For example, in 1966 a loaf of bread cost about fifteen cents. Today it costs almost three times that much.

The causes of inflation

Prices go up for a number of different reasons. Sometimes there are many people who want to buy a certain product, but there is only a small amount available. Some people are then willing to pay higher prices to make sure they get this product. For example, in 1973 there was not enough gasoline in the United States for everyone who wanted to buy it. (See pages 102-103.) This helped cause the price of gasoline to go up very rapidly.

Sometimes a business company will raise the price it charges for a certain

Buying groceries. The problem of rising prices makes it difficult for many people to meet their needs. They have to pay higher prices than they used to for groceries and other things they buy.

product. It does this to make more money. If there are many different companies that make the same product, each company will be slow to raise its prices. Otherwise, it may lose customers to companies whose prices are lower. But in many industries, a few companies make nearly all of a certain product. If one company raises its prices, the others often do the same.

Labor* unions may also bring about a rise in prices. If a union feels that its members are not being paid enough money, it can call a strike.* In this way, it can sometimes force a company to pay more money to its workers. When

this happens, the company may have to raise its prices to stay in business.

Our government also helps cause inflation. Each year, the federal government spends many billions of dollars. Some of this money is used to defend our country against possible enemies. Much is spent for new schools, better health care, and other services.

Usually, the federal government spends more money each year than it receives in taxes. When this happens, the government simply issues more money. Then people have more money in their pockets to buy the things they need and want. But there are not enough goods and services for all the people who want to buy them. As a result, prices go up.

How inflation affects our lives

Inflation hurts nearly everyone in our country. However, some people are hurt worse than others. These are people whose incomes* have not been rising as fast as prices. Some of these people work at jobs that pay little more than they did ten years ago. Others are older people who are living on money they saved when they were younger. Although their income stays about the same, they have to pay more money for the things they buy. As a result, they cannot buy as many things as they could before.

Inflation also hurts business companies. They must pay higher wages to keep their workers happy. Also, they must pay more money for the goods they use. If they charge higher prices for their products to meet these costs, they may lose some of their customers. It is hard for some companies to stay in business during times of inflation.

The fight against inflation

Today, government leaders and other people in the United States are studying ways to stop inflation. Some people believe the government should pass laws to control wages and prices. Then workers could not get raises without the government's permission. Also, companies would need the government's permission to raise prices.

Wages and prices have been controlled by the government at certain times in the past. But many Americans are against wage and price controls. They believe people should be free to decide on wages and prices without being told what to do by the government.

Some people think inflation cannot be stopped as long as our government spends more money than it receives. These people say the government should either spend less money or raise taxes, or both. If the government cut down on its spending, it would not have to issue so much new money. People would then have less money to spend for goods and services. The same thing would happen if taxes were raised. In either case, prices would go up more slowly than they did before.

There is still much that people need to learn about inflation. Only as we gain more facts will we be able to make much progress toward solving this important problem.

A Citizenship Project

Many of the problems that we face today have come about because people were not living by the seven important beliefs of a democracy. To understand this more clearly, you may want to carry out the following project.

When you go home tonight, read your daily newspaper. Or listen to a news report on radio or television. Take notes about some of the news stories of the day. Bring your notes to class, and be prepared to answer the following questions about each story:

- How does this news story relate to the seven beliefs that make democracy possible?
- Are the people in the news story being loyal to the seven beliefs? Or are they acting against these beliefs? Explain your answer.
- Are the actions of these people making life better or worse for other citizens of our country? Give facts to support your answer.

7 The Arts

A Problem To Solve

How do the arts of the Northeast help us to understand our country's history? In forming hypotheses* to solve this problem, you will need to consider the works of art created since colonial times by each of the following:

a. writers of the Northeast
b. painters of the Northeast
c. composers of the Northeast

As you try to solve this problem, you may wish to do research in this book as well as in other books.

See Skills Manual, "Thinking and Solving Problems"

In New York City's Guggenheim Museum, visitors can view paintings by many of the artists of our own time. The Northeast offers opportunities for people to enjoy many different kinds of art. Cities throughout the region have fine museums, art galleries, theaters, and concert halls.

The arts help tell America's story

The arts are much more than collections of paintings, books, and music for people to enjoy. The arts also tell us about a country's way of life and about people's thoughts, feelings, and goals. Learning about America's arts and artists can bring us to a richer understanding of our country and its history.

Many of America's greatest artists have lived in the Northeast. In the early years of our country, almost all of our large cities were in this region. Painters, writers, and musicians came to study and to work in some of these early cities, such as New York and Boston.

The Arts in Early America

During the early years of our country's history, most people had little time for the arts. When they were not hard at work, the early settlers spent a great deal of time in church. Most writing was about religion, and hymns were almost the only kind of music. A number of artists were able to earn their living by painting people's pictures, however. John Singleton Copley is considered the best American painter of these early times.

During the Revolutionary War,* American writers became less interested in writing about religion and more interested in writing about our country and its leaders. Thomas Paine, for example, wrote articles to encourage the American people in their fight for independence. One of his writings is called *Common Sense*.

The interest that Americans felt in their history and their leaders was also shown in paintings. Gilbert Stuart and Charles Willson Peale were two of the many artists who painted pictures of George Washington and other great Americans. John Trumbull painted some of the great events in American history. Among his paintings are *The Battle of Bunker's Hill* and *The Declaration of Independence*.

The Arts in the 1800's

Painting

Three of the leading American painters of the 1800's were George Inness, James McNeill Whistler, and Mary Cassatt. Inness painted peaceful, dreamy pictures of the countryside. Whistler's paintings were known for their unusual use of color. Cassatt was best known for her paintings of mothers and children. Although Whistler was a native of

*See Glossary

A nineteenth-century painting called *The Lackawanna Valley*, by George Inness. What feelings do you suppose the artist was trying to express in this painting? How does the picture make you feel?

New England and Cassatt was born near Pittsburgh, both artists spent much of their lives in Europe.

Two other leading artists were Thomas Eakins and Winslow Homer. Eakins painted pictures of hospital scenes and sporting events. Homer, one of our country's best-known artists, painted pictures that showed the might and power of the sea.

Music

The well-known songwriter Stephen Foster lived in the Northeast, but he wrote mostly about the South. His songs include "Old Folks at Home" and "Oh! Susanna."

Edward MacDowell was one of America's greatest composers of the 1800's. He was born in New York City. MacDowell wrote piano and orchestra music. Two of his works are *Indian Suite* and *New England Idyls.*

Writers of fiction*

Washington Irving lived in New York State during the early 1800's. He wrote several well-liked books about American life. One of these was a group of stories called *The Sketch Book.* This book includes "The Legend of Sleepy Hollow" and "Rip Van Winkle." James Fenimore Cooper was also a great writer of the early 1800's. Cooper wrote several novels* about life on the frontier.*

Nathaniel Hawthorne, who wrote during the mid-1800's, was one of New England's best-known writers. He wrote several novels, including *The House of Seven Gables*, and also many short stories. Herman Melville wrote a number of books. His *Moby Dick* is one of the greatest American novels. Edgar Allan Poe wrote both short stories and poetry. Some of his stories, such as "The Fall of the House of Usher," are spooky and scary. Another author of the mid-1800's was Louisa May Alcott. She wrote *Little Women* and other stories about young people.

Stephen Crane and Henry James also lived in the Northeast. In *The Red Badge of Courage*, Crane described the fear and the courage of soldiers in the Civil War. James wrote many novels about Americans in Europe, describing the lives of wealthy people.

Poets

Several of America's best-loved poets of the 1800's lived in the Northeast. William Cullen Bryant was important both as a poet and a newspaper writer. Perhaps you have read his poem "To a Waterfowl." John Greenleaf Whittier wrote "Snow-Bound" and many other well-known poems. You might know some of Henry Wadsworth Longfellow's poems. These include "The Village Blacksmith" and "Paul Revere's Ride."

Emily Dickinson and Walt Whitman wrote poetry that was very different from that of other American poets. Dickinson wrote hundreds of poems that describe her own feelings about life and death. In many poems she used words in unusual ways. Whitman's poems show his love of America and democracy. His poetry was very different because he wrote in a freer style than earlier poets. He did not always follow the usual rules of writing.

Writers of nonfiction*

Several of America's leading writers of nonfiction during the 1800's lived in the Northeast. George Bancroft and Francis Parkman wrote important books about our country's history. Ralph Waldo Emerson and Henry David Thoreau were thinkers who believed that all people are good and should follow their own best feelings. Emerson's essay* "Self-Reliance" and Thoreau's book *Walden* are among our country's best-known writings.

The Arts in the 1900's
Literature

Eugene O'Neill is one of America's greatest playwrights. Many of his plays, such as *The Emperor Jones* and *Long Day's Journey Into Night*, show people living unhappy and hopeless lives.

One of the best-known American poets of the 1900's is Robert Frost.

Although Frost was born in San Francisco, he spent much of his life in New England. His poetry shows both the beautiful and the unhappy sides of life.

Many other poets of the 1900's have made their homes in the Northeast. Among these writers are Marianne Moore, Wallace Stevens, Amy Lowell, William Carlos Williams, and E.E. Cummings. In their poems, they often used unusual groups of words to tell their own ideas about life and art. Edwin Arlington Robinson wrote clever poems about people who are mixed-up and lonely. Well-known black poets who have lived and worked in New York City are Langston Hughes, Countee Cullen, and Claude McKay.

Other important writers of the Northeast, such as John O'Hara and John Marquand, wrote novels and short stories that tell about America's changing values. Conrad Richter and Kenneth Roberts wrote interesting stories about the history of the Northeast. In novels such as *Go Tell It on the Mountain*, James Baldwin has described the hopes and problems of

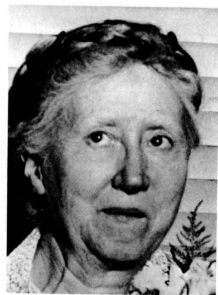

Language

See Great Ideas

Four of the many important writers of the 1900's who made their homes in the Northeast are shown in these pictures. Robert Frost (upper left) and Marianne Moore (upper right) are two of America's best-known poets. The plays of Eugene O'Neill (lower left) are famous all over the world. James Baldwin (lower right) is noted for his powerful novels about black Americans. Writers use words to tell about their ideas and feelings. What are some other ways in which people express their ideas and feelings?

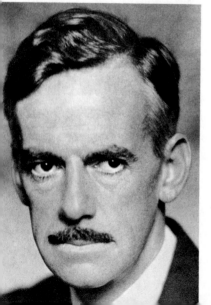

Beverly Sills is a world-famous opera singer who was born in New York City and has performed in many operas there. What other well-known artists have lived and worked in the Northeast?

black people living in large cities. Bernard Malamud has written about the lives of Jewish Americans.

Painting

Important painters of the Northeast during the 1900's are John Marin, Anna Mary ("Grandma") Moses, and Andrew Wyeth. Marin painted many pictures of the Maine seacoast and New York City. "Grandma" Moses, who began painting at the age of seventy-six, painted many simple, colorful scenes of country life. Wyeth also painted pictures of country life in Pennsylvania and Maine.

Music

One of America's greatest composers of the 1900's is Charles Ives. He was a New York businessman who wrote music in his spare time. Other important composers from the Northeast are Aaron Copland and George Gershwin. Copland's works include the music for three ballets, *Appalachian Spring, Billy the Kid,* and *Rodeo.* Gershwin wrote the musical play *Porgy and Bess.*

Express Your Opinion

Read one of the following poems in class:

"Annabel Lee," by Poe
"I Never Saw a Moor," by Dickinson
"Richard Cory," by Robinson
"The Runaway," by Frost

Discuss the following questions.

1. How did the poem make you feel?
2. Did you like the poem? Why? Why not?

Part 3

Earning a Living

In the Northeast, as in other parts of our country, people earn their living in many different ways. The Northeast is one of the most important manufacturing regions of our country. This region is also good for farming, and it has many valuable natural* resources. Below is a list of just a few ways people in the Northeast earn their living.

- mining coal
- tree farming
- fishing for lobsters
- raising vegetables
- raising dairy cattle
- working in an office in a steel plant
- working in a clothing factory
- working in a department store

As you do research in Part 3, make a list of additional ways in which people in the Northeast earn their living. You may wish to compare your list with the lists made by the other members of your class.

A nuclear* power plant in Pennsylvania. About 3% of the energy we use in the United States is nuclear energy. It produces electricity that is used by many people working in business and industry.

Planting celery on a truck farm in Pennsylvania. Truck farming is an important way of earning a living in the Northeast. What are some of the other types of farming in this region?

8 Farming

A Problem To Solve

Farmers in the Northeast earn more money from milk than from any other product. <u>Why is dairying the most important type of farming in this part of our country?</u> In forming hypotheses,* you will need to consider the following:

a. climate of the Northeast
b. land features of this part of our country
c. markets for dairy products

See Skills Manual, "Thinking and Solving Problems"

A New Jersey truck farm

It is a hot summer afternoon. As we drive across the level countryside of southern New Jersey, we see many green fields of crops. A sign along the road tells us that there is a vegetable stand at the farm ahead.

We stop at the stand and pick out some nice, ripe, red tomatoes. As we

*See Glossary

are paying for the tomatoes, the woman who owns this farm comes over to talk with us. We ask her whether she grows any crops besides tomatoes. The farmer says that she also raises green beans, peppers, and cauliflower. She explains that raising vegetables for sale is known as truck farming.

We learn that this farm is very small compared with many farms in the United States. It covers only 50 acres (20 ha.).[†] But the farmer knows how to earn a good living from this small piece of land. First, she grows crops that sell for high prices. Second, she makes sure that each acre of land produces as much as possible.

The farmer tells us that vegetables are a profitable crop. She explains that her farm is only 40 miles (64 km.)[†] from Philadelphia and 100 miles (161 km.) from New York City. In both of these cities, there are many people who will pay a good price for fresh vegetables. The farmer never sees most of these people because she sells her crops mainly to large grocery stores. Trucks can deliver the farmer's vegetables to stores in New York on the same day they are picked.

To produce good crops, the farmer must give them a great deal of care. In the spring, she and her son and daughter plow and fertilize the land. Then they set out the young vegetable plants. As the plants grow, they are weeded. They are also sprayed with chemicals that kill harmful insects. If the weather is dry, the plants must be irrigated.* At harvesttime, the farmer has to hire more workers to pick the vegetables before they spoil.

As we tell the farmer good-bye, she smiles and says she wishes all her sales were this easy. She tells us that in order to be a truck farmer she also needs to understand business. She must have enough money to buy fertilizer and insect spray. At times, she must buy a new piece of farm machinery. To make a profit, she needs to sell her crops at the highest possible prices.

Other kinds of farms

Not all farms in the Northeast are like the one we have just visited. Some of them are much larger. There are farms that raise fruit or other crops. Many farms raise only livestock, such as cattle or poultry. In spite of these differences, many northeastern farms have certain things in common. You will learn what some of

† ha. means hectare
† km. means kilometer

these things are as you read more about farming in the Northeast.

Efficient farming methods

Although less land in the Northeast is being used for farming today than in the past, this region produces more farm products than ever before. Northeastern farmers are able to get large yields because they use their land very efficiently. They try to choose the best kinds of plants and livestock. They use large amounts of fertilizer, and chemicals are used to kill weeds and insects. When the weather is dry, the farmers irrigate their fields.

Farmers in the Northeast have machines to help them do much of this work. For example, milking machines are used on most dairy farms. Many kinds of vegetables can be planted and harvested by machine. But people are still needed to run the machines. They are also needed to do work that machines cannot yet do, such as harvesting peaches and other fruits that are easily damaged.

Long growing season

Another reason why some farmers in the Northeast are able to harvest more crops is that they live in areas where the growing season is long. (See map on page 32.) In some places along the Atlantic coast, the frost-free period is long enough for growing two crops on the same land in a single year. A truck farmer in Delaware may plant green

Using Tools

See Great Ideas

A truck farmer in Delaware harvesting lima beans with modern machinery. Today, there are fewer farmers in the Northeast than there were in the past. Yet they produce larger amounts of crops than ever before. One reason for this is that farmers now use many farm machines. What are some of these machines? How do these machines help each farmer to produce more crops? How has this change in farming affected the lives of nearly everyone in the United States?

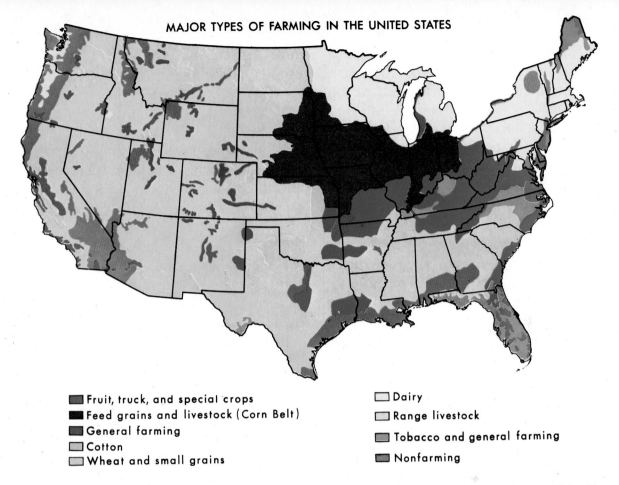

- ▨ Fruit, truck, and special crops
- ■ Feed grains and livestock (Corn Belt)
- ■ General farming
- ☐ Cotton
- ☐ Wheat and small grains
- ☐ Dairy
- ☐ Range livestock
- ▨ Tobacco and general farming
- ▨ Nonfarming

beans as soon as the soil warms up in the spring. By the end of June, the beans will be ready to pick. After they have been harvested, the land will be plowed again and fertilized. Then the farmer will plant some other vegetable that will ripen before the first frost of autumn.

The use of labor, machinery, and efficient methods to produce a large harvest in a small area is called intensive farming. Much of the farming done in the Northeast is intensive.

Markets for farm products

Farmers in the Northeast have been helped by their location in the most heavily populated part of our country. Millions of people live in the great cities of the Northeast. Each day these people buy huge quantities of food such as milk, eggs, vegetables, and fruit. All of these products must be sold and used quickly before they spoil. Therefore, farms that are close to cities have an advantage over farms that are located farther away. It is no surprise that there are many dairy and poultry farms, orchards, and truck farms in the Northeast. Farmers here use trucks and trains to rush their products to customers in the cities.

Livestock

Dairy cattle

Raising cows for milk is the most important type of farming in the Northeast. Farmers here earn more money from milk than from any other product. Dairy farms can be found in nearly all parts of this region. (See map on page 85.)

There are several reasons why dairying is so important in the Northeast. People in the large cities of this region use huge quantities of fresh milk every day. Milk spoils quickly. Even with fast, refrigerated trucks and trains, fresh milk is usually not shipped farther than 200 miles (322 km.). Because of this, most dairy farms are near cities or towns.

The land and climate of the Northeast also help to explain why there are so many dairy farms here. Land that is too rough for growing crops can often be used as pasture for dairy cows. Grasses used for hay and grazing grow well where summers are too short and cool for raising most other kinds of crops. Cows give more milk if the weather is not too hot. In the Northeast, there is usually enough rainfall to provide drinking water for cattle.

Most dairy farms in the Northeast are rather small. A typical farm covers about 100 acres (40 ha.). Dairy farmers use most of their land for pasture, or for growing hay and other feed crops. Also, some farmers feed their cattle grain from the Midwest.* In this way, they do not need to own as much land as they would if they grew their own feed crops.

Dairy farming requires skill and care. On most farms, there may be as many

Milking time on a modern dairy farm in the Northeast. Dairy farms can be found in nearly all parts of the Northeast. Farmers here earn more money from milk than from any other farm product.

as forty cows. These cows must be milked twice a day all through the year. Milking machines and other equipment must be kept very clean. The cows must be given just the right amounts of certain feeds if they are to produce large amounts of good milk.

Farmers sell most of their milk to dairies. Here it is pasteurized* and put into bottles or cartons. Most of this milk is sold to grocery stores or is delivered to people's homes. Dairies also use some of the milk to make butter, cheese, or other products.

Poultry

Poultry and eggs are second in value among the farm products of the Northeast. Like dairy cows, poultry can be raised in areas where the land is too poor for growing most crops. Also, farmers can raise a lot of poultry on only a few acres of land. There is a huge market for eggs and fresh poultry in the large cities of the Northeast. Broiler chickens are among the main types of poultry raised in this region of our country.

Many farmers in the Northeast raise chickens for their eggs. Pennsylvania and New York are the main egg-producing states in this region. There are also many chicken farms in the southern part of New England. Each day, these farms supply many thousands of eggs to customers in nearby cities.

Other kinds of poultry are also raised in the Northeast. Farms on Long Island produce about half of the ducks raised in the United States. Large numbers of turkeys are raised in Pennsylvania and West Virginia.

People who specialize in other kinds of farming sometimes raise a few chick-

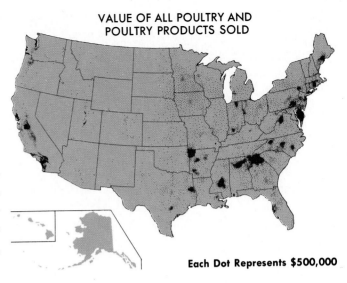

VALUE OF ALL POULTRY AND POULTRY PRODUCTS SOLD

Each Dot Represents $500,000

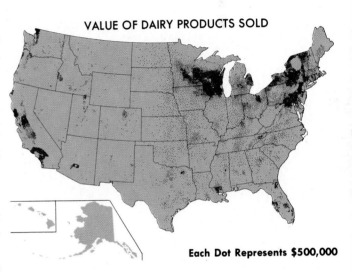

VALUE OF DAIRY PRODUCTS SOLD

Each Dot Represents $500,000

ens. However, most poultry farming in the Northeast today is a full-time business. Some farmers care for many thousands of birds. To do this, farmers must have a great deal of knowledge and skill. They must select the kinds of birds that will provide the most meat or eggs at the lowest cost. They must spend much money to build poultry houses and to equip them with automatic feeders and other modern machinery. The farmers must make sure that their birds receive the right amounts of food and water. They must protect the birds from disease by giving

A turkey farm in the Northeast. Poultry and eggs are second in value among the farm products of the Northeast. In addition to turkeys, what other kinds of poultry are raised in this region?

them "shots" and keeping their houses clean. It is also important for farmers to know how to sell their poultry and eggs at a good price so that they can make a profit.

Beef cattle

The raising of cattle for beef is less important in the Northeast than the raising of dairy cattle. However, many herds of beef cattle graze on hillside pastures in West Virginia. Much of the land in this state is too rough for growing crops, but it can be used for pasture.

The cattle raised in West Virginia are usually thin, because they feed mainly on grass. They must be fed corn and other grains to fatten them before they can be sold for meat. Although it is difficult to grow corn and other grains on the rough land of West Virginia, these crops grow well on the fertile, rolling Piedmont Plateau. Each fall, large numbers of beef cattle are shipped by train or truck from West Virginia to farms on the Piedmont in Maryland and southeastern Pennsylvania. There they are kept in feedlots* and fed a rich diet of hay and grain. When they are fat enough, they are shipped to meat-packing plants in New York and other cities of the Northeast.

Vegetables

In the Northeast, there are thousands of truck farms like the one we visited at the start of this chapter. Many truck farms are located on Long Island, on the Delmarva Peninsula,* and in southern New Jersey. All three of these areas are in the Coastal Plain region of our country.

The land and climate of the Coastal Plain help explain why truck farming is so important here. Most of the land is level enough for growing crops. The loose, sandy soil is easy to cultivate, even though it must be fertilized heavily to produce good harvests. This kind of soil is very well suited to growing root crops, such as carrots and beets. The Coastal Plain has a long growing season. Also, the sandy soil warms up quickly in the spring. As a result, farmers here can plant their crops earlier than farmers in other parts of the Northeast. They can harvest their vegetables and send them to market earlier in the season. In this way, they are likely to get a better price.

Many different kinds of vegetables are raised on the Coastal Plain. Among the most important are tomatoes, potatoes, beans, peas, and cucumbers. A large part of the vegetable crop is sold fresh in nearby cities. The rest is sent to canning or freezing plants.

Not all truck farms are as small as the one we visited. Some of them cover thousands of acres. These large farms may grow only one vegetable, or they may raise many crops. Some of them are owned by food companies. The large farms use many kinds of machinery for planting, cultivating,* and harvesting their crops.

The Coastal Plain is not the only truck-farming area in the Northeast. Large crops of cabbages, beans, and other vegetables are grown on the Lake Ontario plain in New York State. Northern Maine is one of the best potato-farming areas in the United States.

Fruits

In some parts of the Northeast, fruit growing is an important kind of farming. There are many orchards on the Erie-Ontario Lowland in western New York and Pennsylvania. The climate here is very good for growing fruit. Among the kinds of fruit grown here are apples, peaches, pears, and cherries. In western New York, grapes are also grown. These are used mainly for grape juice and wine.

Apples are grown in every state of the Northeast. They can be raised in places where the climate is too cold for other kinds of fruit. In fact, they grow best where summers are not extremely hot. Some of our country's best apple-growing areas are in the Appalachian Ridges and Valleys section in Pennsylvania, Maryland, and West Virginia. In the springtime, many hillsides and mountain slopes here are covered with white rows of blossoming apple trees.

Among the other fruit crops grown in the Northeast are blueberries and cranberries. Large amounts of blueberries are grown in New Jersey. They are also grown along the eastern coast of Maine. In these places, the soil is well suited for growing this crop. Massachusetts is our country's leading producer of cranberries. Large amounts of this crop are grown in the southeastern part of the state.

Other Crops

In addition to vegetables and fruits, many other crops are produced in the Northeast. Among these are wheat, corn, oats, hay, and tobacco.* In some parts of the Northeast, several different crops are grown on the same farm. This kind of farming is called mixed farming.

Farming in Lancaster County

To learn more about mixed farming, we will visit Lancaster County in southeastern Pennsylvania. This part of Pennsylvania is one of our country's most fertile farming areas. The soil is rich, and the land is gently rolling. Rainfall is plentiful, and the growing season is long enough for many kinds of crops.

It is a bright morning in June as we drive through the countryside of Lancaster County. Here we see golden fields of wheat and green rows of corn and tobacco plants. There are neat farmhouses and sturdy barns. The people who own these farms are mainly of German descent. Many are members of a religious group known as the Amish. They are noted for their hard work and their love of farming.

The main crops grown in Lancaster County are wheat, potatoes, corn, hay,

Farming in Lancaster County, Pennsylvania. This county lies in one of the most fertile farming areas in the United States. Farmers here grow several different kinds of crops. In Lancaster County, members of certain religious groups, such as the Amish, still use horses instead of tractors.

and tobacco. To help keep the soil fertile, farmers practice crop* rotation. Many farmers in Lancaster County raise beef cattle. In the fall, after their crops are harvested, they buy lean cattle from West Virginia and other states. They feed the cattle corn and other grains that they have grown on their own farms. When the cattle are fat enough, the farmers sell them for meat.

Grain crops

As you have learned, much of the Northeast is not well suited to growing corn, wheat, and other grains. However, these crops are important in some areas. Wheat is raised on the lowland that borders Lake Erie and Lake Ontario. It is also raised on the Piedmont Plateau. Some of it is used in making flour, and some is fed to livestock. In many parts of the Northeast, dairy farmers raise corn for silage.* Other grain crops grown in the Northeast include barley, oats, and rye.

Nurseries and greenhouses

Near the large cities of the Northeast, there are many nurseries and greenhouses. Nurseries are places where trees, shrubs, and flowering plants are grown for sale. People buy these plants for their lawns and gardens. Flowers, vegetables, and other plants are raised in greenhouses the year around. Many of the orchids, carnations, and gardenias sold in the United States come from greenhouses in southeastern Pennsylvania. This is also the chief mushroom-growing area in the United States.

Explore Truck Farming in the Northeast
Imagine that you are a truck farmer in the Northeast and have been asked to write a story about your farm for a leading farm magazine. Before writing your story, you will need to do research. Take careful notes and then make an outline before you begin to write. Some of the things your readers will be interested in are:
1. where your truck farm is located
2. why this is a good location
3. what crops you grow
4. how your farm products are sent to market and who buys them
5. what kinds of work you do on the farm

This chapter provides much useful information for this project. For help in finding additional information, see "Learning Social Studies Skills" in the Skills Manual.

9 Natural Resources and Energy

A Problem To Solve

How have the natural resources of the Northeast affected the development of manufacturing in this region? To solve this problem, you will first need to know what natural resources are found in the Northeast. Then you will need to make hypotheses* that explain how these resources have affected:

a. the location of industries in the Northeast
b. the types of manufacturing that have developed here

See Skills Manual, "Thinking and Solving Problems"

Natural Resources

If you take a trip on the Ohio River, you will see many towboats pushing long barges upstream. Some barges are loaded with coal. Others are filled with crushed limestone. Both the coal and the limestone will be used by steel mills in or near the city of Pittsburgh.

Coal, limestone, and other minerals are valuable gifts from nature. These gifts are called natural resources. The people of the Northeast have used their natural resources to develop many important industries.

In addition to minerals, there are many other valuable natural resources in the Northeast. Forests cover more than half of the land. Each year, millions of pounds of fish are caught in the waters along the coast of this region. Rivers and lakes generally supply the Northeast with enough water for its great cities and industries. Fertile soil, sunny days, and rainfall are also valuable natural resources. (See Chapters 2 and 3.) They help farmers provide much of the food needed by the people who live in this part of our country.

Water Resources

Water is a valuable resource

The people in the Northeast, like people everywhere, use water in many ways. In their homes, they need water for drinking, cooking, and other uses. On warm summer days they enjoy sports such as swimming and boating. Farmers in the Northeast need water in order to raise crops and livestock.

*See Glossary

Robert Moses Power Dam at Niagara Falls, in New York State. Water is one of the most valuable natural resources of the Northeast. People in this region, like people everywhere, need water for drinking, bathing, and many other uses. Large amounts of water are also used on farms and in factories. The force of running water is also an important source of energy. Do research in this chapter to discover how waterpower is used to produce electricity.

Water is also important to the industries of the Northeast. It is used in the manufacture of most products. For example, as much as 65,000 gallons of water are used to make one ton of steel. Water is also a source of some of the electric energy in the Northeast. (See feature on page 107.)

Using water wisely

The rivers and lakes of the Northeast supply most of the water needed by the people who live here. However, many rivers and lakes that could be used to supply water have become polluted* with wastes from factories and homes. For example, factories often dump harmful wastes into nearby rivers and lakes.

Most people in the Northeast understand that water is a valuable resource and that it must be used wisely. Like people in other parts of our country, they are trying to reduce pollution in their rivers and lakes. Industries in the Northeast must follow new laws that limit the amount and kinds of wastes that can be dumped into the water. If the pollution of lakes and rivers can be controlled, the Northeast will become a healthier as well as a more beautiful place in which to live.

Mineral Resources

There are only a few important mineral deposits in the Northeast. Many of the minerals needed by industries in this region are brought in from other

Mining coal in Pennsylvania. Coal is one of our country's most valuable mineral resources. Do research in this book and other sources to find some of the different ways we use coal.

parts of the United States. Some are brought in from other countries.

Coal in the Northeast

Coal is the most important mineral resource of the Northeast. Deposits of high-grade soft coal, called bituminous coal, are found in the Appalachian Plateau. Deposits of anthracite, or hard coal, are found in eastern Pennsylvania. Industries in the Northeast use much of the region's coal. Some coal is transported to Lake Erie for shipment to steel plants in the Midwest.

More bituminous coal than anthracite is mined in the Northeast. Anthracite was once used widely for heating homes. Today, oil or natural gas is used in most homes and there is little demand for anthracite. However, bituminous coal is used for many purposes. For example, it is needed in the manufacture of steel, chemicals, and many other products.

A coal mine in West Virginia

We are visiting a coal mine in the northern part of West Virginia. The main tunnel of the mine leads into the side of a large hill. This kind of mine is called a drift* mine.

The workers in the mine are running machines. One of the machines tears pieces of coal from a wall of the tunnel. The pieces fall onto a conveyor* belt. This belt carries the coal to a "shuttle car," which looks like a long, open trailer.

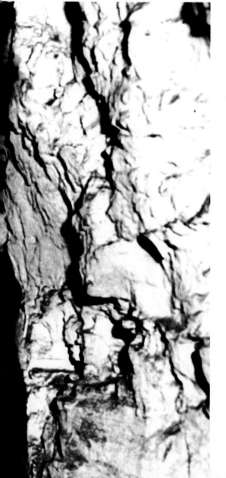

COALFIELDS OF THE UNITED STATES

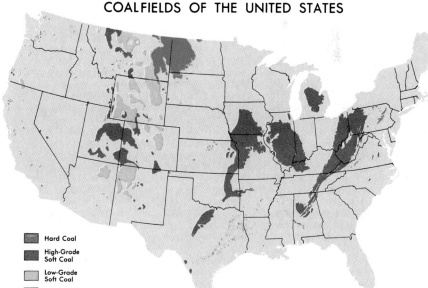

Hard Coal

High-Grade Soft Coal

Low-Grade Soft Coal

Lignite

The map above shows the main coal deposits in the conterminous* United States. Deposits of high-grade soft coal are found in West Virginia and western Pennsylvania. They are part of a huge coalfield in the Appalachian Plateau. Hard coal is found in eastern Pennsylvania. West Virginia and Pennsylvania are two of the most important coal-producing states in our country.

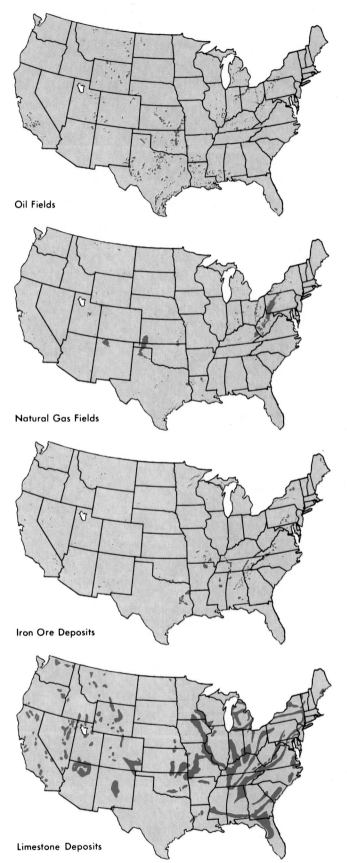

Oil Fields

Natural Gas Fields

Iron Ore Deposits

Limestone Deposits

When the car is loaded, it is driven to a large building near the front of the mine. Here, machines wash and sort the pieces of coal by size. Then the coal is taken by train to a river, a few miles away. There it is put on barges and taken down the river to large steel mills in the Pittsburgh area.

Changes in coal mining

Early in the 1900's, hundreds of thousands of people worked in the coal mines of West Virginia. These people worked long hours for very little pay. Their job was hard and dangerous. Sometimes gases or coal dust would collect in the mines and cause an explosion, or the ceiling of a mine would cave in. When such accidents happened, many miners lost their lives.

As time passed, coal-mining companies found it more and more difficult to make any money. Many Americans had begun to use oil or natural gas, instead of coal, to heat houses and other buildings. Oil also replaced coal as the main fuel for railroad engines. Since there were fewer customers for coal, some of the mines were shut down and thousands of people lost their jobs. Meanwhile, new machines had been invented to do much of the work once done by miners using picks and shovels. As more machinery was used, fewer miners were needed.

The unemployed miners had a hard time finding other work in the coal-mining areas. Many of them left home to find jobs in other parts of our

These maps show deposits of four valuable minerals in the conterminous United States. It is important to remember that these maps show both developed and undeveloped deposits.

country. Those who stayed behind often lived in poverty. They received just enough money from the government for their most important needs.

Today there are signs of growing prosperity in the coal-mining areas. Our country faces a shortage of oil and natural gas to meet its needs for energy. (See pages 102-113.) These fuels can be imported from other countries, but only at a high price. Since the United States has huge deposits of coal, there is growing interest in this mineral as a source of energy. New mines are being opened, and more workers are being hired. Also the miners now earn higher wages and enjoy safer working conditions than they did before.

Petroleum and natural gas

There are deposits of petroleum, or oil, and natural gas in several states of the Northeast. America's first oil well was drilled in northwestern Pennsylvania in 1859. Ways of pumping and refining crude* oil were also developed here. Until 1895, the Northeast produced more oil than any other part of the United States.

Today, other parts of our country are far ahead of the Northeast in petroleum production. However, the oil found in the Northeast is valuable because of its high quality. It is used to make gasoline, kerosene,* and other products.

West Virginia leads the Northeast in the production of natural gas. This resource has many uses. Some of it is carried by pipes to homes where it is used for heating and cooking. Chemicals made from natural gas are used in manufacturing many products, such as medicines and plastics.

Metal ores

There are only a few deposits of metal ores in the Northeast. The main deposits of iron ore in this region are found in the Adirondack Mountains of New York. Zinc ore is mined in New York, New Jersey, Maine, and Pennsylvania. New York is one of our country's leading producers of zinc. This metal is combined with copper to make brass, and it is also used as a coating to prevent rust.

Other minerals

There are large deposits of limestone in several states of the Northeast. This nonmetallic* mineral has many important uses. In the Northeast, large amounts of limestone are used to make steel. This mineral is also used in making cement. Pennsylvania and New York, which have large deposits of limestone, are among our nation's leading producers of cement. Blocks of limestone are used in the construction of buildings.

Several other nonmetallic minerals are also produced in the Northeast. Sand and gravel, which are found in every state of this region, are used mainly as construction materials. Some high-quality sand is used in the manufacture of glass. Vermont produces large quantities of granite and marble. These are used in the construction of buildings. Several states of the Northeast also produce slate.*

Among the other minerals produced in the Northeast are salt and clay. New York produces large amounts of salt. Various types of clay are found throughout the region. These are used in making pottery, china, tile, bricks, and many other products.

Forest Resources

Although the Northeast is our country's most densely populated region, more than half of the land is forested. Large forests are found in nearly every part of this region.

Many different kinds of trees grow in the Northeast. Softwoods, such as spruce and fir, grow mainly in the north. Hardwoods, such as oak, birch, and maple, are found throughout this region. (See map on page 99.) To learn more about the trees in the Northeast, let us visit a tree farm.

A tree farm in Maine

It is a cool fall day, and we are visiting a tree farm in northern Maine. Many acres of the farm are green with fir

Harvesting timber. Forests are an important resource in the Northeast. Large amounts of timber are harvested here every year. Loggers use big power saws to cut down the trees. They also use other tools to lift the heavy logs and to move them from the forests to mills and factories. What tools do you see in this picture? Do you think it would be possible to harvest so much timber without the use of tools like these? Why do you think this? Do you think it would be possible to make forest products such as lumber and newsprint without the use of tools? Give reasons for your answer.

trees. There is also a large grove of brightly colored beech and maple trees. The farmer tells us that the beeches and maples were growing here when he bought the land. However, he planted and raised the fir trees, just as other farmers raise crops such as wheat or oats.

The farmer says that he began raising trees nearly twenty-five years ago. The first fir trees that he planted have just been sold. They will be made into wood pulp.* Through the years, he has sold many of his beech and maple trees to a nearby lumber company.

We ask the farmer if tree farming takes much time and work. He tells us that after the trees are planted, they must be protected against fire and other enemies. Sometimes the trees must be sprayed to prevent damage from insects or disease. The farmer also says he spends long hours pruning* and cutting the trees. However, he does have enough time to raise some livestock to sell.

As it is getting late, we thank the farmer and leave for home.

Forest products

When European settlers first came to the Northeast, they discovered that the vast forests in this region were a valuable resource. They cut down trees and used the lumber to build homes, schools, churches, and ships. Much lumber was exported to other countries.

Today, many products are made from wood. One of the most important forest products of the Northeast is wood pulp. It is used to make newsprint, cardboard boxes, and other paper products. Some of the wood from the Northeast is cut into lumber, which is used to make furniture and to build homes and other buildings.

Maple syrup and maple sugar are also forest products of the Northeast. In late winter, when days become warmer but nights are still cold, the sap begins to flow in sugar maple trees. This sap is collected and made into maple syrup and maple sugar. New York and Vermont lead all of our states in the manufacture of these two products.

Other uses of forests

In addition to providing the raw materials for many products, forests are valuable in other ways. The roots of trees help hold the soil in place, preventing erosion.* Forests also give shelter and food for wildlife.

Forests help in saving water. During a heavy rainfall in open country, water often flows away quickly in ditches and streams. Where there are trees, however, rain must fall through leaves and branches. Therefore, a heavy rainfall reaches the ground more slowly in a forest than it does in open country. This gives the ground time to soak up the water. In addition, snow melts slowly in a forest and is soaked up by

Collecting maple sap in New York. The forests of the Northeast provide raw materials that are used in making a variety of products. In what other ways are forests valuable to the people of the Northeast?

the soil. Much of the rain and melted snow that collects in the ground beneath the forest drains slowly into rivers and lakes, helping to give them a steady supply of water.

Forests are also important to the tourist industry of the Northeast. They provide beautiful scenery for the people of this region and for visitors from other parts of our country. People can hike, camp, or hunt in the Northeast's many state and national forests.

Conserving the forests

In the past, the forests of the Northeast were not used wisely. Trees were cut until much of the land was barren. Soil once protected by trees was carried away by wind and water. Some forests were destroyed by fire. No efforts were made to replace the trees that were lost.

Today, people in the Northeast are trying to conserve forest resources. When forests are cut, new trees are usually planted. Sometimes several large healthy trees, called "seed trees," are left standing. These trees drop their seeds, and new trees begin to grow where others were cut. Better ways of controlling insects and disease are being discovered. Also, much land that is not good for growing food crops is now used for raising trees. For these reasons, forests will be an important natural resource in the Northeast for many years.

Fishing Grounds

The Atlantic coast of the Northeast is an important fishing area. There are several reasons why this is so. One of the world's best fishing grounds lies in the coastal waters that extend northward from Massachusetts. There are also many fish in Chesapeake Bay and other inlets along the Atlantic coast. In addition, the Northeast has fine natural harbors where fishing boats can anchor.

Fishing in the Middle Atlantic states

Fishing is important in several Middle Atlantic states. Boats sailing from ports in New York State bring back large catches of fish from Long Island Sound. Off the Atlantic coast of New York and New Jersey is one of the most important clam-producing areas

Natural Forest Regions

River bottom hardwoods and cypress
Longleaf — loblolly — slash pine
Mangrove or subtropical forest
Oak — hickory
Oak — pine
Oak — chestnut — yellow poplar
Spruce — fir with some hardwoods
Birch — beech — maple — hemlock
White, red, and jack pine

in the United States. Each year, Maryland fishers bring in thousands of tons of oysters. They also harvest other shellfish from Chesapeake Bay.

Large amounts of menhaden* are caught in the coastal waters of the Middle Atlantic states. The oil from menhaden is used in making soap and paint. Menhaden are also ground up and used as fertilizer.

Fishing in New England

Fishing is an important occupation along the Atlantic coast of New England. Massachusetts leads all the states of the Northeast in the value of fish caught. (See graph below.) New Bedford, Gloucester, and Boston are the leading fishing ports in this state. Other important fishing ports are Point Judith, Rhode Island, and Portland, Maine. Some of the fish that are brought to ports in New England are sold fresh in the cities of the Northeast. Others are frozen or canned and sold throughout our country.

Many different kinds of fish are caught off the coast of New England. Whiting, ocean perch, haddock, cod, and menhaden are brought to the ports at Boston and Gloucester. Flounder and scallops are important types of fish brought into the port of New Bedford. Thousands of tons of lobsters and clams are also caught off the coast of New England.

A visit to Gloucester Harbor

We are visiting the busy harbor of Gloucester, Massachusetts. Several fishing boats are entering or leaving the harbor. Others are docked here. Many of the boats

This graph shows the value in dollars of the 1974 fish catch in six northeastern states. Massachusetts leads the Northeast in the value of fish caught, and ranks sixth among all states. Ships from this state bring in huge catches of haddock, ocean perch, and other fish. Each year, Maine fishers catch thousands of tons of lobsters. Maryland fishers take large quantities of oysters from Chesapeake Bay.

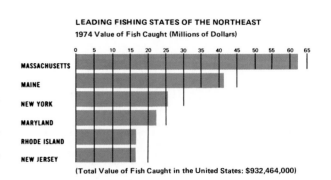

LEADING FISHING STATES OF THE NORTHEAST
1974 Value of Fish Caught (Millions of Dollars)

0 5 10 15 20 25 30 35 40 45 50 55 60 65

MASSACHUSETTS
MAINE
NEW YORK
MARYLAND
RHODE ISLAND
NEW JERSEY

(Total Value of Fish Caught in the United States: $932,464,000)

Maine lobster fishers. The Atlantic coast of the Northeast is an important fishing area. Massachusetts and Maine are the region's leading fishing states. What kinds of fish do Northeast fishers catch?

that we see are trawlers. Some of these boats are as long as one hundred feet and are powered by diesel* engines.

A fisher working on the deck of his trawler invites us to come aboard. He shows us a huge net called an otter trawl. This net is towed along the bottom of the ocean with long cables. Two boards, called otter boards, keep the mouth of the net open so that fish can

swim in. When the net is full, it is pulled into the boat with a machine called a winch.

The fisher tells us that he and his crew travel northward toward Newfoundland to fish for haddock, cod, and ocean perch. As soon as the fish are caught, they are refrigerated. This keeps them fresh until the ship arrives in port.

Energy

The Gasoline Shortage

In 1973, something happened that surprised many people in the United States. There was a shortage of gasoline. Gas stations could no longer get all the gas they needed from the companies that had always supplied them. Some stations had to close down because they did not have any gas to sell. Others stayed open for only a few hours each day. Sometimes drivers had to wait in line for hours to buy gas for their cars.

This was a new experience for most Americans. In the past, there had always been plenty of gasoline. What caused the gasoline shortage?

Where our gasoline comes from

As you discovered earlier, gasoline is made from petroleum, or oil. This dark-colored liquid is found in layers of rock far beneath the ground. To get oil, people drill wells deep into the earth. Then they pump the oil to the surface. The oil is sent to factories called refineries. There it is made into gasoline, fuel oil, and other kinds of fuel. Much of the fuel oil is burned to make electricity. Oil is the most important source of energy in the United States today. (See chart at right.)

A growing need for oil

In the past, the United States produced most of the oil it needed. There were thousands of oil wells in Texas, California, and other parts of our country. As time passed, many of these wells ran out of oil. New deposits of oil were discovered from time to time. However, these were not large enough to take care of all of our country's needs. This was because Americans were using larger amounts of gasoline and other fuels.

Oil from the Arab* nations

To get the oil it needed, the United States began buying oil from other countries. Some of these countries were Saudi Arabia, Iraq, and other Arab

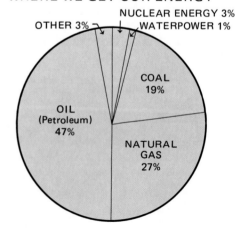

WHERE WE GET OUR ENERGY

OTHER 3%
NUCLEAR ENERGY 3%
WATERPOWER 1%
COAL 19%
OIL (Petroleum) 47%
NATURAL GAS 27%

Traffic in New York City. The many cars, trucks, and buses in our country use huge amounts of gasoline. This fuel is made from petroleum, or oil. Where does our country get the oil it needs?

nations. These nations have the largest deposits of oil in the world.

In 1973, some of the Arab nations were at war with the neighboring country of Israel. They were angry because the United States seemed to be taking Israel's side in this war. In the fall of 1973, the Arab nations stopped selling oil to the United States. This caused problems for the American refineries. They could not get enough oil to make gasoline for all the people who wanted it.

An unsolved problem

The gasoline shortage lasted for several months. Then the Arab nations began selling oil to the United States again. Americans could again buy all the gasoline they wanted. But they had to pay a much higher price than they had paid before.

The gasoline shortage was over for the time being. But the United States still faces a serious problem. The world's supply of oil is growing smaller each day. Scientists say that most of the known oil deposits will be used up within the next forty years. Before this happens, the United States and other countries will have to find new ways of producing the energy they need.

Otherwise, people's lives will be much less comfortable than today.

What Is Energy?

Why is energy so important to people? To answer this question, we need to know what energy is.

Energy is power that can be used to do work. For example, we use energy in the form of heat to cook our meals.

The port of New Orleans in the 1880's. Long ago, people knew only a few ways of getting the energy they needed. They depended mostly on their own muscles or the muscles of animals to do work. Later, they found out how to use other sources of energy. What sources of energy does this picture illustrate?

We also use energy to keep our houses warm. We use other kinds of energy to run cars, boats, trains, and airplanes. Energy is needed to build houses and other buildings. It is needed to plant and harvest the farm crops so we have food. Electric energy is needed to light our homes. It is also needed to run the machines that make all the different kinds of goods we use. We could not live at all without using some form of energy.

Changes in the Use of Energy

Muscle power

Long ago, people knew only a few ways of getting the energy they needed. For thousands of years, they depended largely on their own muscles to do work. They lifted, carried, pushed, and pulled heavy objects. They hunted wild animals with simple weapons. These weapons were made from stone, wood, and bones. People built fires out of wood to keep warm and to cook their food.

Thousands of years ago, people began using animals to help them do work. They rode on the backs of horses and camels. They used donkeys or oxen to pull their plows and wagons. Sometimes they hitched these animals to simple machines. These machines ground grain or did other jobs.

Wind and water

As time passed, two new sources of energy were discovered. These were wind and water. People began to build sailboats. These boats depended on the wind to move them from place to place. Later, windmills were invented. They were used for such tasks as grinding grain and pumping water out of the ground. People also built gristmills* along the banks of rivers. The flowing water turned a large wooden wheel. This provided energy to run machinery for grinding grain.

The steam engine

During the 1700's, the steam engine was developed in Great Britain. A steam engine works in this way: Coal or some other fuel is burned to heat water in a large tank. The water turns to steam and expands. This means it takes up more space. The power of the expanding steam can be used to run machinery. The steam engine was soon being used to run many kinds of factory machines. It was also used to run ships and trains.

The gasoline engine

In the 1800's, another new source of energy was discovered. Scientists found that oil could be used to make kerosene, gasoline, and other kinds of fuel. Soon many people were using kerosene for lighting their houses and cooking food. Then inventors in Europe developed a new kind of engine that ran on gasoline. This engine was lighter than the steam engine. Also, it took up less space. By the end of the 1800's, it was being used to run the world's first automobiles.

Electricity

For years, scientists had been studying the strange force known as electricity. Then inventors developed machines that could produce electric power. They also found ways to use electricity in homes and factories. One of these people was an American named Thomas Edison. In 1879 he invented an electric light bulb that was cheap and easy to make. Later, Edison built our country's first electric power plant. The electricity produced here was used to light nearby houses, stores, and offices. As the years passed, people began using electricity to run many different kinds of machines.

Meeting Our Energy Needs Today

In the United States today, people get energy from several different sources. The most important of these are named on the chart on page 102. They are oil, natural gas, and coal. These three provide about 93 percent of the energy we use. They are called fossil* fuels. They were formed from the remains of plants and animals that lived on the earth millions of years ago.

Fossil fuels

Nearly one half of all the energy we use in the United States today comes from oil. As you have seen, oil is made into gasoline and other kinds of fuel. Some of these are used to run cars, boats, trains, and airplanes. Petroleum is also made into fuel oil. Fuel oil is used mostly to heat houses and to produce electricity.

Natural gas is the second most important source of energy in our country today. Millions of Americans burn natural gas to heat their houses. Many of them also use gas for cooking food and heating water. Factories use natural gas as a fuel in making hundreds of different things.

Coal provides about one fifth of our country's energy needs. It is used mostly as a fuel in power plants that produce electricity. But some coal is also used to heat schools and other buildings.

Waterpower

Another source of energy used in the United States today is waterpower. Dams and power plants have been built on many rushing rivers in our country.

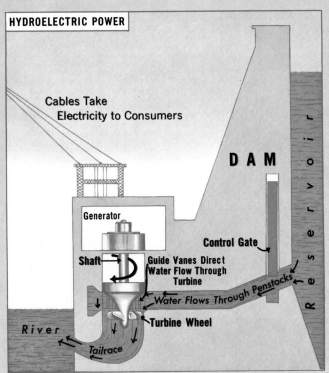

HYDROELECTRIC POWER

Cables Take Electricity to Consumers

D A M

Generator

Shaft

Control Gate

Guide Vanes Direct Water Flow Through Turbine

Water Flows Through Penstocks

Turbine Wheel

River

Tailrace

Reservoir

Most electricity is produced in power plants by large machines called generators.* These generators are usually driven by turbines.* There are two main kinds of turbines. One kind is powered by steam. The other is powered by falling water.

Steam-powered turbines are used in producing almost nine tenths of the electricity generated in the Northeast. To make steam for the turbines, water is heated in large boilers. In the Northeast, coal is the fuel most commonly used to heat the water. Oil or natural gas is used in some places. However, a few plants use nuclear energy.

About one tenth of the Northeast's electricity is produced by generators driven by water turbines. Electric power produced in this way is called hydroelectricity.

The chart on this page shows how waterpower is changed into electrical energy. A dam has been built across a river to hold back the water. This creates a large reservoir.* Turbines are placed at the bottom of the dam. When the control gate is opened, water rushes downward through pipes and turns the turbines. Shafts leading from the turbines turn the generators, which produce electricity.

The power of the moving water is used to run machines that produce large amounts of electricity.

Nuclear energy

During the last few years, people in the United States have begun to use a new source of energy. This is the energy stored in tiny bits of matter called atoms.* When atoms are split or combined in certain ways, huge amounts of energy are given off. This is known as nuclear energy. Today there are a number of nuclear power plants in our country. Here, the energy stored in atoms is used to produce electricity for homes and factories.

Energy and Our Way of Life

Today, most Americans have a better way of life than even the richest people enjoyed in earlier times. This is because we have so many different ways of getting the energy we need. We can produce many more goods and services than people could when they used their muscles for energy.

There is a close connection between people's standard* of living and the amount of energy they use. To see an example of this, look at the chart on page 108. This chart shows that the average person in the United States uses almost twenty times as much energy as the average person in China. At the same time, the average American produces more than twenty-five times as many goods and services each year as the average Chinese.

This helps to explain why the standard of living in our country is one of the highest in the world. We use large amounts of energy to help us meet our needs.

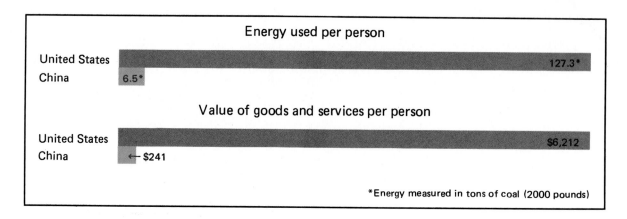

Energy used per person		
United States		127.3*
China	6.5*	

Value of goods and services per person		
United States		$6,212
China	← $241	

*Energy measured in tons of coal (2000 pounds)

Many Americans wonder how long we will be able to enjoy our present way of life. They point out that we are rapidly using up the natural resources that supply most of our energy.

The Energy Problem

As you have discovered, about 93 percent of the energy we use each year comes from the fossil fuels. These are oil, natural gas, and coal. It is becoming harder to find new deposits of oil. Our country is also starting to run out of natural gas. Scientists say that the natural gas we now have will only last for another twenty or thirty years.

As energy fuels become harder to find, they also become more costly. Today, Americans are paying much higher prices for gasoline than they did in the past. They are also paying more for fuel oil and natural gas to heat their houses. This is because much of our electricity is produced by burning fuel oil or natural gas.

Dark houses and empty factories

Unless we can find new ways to meet our need for energy, we will likely face a number of serious problems. For example, factories might have to shut down because they could not get fuel oil or natural gas for heating. Also, they could not get electricity to run their machines. If this happened, thousands of people might be left without jobs. Also, many Americans might have to stop using their cars because gasoline prices were too high. And, there might not be gasoline to buy.

A shortage of fuel might cause power companies to cut off electricity to some of their customers for hours or days at a time. If this happened, lights would go out. People would not be able to use any electrical appliances such as stoves and refrigerators. Blackouts* have already taken place in New York and other cities.

Solving the Energy Problem

What can be done to make sure that our country has enough energy to meet its needs? Let us explore some of the different answers to this question.

Finding more oil and natural gas

Today, people who work for oil companies are trying hard to find new deposits of oil and natural gas. They are going to far-off places to search for them. And they are using new tools that make it easier to find these deposits that lie deep in the earth.

The Alaskan pipeline. A few years ago, a huge deposit of oil was found along the coast of northern Alaska. Oil from this deposit is now being shipped to refineries in other parts of our country.

In some cases, their search has been successful. A huge deposit of oil was discovered a few years ago along the coast of northern Alaska. Oil from this deposit is now being shipped to refineries in other parts of the United States. Scientists believe that other large oil deposits lie under the Atlantic Ocean, near our country's eastern coast. The ocean is not deep there. It would be possible to get the oil.

These new deposits can help to meet our needs for a short time. But they will not solve the energy problem. Sooner or later, we will have to use something other than oil and natural gas.

Coal

The only fossil fuel that we have plenty of today is coal. Some experts believe that there is enough coal in the United States to meet all of our energy needs for the next four hundred years or more. But the use of coal as a fuel leads to certain problems.

First is the problem of removing the coal from the earth. There are two main ways of mining coal. One is to dig tunnels deep under the ground. This is costly. It is often dangerous. The other way is to dig giant holes in the earth with power shovels. This is safer and less costly than underground mining. However, it causes great damage to the land.

Coal has other disadvantages too. In general, it gives off large amounts of smoke when it burns. For this reason, it is a major cause of air pollution. Also, coal cannot be used now to run cars or trucks.

To use coal as our chief energy fuel, these problems must be solved. Scientists are looking for a way to change coal into a new form. They hope to make a kind of fuel that will burn without causing air pollution.

Waterpower

The power of rushing water can be used to make electricity. Waterpower does not cause air pollution, as the burning of fuel does. Also, we won't run out of waterpower as long as rivers flow. But waterpower cannot be used without building large dams and power plants. These are costly. Also, they can be built only in certain places. Water must flow down from a higher level to a lower level. For these reasons, waterpower will never supply more than a small part of our energy needs.

Wind power

For thousands of years, people have been using the wind as a source of energy. The wind is free. It can never be used up. Also, wind power does not cause any pollution. Today, some people are using windmills to produce electricity for farms. But this works only in places where the wind blows strongly for hours at a time.

Solar energy

Every day great amounts of energy come to our earth as sunlight. This is known as solar energy. It does not cause pollution. And it will never run out. If all the solar energy that reaches the earth could be used, it would take care of all of our energy needs for millions of years.

Certain devices are needed to collect the sunlight and change it into heat and electricity. These cost a great deal. They take up a large amount of space.

A solar house. Panels on the roof of this house collect sunlight, or solar energy. This energy is used to provide the house with heat and hot water. Do you think solar energy is an important natural resource? What are some good things about using sunlight as a source of energy? What are some of the drawbacks of this kind of energy?

Also, solar energy cannot be collected at night or when dark clouds hide the sun.

However, many Americans today are interested in making use of solar energy. Thousands of people now use sunlight to heat houses and other buildings. Solar energy is also being used to heat water for homes and business places.

Nuclear energy

As you have discovered, nuclear energy can be used in making electricity. A few years ago, many people believed that nuclear energy would soon be our main source of energy. They thought it would take the place of oil, natural gas, and coal. So far this has not happened.

To understand why, you need to know that there are two main ways of producing nuclear energy. One is by splitting atoms into smaller parts. This is called fission.* The other way is by combining atoms into larger ones. This is known as fusion.*

At the present time, only fission is being used to produce nuclear energy. Fission has a number of disadvantages. First, fission power plants are costly to build. Second, it is difficult to keep them working properly. Also, a mineral called uranium* is needed as a fuel in these plants. Uranium is costly, and new deposits are becoming hard to find.

Many people believe that fission power plants are unsafe. They are afraid that an accident might kill or

Inside a nuclear power plant. Here, nuclear energy is made into electricity. What mineral is used as a fuel in nuclear power plants?

hurt thousands of people. Also, fission makes large amounts of harmful waste matter. These wastes can cause illness or death to people unless they are stored carefully.

Scientists are now working on these problems. They are also trying to find a cheap, practical way of using fusion to produce nuclear energy. This will be much safer than fission. Also it will not leave harmful waste matter. With fusion, water can be used as a fuel instead of uranium. As a result, our supply of fuel would never run out.

Using Energy More Wisely

Someday, we may have all the energy we need. Perhaps we will find ways to produce nuclear energy cheaply and safely. Or we may find practical ways of using solar energy. Until then, we cannot take a chance on running out of oil and other energy fuels. We must be more careful in using the energy we have.

In the past, the United States has always had enough energy. Americans have been more wasteful of energy than people in most other countries.

There are many things that Americans can do to make better use of their energy. For instance, engineers can develop new machines that will run on less electricity. Builders can construct buildings that do not need so much fuel to keep them heated.

How we can do our part

All of us can help to save energy in a number of different ways. For example, we can buy smaller cars. We can drive them more slowly. In this way, we can go farther on every gallon of gasoline. We can also save energy by riding buses or trains instead of driving our own cars. We can make sure that our houses are well insulated to save heat during the winter. We can turn down our furnaces in the wintertime. We can use less air conditioning in the summertime. We can turn out all electric lights that are not being used. And we can save energy in the ways we use stoves and other appliances.

All citizens of the United States must work together to help solve the energy problem. Our way of life in the future will depend on the steps we take to save energy today.

Energy and You

All of us can help to save energy in a number of different ways. For example, we can turn off the TV set when no one is watching it. We can ride a bike instead of asking someone to take us in a car. Prepare to discuss the following questions with the other members of your class.

1. What things do you and your family use that need energy?
2. What are some of the ways you can help to save energy?

To prepare for your discussion, list the things you and your family use that need energy in order to work. Your list might include appliances, such as a refrigerator and a stove. It might also include means of transportation and sports or recreational equipment. Think about the energy each of these things uses. What are some things you and your family could do to save some of this energy?

10 Industry

A Tour Through a Steel Plant

We are driving along a highway in Pennsylvania, about 30 miles (48 km.)† northeast of Philadelphia. In the distance, we see a row of smokestacks and the towers of three giant blast* furnaces. These are part of one of the largest steel plants in the Northeast. To learn how steel is made, we will take a tour of this plant. (See page 116.)

This plant is owned by a large steel company. Before the tour starts, our guide tells us about the plant we are visiting. He says that the plant belongs to the United States Steel Corporation. This is a huge company. It has factories and offices in many parts of our country. Only a company with large amounts of capital* could build a plant like this one. This plant cost about 400 million dollars.

Our guide tells us this company began over seventy years ago. It was started by a group of people in the Northeast and the Midwest.* Several small steel companies were joined to form one larger company. Shares of stock* were bought by the people who started the company. More shares were sold to other people who wanted to invest* their money. These investments helped the company to grow larger and brought profits* to the people who owned stock. Today, about 250,000 people own stock in the United States Steel Corporation. Much of the money needed to start new plants comes from profits. The company may also borrow money from banks or offer more shares of stock for sale.

Thousands of workers

Many workers are needed to make steel. We learn that about 9,000 people work in this plant. Some

† km. means kilometer
*See Glossary

Inside a steel plant. Hot, melted iron is being poured into a furnace. There it will be made into steel. The making of steel is one of the leading industries in the Northeast. What are some important products that are made from this metal?

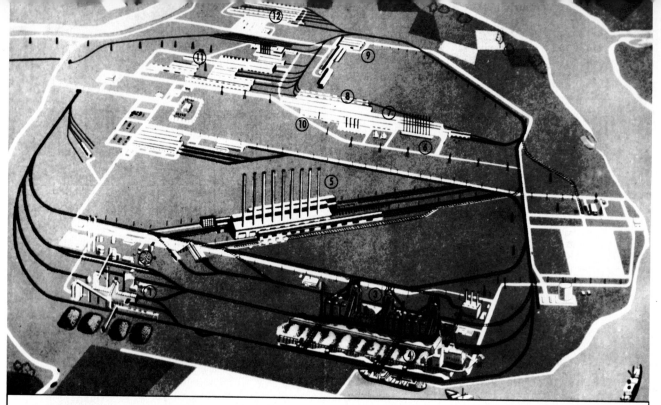

1. Coke Ovens
2. Coal-Chemicals Plant
3. Blast Furnaces
4. Docks and Ore Storage Yard
5. Open-Hearth Building
6. Soaking Pits
7. Slab—Bloom Mill
8. Billet Mill
9. Bar Mill
10. Hot-Strip Mill
11. Sheet and Tin Finishing Mill
12. Pipe Mill

A Steel Plant

Our tour of the steel plant pictured above will show us how three important raw* materials are used in making steel. These raw materials are iron ore, coal, and limestone.

We begin our tour at the coke ovens (1). Here, coal is unloaded from trains and heated in airtight ovens. The heat drives gases from the coal, leaving a hard, gray substance called coke. This is a fuel that burns with a hot flame. Coke is needed in the making of iron and steel. The gases given off when the coal is heated are piped to the coal-chemicals plant (2), where they are made into valuable chemicals.* A conveyor* belt more than a mile long carries the coke from the ovens to the blast* furnaces (3).

Now we visit the docks along the Delaware River (4). Here we watch a ship unloading reddish brown iron ore. Large amounts of iron ore, coke, and limestone are fed into the three giant blast furnaces nearby. Powerful machines then blow a blast of very hot air into each furnace. This air makes the coke burn with a very high heat that melts the iron ore. The limestone mixes with waste materials in the ore to form slag,* which rises to the top. Melted iron containing carbon and other substances settles at the bottom of the furnace. The iron is now ready to be made into steel.

Our next stop is the open-hearth building (5), where steel is made. Here we watch iron ore, limestone, and steel scrap* being loaded into a huge open-hearth furnace. These materials are heated until they melt. Then melted iron is brought from the blast furnace and added to the mixture. Small amounts of special metals may also be added. The mixture is cooked for several hours to burn out some of the carbon and other unwanted materials from the iron. Finally, melted steel is drained from the furnace and poured into molds.* As the steel cools, it hardens into huge blocks called ingots. The molds are removed and the ingots are taken to the soaking pits (6). Here they are reheated until they are an even temperature throughout.

The steel now goes to the mills (7-12). At the mills it will be formed into different shapes that can be used in making steel products. Some of the steel is rolled into thin sheets or strips. Some is formed into other shapes. In one of the mills, sheets and strips of steel are used in making tinplate.* Steel pipes and tubes are made in another mill.

*See Glossary

of these workers run the machines. Others are managers or office workers. Most of them live in towns or cities within 20 miles (32 km.) of the plant.

Raw* materials for steelmaking

We ask where this steel plant gets the iron ore and other raw materials it needs. Our guide says large amounts of iron ore are imported* from other countries. The cheapest way to bring iron ore a long way is by water. Our guide explains that the plant is on the Delaware River. This river empties into Delaware Bay, an arm of the Atlantic Ocean. Ships bringing iron ore from other countries can travel up the river to the plant.

This steel plant is also in a good place for getting the other raw materials it needs. Coal is brought by train from mines in western Pennsylvania and West Virginia. Trucks bring limestone from central Pennsylvania.

Electricity runs the machinery

As we tour the plant, we see that many kinds of machinery are needed for making steel. These machines are run by electric* power. Our guide says the plant has its own powerhouse. There, gas from the blast furnaces and coke* ovens is burned to heat water. The water turns to steam. The steam is used to run generators* that produce electricity for the steel plant. About half of the electricity this plant needs comes from the powerhouse. The rest is bought from a company that supplies power to homes, stores, and factories.

The Delaware River supplies water

Large amounts of water are needed in making steel. Our guide says this plant uses about 250 million gallons of Delaware River water each day. After the water has been used, it is treated to purify* it. Then it is returned to the river.

Many customers

A factory cannot do business without customers to buy its products. In other words, every factory must have a market. This steel plant is in a very good place. It lies between the two largest cities in the Northeast, New York and Philadelphia. There are many factories in this area. Some of them use large amounts of steel in making their products. For example, automobile plants use sheets of steel in making cars. Other plants use steel in making tools. Steel is also used in making electrical appliances such as washing machines.

After the steel has been made, it must be delivered to the people who buy it. This steel plant is near several very good highways and railroad lines. Most of the steel made here is shipped to customers by train or truck.

A Great Manufacturing Region

The plant we just visited is only one of many factories in the Northeast. There are more than 100,000 factories here. They make many kinds of products, from nails and buttons to airplanes and ocean liners. The total value of goods made each year in the Northeast is more than 100 billion dollars. No other part of our country except the Midwest has so much industry.

What industries need

Our tour of the steel plant showed us a factory needs many things. First, capital is needed to start the factory and to keep it going. Skilled people are needed to run machines and work in the factory offices. People are also needed to manage these offices. The factory needs raw materials. It must also have power to run its machinery. Trucks, trains, and other kinds of transportation are needed to bring raw materials to the factory. They are also needed to ship goods to customers. Finally, every factory must have a market for its goods.

The Northeast has most of the things factories need. Some things it does not have. But these can easily be gotten from other regions of the United States or other countries. Let us learn more about why the Northeast has so much industry.

Early history

The history of the Northeast helps explain why it has so much industry today. The first factories in our country were started in the Northeast. Therefore, the people here have long known how to manufacture goods. Also people in other regions are used to buying goods from factories in the Northeast.

All through its history, the Northeast has been the home of skillful people. Some of these people developed new products or new ways of making things. Inventions such as the telephone and the electric light were first tried out in the Northeast. They led to the growth of several new industries in this region.

The capital industries need

The Northeast has long been the home of people who are willing to invest money in new industries. Today it still has the capital industries need. In this region are many banks that lend money to businesses that want to build new factories. Here, too, are large stock exchanges, where people can buy and sell shares in many different companies.

Many workers

The Northeast has many industrial workers, for more than 56 million people live here. Many of these people have the skills needed to run complicated* machinery. Others make beautiful things by hand. New England is noted for its skillful craft workers. The

A worker in a factory in Buffalo. What are some of the things that factories need besides workers? Which of these things does the Northeast have? Which of these does the Northeast lack?

Northeast also has many office workers and managers.

To make good products, workers and managers must be well trained. There are many fine schools in the Northeast that train people for jobs in industry.

Raw materials

The Northeast has a number of raw materials that factories need. The most important of these is coal. Other minerals here include limestone, natural gas, and salt. There are large forests that supply wood for certain industries. Raw materials also come from farms and fishing grounds in the Northeast.

At the same time, the Northeast does not have many raw materials it needs. For example, it does not produce nearly enough oil for its refineries.* It also has little iron ore, bauxite, and other metal ores. Many farm products cannot be raised in the Northeast as the land and climate are not suitable.

Being without these raw materials has not kept industry from growing in the Northeast, however. Industries can get raw materials from other parts of the United States or from other countries. Also, the Northeast has made good use of its resources. New England, for instance, has few mineral resources. But it has many skilled workers. Therefore, many factories in New England make products that need skilled workers but few raw materials. Among these products are clocks, machine tools, and electronic* products.

Well supplied with power

Nearly all machines in northeastern factories are run by electric power. Most of this power comes from steam plants. But some power comes from

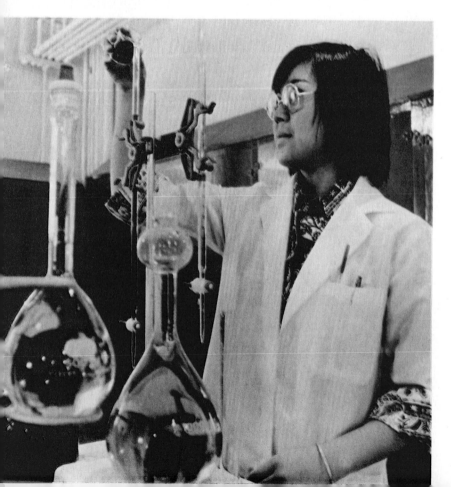

A chemist for a large oil company in the Northeast. The Northeast does not have large deposits of petroleum, or crude oil. But there are many oil refineries in this region. Much of the oil used in these refineries is shipped here from other parts of the United States or from other countries. Where are some of the Northeast's oil refineries located?

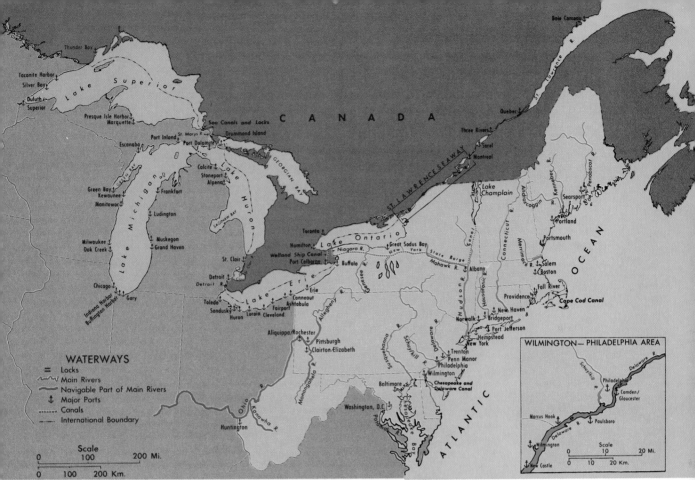

Ports and waterways have helped the Northeast become an important manufacturing region. A number of cities along the Atlantic coast have fine deep-water harbors. Ships from all over the world bring goods of many kinds to these harbors. Ships also carry goods from these harbors to many faraway ports.

Inland waterways are also important in the Northeast. One of these is the Great Lakes–St. Lawrence Waterway.* It connects lake ports in the Northeast, the Midwest, and Canada. It also connects these ports with the Atlantic Ocean. The Ohio River connects the Northeast with parts of the South and the Midwest.

hydroelectric* plants. (See page 107.) Coal from Pennsylvania and West Virginia is used in many steam power plants. There are hydroelectric plants along several rivers in the Northeast.

Industry got an early start in New England. This was partly because of the many small streams here to provide waterpower. In time, New England's factories needed more power than these streams could give. Today, most factories here use electricity made in steam power plants. Coal for these plants is brought by train and ship from Pennsylvania and West Virginia.

Good transportation

The Northeast is served by many good roads, railroads, and airways. The main waterways are also good transportation routes. (See map below.) Because this region is on the Atlantic Ocean, raw materials can be shipped here from all parts of the world. Factories in the Northeast can send their products by ship to other countries.

A huge market

A business person choosing a place for a new factory might decide to build it in the Northeast. For one reason,

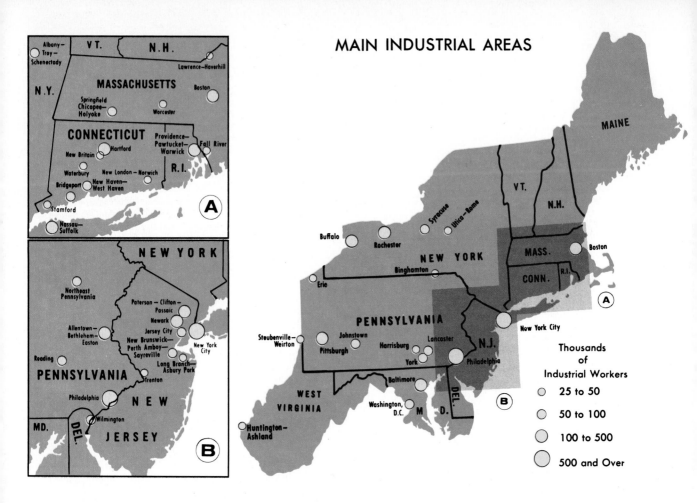

MAIN INDUSTRIAL AREAS

Thousands of Industrial Workers

- 25 to 50
- 50 to 100
- 100 to 500
- 500 and Over

the millions of people here buy many manufactured products. Also, many factories in the Northeast use goods other factories make. This large market helps explain why there is so much industry in the Northeast today.

Main industrial areas

All parts of the Northeast do not have factories. There are few industries in some parts, such as the Adirondack Mountains and northern New England. Other parts have many industries.

The three maps above show the main industrial areas of the Northeast. You can see that many of these areas are along the Atlantic coast, from New Hampshire to Washington, D.C. This is a densely populated area, with many large cities. (See map on page 50.)

Another great manufacturing belt crosses the central part of New York State. It goes from Albany to Buffalo. This area lies along one of the main transportation routes through the Appalachian Highlands. Cities that have grown up here are served by roads, railroads, and the New York State Barge Canal. (See map on page 121.)

There are also many factories in western Pennsylvania and West Virginia. This area is rich in coal, natural gas, and other minerals used in industry.

Products of Industry

Iron and steel

The manufacture of iron and steel is one of the Northeast's most important industries. There are more than three hundred steel plants here. Plants in

Pennsylvania alone make nearly one fourth of our country's steel.

The greatest steelmaking area in the Northeast is around Pittsburgh. Steel plants here can get coal and limestone from large deposits nearby. Iron ore is brought from mines near Lake Superior. Factories in the cities of the Northeast and Midwest buy much of Pittsburgh's steel. The Pittsburgh area is well served by railroads, waterways, and other means of transportation.

Not all of the steel plants in the Northeast are in the Pittsburgh area. There are some plants in eastern Pennsylvania. Also, there are large plants near Buffalo and Baltimore. There are no large steel plants in New England, however. This area does not have enough coal and iron ore for making steel. Factories here must buy most of their steel from plants in other parts of the Northeast.

Machinery

Factories in the Northeast use steel and other metals to make thousands of useful things. More people work in the manufacture of machinery than in any other industry in the Northeast. Electrical machinery such as motors and generators are important products of this region. Air conditioners, washing machines, and other household appliances are also made here.

Many factories in the Northeast make parts for electronic products such as radios and television sets. There

Workers in a television factory. Many of the manufacturing plants in the Northeast make parts for electronic* products. Among these products are radios, television sets, and computers.

are also factories that make different kinds of telephone equipment.

Many other kinds of machinery are also made in the Northeast. Among these are typewriters and other kinds of office equipment. An important industry in New England is the manufacture of machine tools. These are machines that cut, grind, and shape metal. Other types of factory machinery are also made in the Northeast. For example, textile* machinery is made in New England. Printing machinery is made in the New York City area.

Transportation equipment

Some of the metal produced in the Northeast is used in making transportation equipment. Factories in Connecticut, Maryland, and other states make airplanes or airplane parts. There are automobile plants in New Jersey and Delaware. Factories in Pennsylvania, New York, and New Jersey make railroad cars. Shipbuilding has been carried on in the Northeast since colonial days. Today there are large shipyards near Boston, New York, Philadelphia, and Baltimore. They build all kinds of ships, from tugboats to huge naval and passenger ships. Nuclear* submarines and helicopters are made in Connecticut.

Other metal products

Factories in the Northeast make many other products from metal. Steel sections used in building bridges are made in Pennsylvania. Many northeastern factories make nails, locks, and other hardware. Connecticut is noted for products made from copper and brass. Here, too, are factories that make ball and roller bearings* for industry.

Petroleum products

In the Northeast, there are many refineries that make gasoline, fuel oil, and other products from petroleum. Although these plants do not use many workers, the goods they make are very important. There are several huge refineries along the Atlantic coast, near Philadelphia and other cities. They use petroleum shipped in from other states and other countries. There are some small refineries near oil fields in western Pennsylvania and New York.

Chemicals* and chemical products

The chemical industry is another important manufacturing industry in the Northeast. Many plants here make basic chemicals, such as ammonia, sulfuric acid, and chlorine. Basic chemicals are used in making many different products. These include plastics, synthetic* fibers, soap, medicines, paint, and fertilizer.

Chemical plants in the Northeast are usually built near sources of raw materials or power. Many of these plants are around New York City or along the Delaware River. Some of these chemical plants use products from nearby oil refineries to make chemical products. In West Virginia there are plants that use coal, natural gas, and other minerals found nearby. Some chemical plants that need large amounts of electricity are around Buffalo. They get hydroelectric power from Niagara Falls. Some chemical plants in the Northeast also use raw materials that come from other countries.

Textiles, clothing, and shoes

In 1920, textile manufacturing was the most important industry in New

A Connecticut factory that makes products out of brass. Brass is a metal made of copper and zinc. It is used to make hardware, such as screws. Some musical instruments are also made of brass.

England. Then, in the 1920's and 1930's, many New England textile plants had to close. They could not make textiles as cheaply as mills in the South. Even today, however, textile manufacturing is important in New England and other parts of the Northeast. Some textile mills spin natural or synthetic fibers into yarn. Others use yarn to make cloth. There are also factories that use textiles to make such things as sheets, blankets, tablecloths, and clothing.

Much of the clothing worn by people in the United States is made in the Northeast. New York City is the center of our country's clothing industry. Factories here make dresses, slacks, shirts, coats, and many other kinds of clothes. Clothing is also made in Philadelphia and other cities.

Making shoes is another important industry in the Northeast. Boston and New York are among the leading shoe-manufacturing cities in our country. There are also many shoe factories in the smaller cities and towns of New England. Many animal skins used in making shoe leather come by ship from Argentina and other countries.

Food

Food processing* is also a leading industry in the Northeast. The farms and fishing grounds of the Northeast provide many raw materials for this industry. There are canneries and freezing plants in New Jersey, Maryland, and other states. They process fruits and vegetables from nearby farms. Cattle raised on West Virginia and Pennsylvania farms are processed in meat-packing plants. Other factories process chickens raised on nearby farms or seafood caught by northeastern fishers.

Division of Labor

See Great Ideas

Inspecting shirts in a New Jersey factory. Much of the clothing worn by people in the United States is made in the Northeast. Some factories spin wool, cotton, or synthetic fibers into yarn. Other factories weave the yarn into cloth. Still other factories use cloth to make dresses, shirts, and many other kinds of clothing. Do you think it helps to meet people's need for clothing by dividing work in this way? Explain your answer. What do you think would happen if each person in our country tried to make all of his or her own clothing?

Dairy farms in the Northeast send milk to creameries, cheese factories, and ice cream plants.

Some of the factories in the Northeast use farm products from outside this region. There are large sugar refineries in New York, Baltimore, and other seaports. They process raw* sugar that comes by ship from the West Indies. The city of Buffalo is noted for its breakfast-food plants and flour mills. These plants use grain that is shipped on the Great Lakes from farming areas in the Midwest and Great Plains.* Bakeries in many northeastern cities use flour from Buffalo in making bread, cakes, and other products.

An Important Trading Region

Trade is another important way of earning a living in the Northeast. More people here are employed in trade than in any other kind of work except manufacturing. Some people have jobs in the importing and exporting* businesses. Others work in department stores or small shops.

Trade with other countries

Much of the trade between the United States and other countries is carried on by businesses in the Northeast. Many goods made in other parts of the world come by ship to ports in the Northeast. Many goods are also exported from this region to other parts of the world.

Trade with other regions

The Northeast also carries on much trade with other parts of the United States. For example, fresh fruits and vegetables grown in California and Florida are shipped to the Northeast.

A ship docked in New York Harbor. The Northeast has some of our country's largest seaports. They help make this part of our country an important trading region.

Exchange

See Great Ideas

A drugstore in the Northeast. There are many stores in the Northeast that sell goods directly to people. This is called retail trade. Most people get nearly all the goods they need through retail trade. What do people give in exchange for the things they buy? What are some of the things you and your family buy through retail trade? Would you be able to obtain these things without the great idea of exchange? Give reasons for your answer.

This region, in turn, ships many goods to other parts of our country.

Retail* trade

The Northeast has many stores that sell goods directly to the people who use them. Most of this kind of trade is in the Northeast's large cities. Besides large department stores, these cities have many smaller stores that sell unusual things. People come from hundreds of miles away to shop in the great cities of the Northeast. Here they find many goods they cannot buy in their own cities or towns.

A Problem To Solve

The Northeast is one of the most important industrial regions of the United States and also of the world. Why is this true? In forming hypotheses* to solve this problem, you need to know how the growth of industry in the Northeast has been affected by:

a. its location
b. its history
c. the raw materials available here
d. the markets for manufactured goods
e. transportation routes
f. the sources of power available
g. the skills of the people

Information in other chapters of this book will be helpful in solving this problem.

See Skills Manual, "Thinking and Solving Problems"

Index

Explanation of abbreviations used in this Index: *p* — picture   *m* — map

---

PRONUNCIATION KEY: hat, āge, cãre, fär; let, ēqual, tėrm; it, īce; hot, ōpen, ôrder; oil, out; cup, pùt, rüle, ūse; child; long; thin; ᴛʜen; zh, measure; ə represents a in about, e in taken, i in pencil, o in lemon, u in circus.

PRONUNCIATION KEY: hat, āge, cãre, fär; let, ēqual, tėrm; it, īce; hot, ōpen, ôrder; oil, out; cup, pút, rüle, ūse; child; long; thin; ᴛHen; zh, measure; ə represents a in about, e in taken, i in pencil, o in lemon, u in circus.

Acknowledgments

Grateful acknowledgment is made to the following for permission to use the illustrations found in this book:

A. Devaney, Inc.: Pages 92-93
Alpha Photo Associates, Inc.: Pages 28-29; page 112 by J. Zimmerman
Bethlehem Steel: Pages 114-115
Black Star: Pages 60-61 by Dennis Brack
Cyr Color Photo Agency: Page 98
De Wys, Inc.: Pages 46, 70, and 126
Frederic Lewis: Page 33 by Alon Reininger
Freelance Photographers Guild: Pages 36-37 and 102-103; pages 40-41 by Ward Allan Howe; page 58 by Werner Stoy
Gene Ahrens: Pages 12-13 and 22-23
Glass Image: Pages 38-39 by J. Glab
Grant Heilman: Pages 78-79, 80-81, 82, 84, and 86
Grumman Energy Systems: Page 111
H. Armstrong Roberts: Pages 44, 64, 68, 88-89, 96-97, and 123
Hartford Chamber of Commerce: Page 15
Historical Pictures Service: Pages 42-43
James H. Pickerell: Page 77
Joan Kramer and Associates: Pages 26-27
Killington Ski Resort: Pages 2-3
Knox College Library: Pages 104-105

New York State Department of Commerce: Pages 18-19
Pennsylvania Bureau of Travel Development: Page 57
Philadelphia Convention and Visitors Bureau: Pages 10-11
Photo Researchers, Inc.: Pages 72-73; page 128 by Van Bucher
Photo Trends: Pages 24-25
Rapho Guillumette Pictures: Page 127 by Jan Lukas
Sanford Associates: Pages 100-101
Shostal Associates, Inc.: Pages 16-17, 20-21, 45, 48-49, 52-53, 54, 90-91, and 118-119
Sohio: Page 109
Texaco: Page 120 by J. Motiekaitis
The Bettmann Archive: Page 47
The National Gallery of Art, Washington, D.C.: Page 74, painting by George Inness
The White House: Page 63
United States Industrials Chemical Co.: Page 125
Wide World Photos: Page 76 (all)
Williams: Page 35
Zentrale Farbbild Agentur: Page 1 by Kurt Goebel

Grateful acknowledgment is made to Scott, Foresman and Company for the pronunciation system used in this book, which is taken from the Thorndike-Barnhart Dictionary Series. Grateful acknowledgment is made to the following for permission to use cartographic data in this book: Creative Arts: Pages 30 and 31; Base maps courtesy of the Nystrom Raised Relief Map Company, Chicago 60618: Page 14; Rand McNally & Company: Pages 6 and 8-9; United States Department of Commerce: Bureau of the Census: Pages 41 and 85.

States of the Northeast

Ships in the harbor of New York City (left)
The rocky coast of Maine (below)

Connecticut

Connecticut is our third smallest state. It lies mainly in the highlands of New England. There are only two small lowlands in the state. One borders Long Island Sound. The other is the valley of the Connecticut River.

The highlands. Rolling hills and low mountains make up more than three fourths of Connecticut. Forests cover many parts of these highlands. The soil here is mostly stony. It is not well suited to growing crops. But there are many poultry and dairy farms in the highlands. There are also a number of busy manufacturing cities, such as Waterbury and Danbury.

Connecticut is bordered by Long Island Sound, a narrow arm of the Atlantic Ocean. Along the coast of this state are a number of fine harbors.

Facts About Connecticut		
	Number or Value	Rank
Area (square miles)	5,009	48
(square kilometers)	12,973	
Population	3,108,000	24
Capital — Hartford		
Admission Date: January 9, 1788		5
Colleges and Universities	46	21
Farm Products	$ 230,959,000	44
Dairy products	66,660,000	37
Poultry and eggs	61,585,000	27
Greenhouse and nursery	42,331,000	11
Fish	$ 2,812,000	24
Timber Harvested (cubic feet)	7,435,000	46
Minerals	$ 35,362,000	47
Stone	21,134,000	33
Sand and gravel	11,272,000	37
Feldspar	not available	
Manufactures*	$6,956,000,000	16
Transportation equipment	1,249,600,000	9
Nonelectrical machinery	929,200,000	14
Fabricated metal products	920,700,000	11

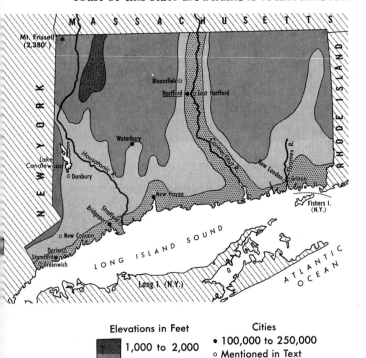

Elevations in Feet
1,000 to 2,000
500 to 1,000
100 to 500
0 to 100
▲ Mountain Peak

Cities
● 100,000 to 250,000
○ Mentioned in Text
Capital Is Underlined

Scale of Miles
0   10   20

More than one thousand lakes and ponds dot the highlands of Connecticut. Most of these were formed by glaciers* long ago. In the summer, people come to these lakes for swimming, boating, and fishing. Some lakes store water for nearby cities and towns.

The lowlands. Along the coast of Connecticut are many bays and river mouths. These provide good harbors for ships. Port cities such as New Haven, Bridgeport, and New London have grown up here. Broad, sandy beaches stretch for miles along the shores of Long Island Sound. They are popular with summer vacationers.

The fertile Connecticut Valley is an important farming and manufacturing area. Farmers here grow tobacco, vegetables, and other crops. In this valley is Hartford, the capital and largest city of Connecticut.

*See Glossary

Delaware

Delaware is smaller than any other state in our country except Rhode Island. It is located mainly in the northeastern part of the Delmarva Peninsula.* On the east, it is bordered by the Delaware River, Delaware Bay, and the Atlantic Ocean.

Nearly all of Delaware lies in the Coastal Plain region of our country. The northernmost tip of the state is in the Piedmont Plateau.

The Coastal Plain. In Delaware, the Coastal Plain is generally low and flat. Hardly any point rises more than sixty feet above sea level. Low marshes and sandy beaches extend along much of Delaware's coast. Along the southern border of the state is a large freshwater marsh called Great Pocomoke Swamp.

The sandy soil of the Coastal Plain in Delaware is good for growing many kinds of crops. If you were to visit this

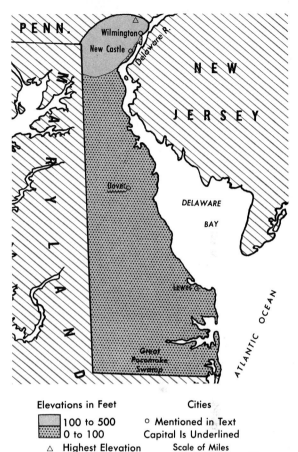

Elevations in Feet
- 100 to 500
- 0 to 100
- △ Highest Elevation (440')

Cities
- ○ Mentioned in Text
- Capital Is Underlined

Scale of Miles
0   15   30

Delaware is located on the Delmarva Peninsula. This state is the second smallest in our country. It is made up mostly of lowlands.

part of the state in the summer, you would see fields of vegetables, soybeans, and other crops. There are also many poultry farms in this area.

The Piedmont Plateau. Rolling hills and fertile valleys make up the Piedmont Plateau section of Delaware. Fine herds of dairy cattle graze on hillside pastures here. The city of Wilmington lies along the Fall Line, which separates the Piedmont from the Coastal Plain. More than two thirds of Delaware's people live in or near Wilmington.

*See Glossary

Facts About Delaware		
	Number or Value	Rank
Area (square miles)	2,057	49
(square kilometers)	5,327	
Population	582,000	47
Capital — Dover		
Admission Date: December 7, 1787		1
Colleges and Universities	7	42
Farm Products	$ 281,562,000	42
Poultry and eggs	157,739,000	15
Corn	38,485,000	26
Soybeans	25,901,000	25
Fish	$ 1,728,000	26
Timber Harvested (cubic feet)	11,808,000	43
Minerals	$ 3,793,000 (Incomplete)	50
Sand and gravel	3,783,000	48
Magnesium compounds	not available	
Clays	8,000	42
Manufactures*	$ 1,308,500,000	38
Chemicals and allied products	297,200,000	26
Food and kindred products	216,000,000	34
Rubber and plastics products	119,200,000	29

District of Columbia

The District of Columbia is a small section of our country that is not part of any state. This area is ten miles long and about seven miles wide. It lies along the Potomac River, between Maryland and Virginia. (See the small inset map below.)

Many years ago, the United States Congress set apart the District of Columbia to be the home of our federal* government. For this reason, the District of Columbia is called a federal district.

The city of Washington, our national capital, has the same boundaries as the District of Columbia. More than 700,000 people live in Washington, D. C. Another 2,300,000 people live in nearby communities in Maryland and Virginia. The large map below shows some of the main places of interest in the Washington area.

PLACES OF INTEREST

1. The Pentagon
2. Senate Office Buildings
3. Supreme Court
4. Library of Congress
5. Capitol
6. House of Representatives Office Buildings
7. White House
8. Department of State
9. John F. Kennedy Center for the Performing Arts
10. Department of the Interior
11. Department of the Treasury
12. Department of Commerce
13. Department of Labor
14. United States Postal Service
15. Internal Revenue Service
16. Department of Justice
17. National Archives
18. Department of Agriculture
19. Department of Health, Education, and Welfare
20. National Gallery of Art
21. National Museum of Natural History
22. National Museum of History and Technology
23. Smithsonian Building (Administration Offices)
24. Washington Monument
25. Jefferson Memorial
26. Lincoln Memorial
27. Grave of President Kennedy
28. Tomb of the Unknowns
29. Department of Transportation
30. Department of Housing and Urban Development

Parks and Cemeteries   Railroads

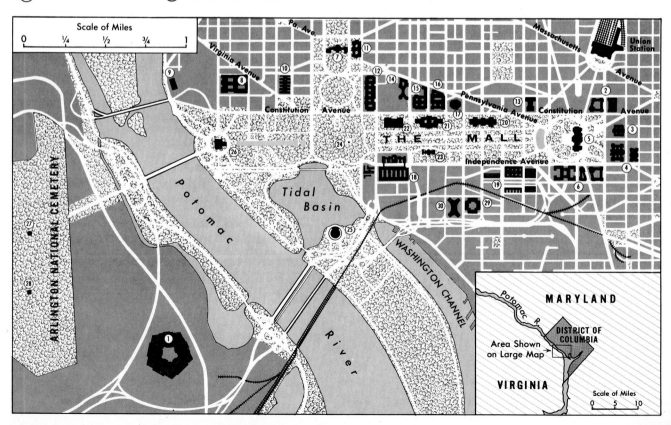

STATE BIRD: Chickadee
STATE FLOWER: White pine cone and tassel
STATE TREE: Eastern white pine

Maine

Facts About Maine		
	Number or Value	Rank
Area (square miles)	33,215	39
(square kilometers)	86,024	
Population	1,085,000	38
Capital — Augusta		
Admission Date: March 15, 1820		23
Colleges and Universities	18	34
Farm Products	$ 443,068,000	37
Poultry and eggs	191,871,000	11
Vegetables	144,694,000	10
Dairy products	67,397,000	36
Fish	$ 41,410,000	8
Timber Harvested (cubic feet)	407,646,000	10
Minerals	$ 36,348,000	45
Cement	not available	
Sand and gravel	10,673,000	38
Zinc	7,485,000	11
Manufactures*	$1,396,600,000	37
Paper and allied products	358,500,000	15
Leather and leather products	194,700,000	5
Food and kindred products	165,200,000	37

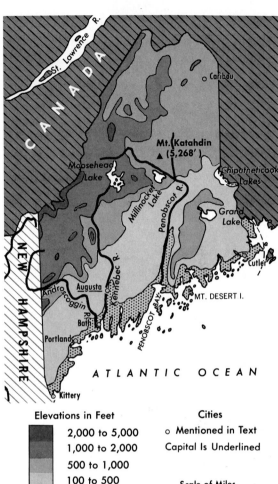

Maine is located in the northeastern corner of our country. Most of the state is hilly or mountainous. A narrow lowland borders the coast.

Maine lies on the Atlantic coast, in the northeastern corner of the United States. Most of the state is in the highlands of New England. A narrow lowland extends along the coast.

The highlands. Mountains, hills, and plateaus make up more than three fourths of the land in Maine. Several mountain peaks rise more than four thousand feet above sea level. Most of the highlands are thickly wooded. More than one thousand sparkling lakes are found here. These lakes were formed by glaciers* long ago. They attract thousands of vacationers each summer.

Most of the land in the highlands is too stony to make good farmland. But there is one fertile farming area. It is in Aroostook County, in the northeastern part of the state. This is one of the most important potato-growing areas in our country.

The coastal lowland. In Maine, the coastal lowland is mostly a level or gently rolling plain. But steep hills rise from the seacoast in some places. In the waters off the coast are more than one thousand islands.

Maine's coastal lowland is famous for its beauty. Many small fishing villages lie along sheltered bays in this area. Most of Maine's people live in the coastal lowland.

*See Glossary

Maryland

STATE BIRD: Baltimore oriole
STATE FLOWER: Black-eyed Susan
STATE TREE: White oak

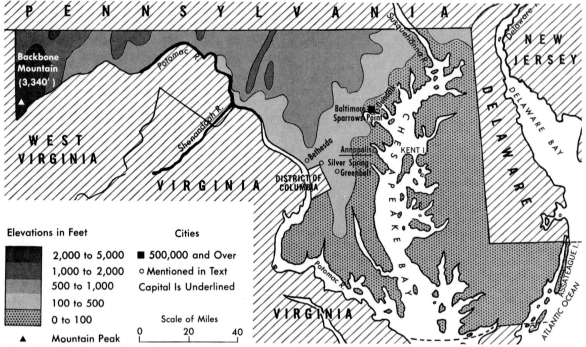

Elevations in Feet

■	2,000 to 5,000
	1,000 to 2,000
	500 to 1,000
	100 to 500
	0 to 100
▲	Mountain Peak

Cities

■ 500,000 and Over
○ Mentioned in Text
Capital Is Underlined

Scale of Miles
0   20   40

Maryland is located in the southern part of the Northeast. The eastern half of the state lies in the Coastal Plain region of our country. The rest of Maryland is in the Appalachian Highlands.

Maryland lies in two of our country's main regions. The eastern half of the state is in the Coastal Plain. The rest of the state is in the Appalachian Highlands.

The Coastal Plain. In Maryland, the Coastal Plain is divided into two parts by a long arm of the Atlantic Ocean called Chesapeake Bay. The area that lies east of the bay is called the Eastern Shore. The land here is low, flat, and generally fertile. West of the bay is the Western Shore. The land here is slightly higher in elevation. In the northern part of this area are many cities and towns.

The Appalachian Highlands. Four sections of the Appalachian Highlands region extend through Maryland. These are the Piedmont Plateau, the Blue Ridge, the Appalachian Ridges and Valleys, and the Appalachian Plateau. In the Piedmont Plateau and in the Appalachian Ridges and Valleys sections, there are fertile farming areas.

Facts About Maryland		
	Number or Value	**Rank**
Area　(square miles)	10,577	42
(square kilometers)	27,393	
Population	4,139,000	18
Capital — Annapolis		
Admission Date:		
April 28, 1788		7
Colleges and Universities	47	20
Farm Products	$ 683,363,000	36
Poultry and eggs	203,472,000	10
Dairy products	156,503,000	20
Corn	108,310,000	16
Fish	$　22,379,000	12
Timber Harvested (cubic feet)	59,435,000	29
Minerals	$ 172,880,000	33
Coal	48,630,000	13
Stone	47,630,000	19
Cement	not available	
Sand and gravel	29,386,000	19
Manufactures*	$4,686,400,000	24
Food and kindred products	683,700,000	18
Primary metals industries	626,000,000	10
Electrical equipment and		
supplies	508,900,000	19

*See Glossary

Massachusetts

Massachusetts extends across New England from the Atlantic Ocean to New York State. A coastal lowland makes up the eastern third of the state. The state's only other lowland area is the Connecticut River valley.

The highlands. The highlands west of the Connecticut Valley make up the highest part of Massachusetts. East of the valley, the highlands are lower. The land here slopes gradually downward to the coastal lowland.

The lowlands. The coastal lowland of Massachusetts is cut by many bays and inlets. Boston and several other manufacturing cities are located here. The broad, flat Connecticut Valley contains the most fertile farmland in Massachusetts.

Facts About Massachusetts	Number or Value	Rank
Area (square miles)	8,257	45
(square kilometers)	21,385	
Population	5,782,000	10
Capital — Boston		
Admission Date: February 6, 1788		6
Colleges and Universities	118	6
Farm Products	$ 214,723,000	45
Dairy products	65,882,000	38
Greenhouse and nursery	38,392,000	14
Poultry and eggs	30,446,000	36
Fish	$ 62,290,000	6
Timber Harvested (cubic feet)	25,786,000	38
Minerals	$ 62,109,000	43
Stone	30,103,000	25
Sand and gravel	26,565,000	22
Lime	4,972,000	13
Manufactures*	$10,721,500,000	11
Nonelectrical machinery	1,740,300,000	8
Electrical equipment and supplies	1,315,800,000	8
Instruments and related products	874,400,000	3

*See Glossary

Massachusetts extends across the middle of New England. The eastern third of Massachusetts and the Connecticut River valley are lowland areas. The rest of the state is made up of highlands.

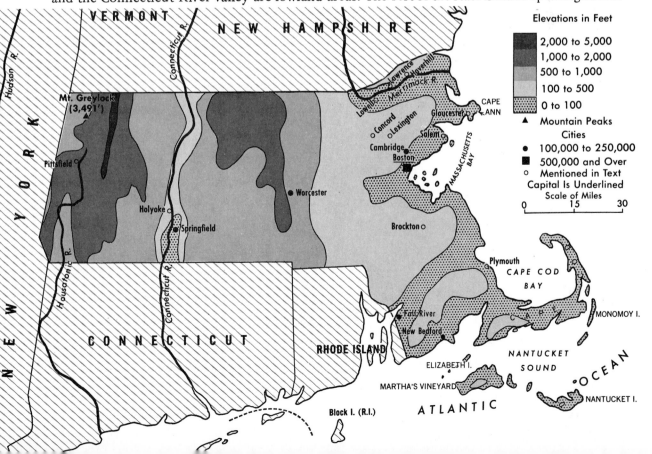

New Hampshire

STATE BIRD: Purple finch
STATE FLOWER: Purple lilac
STATE TREE: White birch

New Hampshire lies almost entirely in the highlands of New England. A narrow plain extends along the state's short coastline.

The White Mountains. The White Mountains include several rugged ranges in northern New Hampshire. The highest peak in the Northeast, Mount Washington, is located here. Few people live in this section of the state.

The plateau section. Most of southern New Hampshire is a hilly plateau. Long ago, this area was quite mountainous. Through the centuries, most of the mountains have been worn away by wind and rain. A few peaks remain, however. In the plateau section are hundreds of lakes and ponds that were formed by glaciers. Most of the soil in the plateau section is too stony for

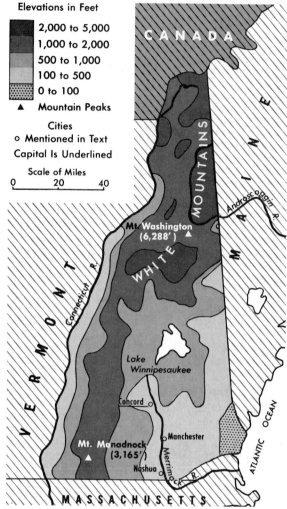

Elevations in Feet
- 2,000 to 5,000
- 1,000 to 2,000
- 500 to 1,000
- 100 to 500
- 0 to 100
- ▲ Mountain Peaks

Cities
- o Mentioned in Text
- Capital Is Underlined

Scale of Miles
0   20   40

New Hampshire is a small state in northern New England. Nearly all of this state is made up of hills and mountains. A coastal plain borders the Atlantic Ocean.

Facts About New Hampshire		
	Number or Value	Rank
Area (square miles)	9,304	44
(square kilometers)	24,096	
Population	849,000	42
Capital — Concord		
Admission Date: June 21, 1788		9
Colleges and Universities	25	29
Farm Products	$ 79,298,000	48
Dairy products	35,572,000	42
Poultry and eggs	16,187,000	39
Fruits and nuts	7,445,000	30
Fish	$ 1,077,000	30
Timber Harvested (cubic feet)	51,191,000	32
Minerals	$ 13,691,000	48
Sand and gravel	8,223,000	44
Stone	5,371,000	44
Clays	55,000	40
Manufactures*	$ 1,297,400,000	39
Nonelectrical machinery	183,300,000	29
Electrical equipment and supplies	172,800,000	29
Leather and leather products	125,800,000	6

growing crops. The only fertile soil is in the narrow valleys of the Connecticut and Merrimack rivers. Both of these rivers provide waterpower for industry.

The coastal lowland. Sandy beaches stretch along New Hampshire's Atlantic coast, which is only about fifteen miles long. A gently rolling lowland dotted with towns and farms extends inland for about this same distance.

*See Glossary

New Jersey

Slightly more than half of New Jersey is located in the Coastal Plain region of our country. The rest is in the Appalachian Highlands. On the west and south, the state is bordered by the Delaware River and Delaware Bay. To the east, it is bordered by the Hudson River and the Atlantic Ocean.

The Coastal Plain. The low, sandy Coastal Plain extends across southern New Jersey. The state has many miles of beaches lined with seaside resorts. Off the Atlantic coast lies a long chain of narrow, sandy islands. Marshes and forests cover large parts of New Jersey's Coastal Plain. These areas are very poor for farming. However, the soil in the western part of this lowland is good for growing vegetables.

The Appalachian Highlands. North of the Coastal Plain, the Piedmont Plateau section of the Appalachian Highlands extends across New Jersey. This gently rolling plateau makes up about one fifth of the state. The eastern part of the Piedmont includes Newark and several other large cities. The western part has fertile farmland and many small towns.

Northwestern New Jersey is made up of ridges and valleys. In the valleys are fertile farmlands. Hundreds of lakes and ponds in this area attract vacationers.

New Jersey is located along the Atlantic coast. Waterways form most of the state's boundaries.

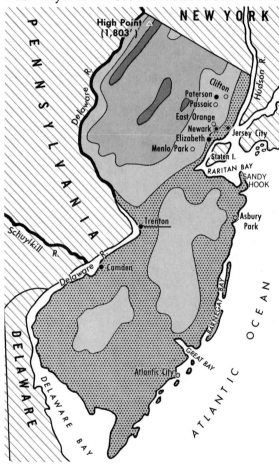

Elevations in Feet
- 1,000 to 2,000
- 500 to 1,000
- 100 to 500
- 0 to 100
- △ Highest Elevation

Cities
- ● 100,000 to 250,000
- ◉ 250,000 to 500,000
- ○ Mentioned in Text
- Capital Is Underlined

Scale of Miles
0 15 30

Facts About New Jersey		
	Number or Value	Rank
Area (square miles)	7,836	46
(square kilometers)	20,294	
Population	7,329,000	9
Capital — Trenton		
Admission Date: December 18, 1787		3
Colleges and Universities	61	14
Farm Products	$ 334,320,000	40
Vegetables	88,226,000	16
Dairy products	56,627,000	40
Greenhouse and nursery	49,993,000	7
Fish	$ 16,609,000	16
Timber Harvested (cubic feet)	14,474,000	41
Minerals	$ 140,748,000	37
Stone	52,456,000	18
Sand and gravel	47,292,000	7
Zinc	23,585,000	6
Manufactures*	$16,318,600,000	7
Chemicals and allied products	3,939,000,000	1
Electrical equipment and supplies	1,599,800,000	7
Food and kindred products	1,544,900,000	7

*See Glossary

New York

STATE BIRD: Bluebird
STATE FLOWER: Rose
STATE TREE: Sugar maple

Facts About New York		
	Number or Value	Rank
Area (square miles)	49,576	30
(square kilometers)	128,397	
Population	17,924,000	2
Capital — Albany		
Admission Date: July 26, 1788		11
Colleges and Universities	259	1
Farm Products	$ 1,698,371,000	22
Dairy products	992,316,000	3
Vegetables	180,435,000	7
Poultry and eggs	109,430,000	21
Fish	$ 25,468,000	11
Timber Harvested (cubic feet)	99,676,000	26
Minerals	$ 440,573,000	25
Cement	not available	
Stone	87,724,000	10
Zinc	66,829,000	1
Manufactures*	$30,744,600,000	2
Printing and publishing	4,234,500,000	1
Instruments and related products	3,507,900,000	1
Apparel and other textile products	3,160,300,000	1

New York, like most states in the Northeast, lies mainly in the Appalachian Highlands region of our country. Lowlands make up less than one fourth of the state. However, most of the people of New York live in the lowland areas.

There are four main lowlands in New York. These are the Erie-Ontario Lowland, the St. Lawrence Valley, the Hudson-Mohawk Lowland, and the Coastal Plain.

The Erie-Ontario Lowland. In western New York, fertile plains extend along the shores of Lake Erie and Lake Ontario. The plain that borders Lake Ontario is about thirty miles wide, while the Lake Erie plain is much narrower. Most of the Erie-Ontario Lowland is flat or gently rolling. In this area are many orchards and truck farms. There are also large industrial cities here.

At the western end of the Lake Ontario plain is the Niagara River, which flows from Lake Erie into Lake Ontario. At one point, the river plunges over a steep cliff, forming beautiful Niagara Falls.

The St. Lawrence Valley. A gently rolling plain extends northeastward from Lake Ontario along the St. Lawrence River. This is the St. Lawrence Valley. Low-cost hydroelectric power produced here is attracting new industry to the area.

The Hudson-Mohawk Lowland. The valleys of the Hudson and Mohawk rivers form another important lowland in New York. The Hudson begins in northeast-

ern New York and flows southward for more than three hundred miles before it empties into the Atlantic Ocean at New York City. The Mohawk is the Hudson's largest tributary. It flows southeastward from central New York and joins the Hudson near the city of Albany. The Hudson-Mohawk Lowland is a natural passageway through the Appalachian Highlands. This passageway is an important transportation route.

The Coastal Plain. Another major lowland area in New York is Long Island, which is part of the Coastal Plain. This island extends eastward into the Atlantic Ocean for a distance of about one hundred twenty miles. The land on Long Island is generally low and level.

*See Glossary

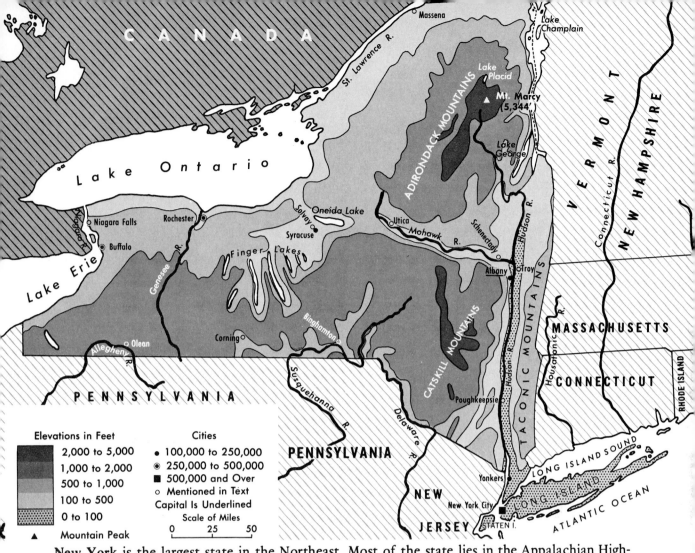

New York is the largest state in the Northeast. Most of the state lies in the Appalachian Highlands region of our country. Lowlands in New York include the Erie-Ontario Lowland, the St. Lawrence Valley, the Hudson-Mohawk Lowland, and the Coastal Plain.

The western end of the island is part of New York City. The eastern part of the island is an important farming area.

The Adirondack Mountains. The Adirondacks make up about one fourth of the land in New York. These forest-covered mountains are located in the northeastern part of the state. The highest mountain in New York is in the Adirondacks. This is Mt. Marcy, which rises 5,344 feet above sea level. Although few people live in the Adiron-

dacks, the rugged beauty of these mountains attracts many vacationers.

The Appalachian Plateau. Most of southern New York lies in the Appalachian Plateau. The Catskill Mountains are the highest part of this area. Because these mountains are not far from New York City, they are a popular resort area. West of the Catskills, the Appalachian Plateau is made up of ridges, valleys, and rounded hills. Dairy farming is important here.

Pennsylvania

STATE BIRD: Ruffed grouse
STATE FLOWER: Mountain laurel
STATE TREE: Eastern hemlock

Almost all of Pennsylvania lies in the Appalachian Highlands region of our country. The only areas outside of this region are two small lowlands.

The highlands. The Appalachian Plateau covers most of western and northern Pennsylvania. It is made up largely of forest-covered mountains and narrow, steep-sided valleys. Most of the land here is too rugged for growing crops. But there are rich deposits of coal and limestone beneath the ground. The great manufacturing city of Pittsburgh is located in the Appalachian Plateau section.

South and east of the Appalachian Plateau is the Appalachian Ridges and Valleys section of Pennsylvania. Many

Facts About Pennsylvania		
	Number or Value	**Rank**
Area (square miles)	45,333	33
(square kilometers)	117,408	
Population	11,785,000	4
Capital — Harrisburg		
Admission Date: December 12, 1787		2
Colleges and Universities	146	3
Farm Products	$ 1,800,478,000	18
Dairy products	777,522,000	5
Poultry and eggs	269,008,000	8
Cattle and calves	152,920,000	31
Fish	$ 171,000	34
Timber Harvested (cubic feet)	158,334,000	20
Minerals	$ 2,374,512,000	6
Coal	1,782,089,000	3
Cement	206,236,000	3
Stone	159,615,000	1
Manufactures*	$ 23,532,200,000	5
Primary metals industries	3,689,000,000	1
Nonelectrical machinery	2,342,800,000	6
Electrical equipment and supplies	2,277,700,000	5

*See Glossary

Pennsylvania is the second largest state in the Northeast. Almost all of the state lies in the Appalachian Highlands region of our country. The only areas outside of this region are two lowlands. One of these lies along Lake Erie, and the other is along the Delaware River.

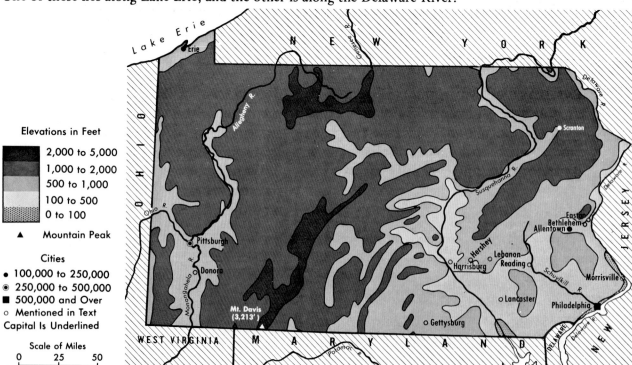

Harrisburg, the capital of Pennsylvania, is in the Great Valley. This is a long chain of river valleys in the eastern part of the United States. The Great Valley is a fertile farming area.

of the ridges here are steep and forest-covered. Between the ridges are long valleys. Some of them are part of a fertile farming area known as the Great Valley.* Here there are fine orchards of apple and peach trees. Many cities and towns are in the Great Valley of Pennsylvania. Among them is Harrisburg, the state capital.

The Piedmont section lies southeast of the Appalachian Ridges and Valleys. This gently rolling plateau slopes downward to the Coastal Plain. Some of the most fertile farmland in our country is found in this part of Pennsylvania.

The lowlands. Along the Delaware River in southeastern Pennsylvania is a narrow lowland. It is part of the Coastal Plain region of our country. The land here is level or gently rolling. Philadelphia, the state's largest city, is a seaport located along the Delaware River.

Another narrow strip of lowland extends along Lake Erie, in northwestern Pennsylvania. This is an important fruit-growing area.

Rhode Island

STATE BIRD: Rhode Island red hen
STATE FLOWER: Violet
STATE TREE: Red maple

Rhode Island is the smallest state in our country. It would fit into Alaska, our largest state, almost five hundred times. Despite Rhode Island's small size, nearly one million people live here. It is one of our most densely populated states.

Rhode Island is made up of lowlands and highlands. More than half the state lies in the lowlands. Highlands make up most of western Rhode Island.

The lowlands. Rhode Island's lowlands include the land bordered by the Atlantic Ocean and by Narragansett Bay. A number of islands in the bay, as well as Block Island in the Atlantic Ocean, are also part of the lowlands. These lowlands are generally flat and sandy. Most of the land here is less than one hundred feet above sea level. Many wide, sandy beaches line the shores of the bay

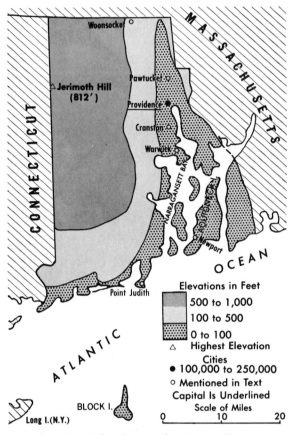

Rhode Island is the nation's smallest state. Although much of western Rhode Island is hilly, the state's highest point is only about eight hundred feet above sea level.

and the ocean. However, in some places, rocky cliffs rise above the sea. Farther inland, the land is higher and gently rolling.

Most of Rhode Island's cities are located in the lowlands. Providence, which lies at the head of Narragansett Bay, is the capital of the state.

The highlands. The highlands of Rhode Island are made up of rough hills covered with forests of oak, cedar, and maple. Most of these hills do not rise very high above sea level.

Facts About Rhode Island		
	Number or Value	**Rank**
Area (square miles)	1,214	50
Area (square kilometers)	3,144	
Population	935,000	39
Capital — Providence		
Admission Date: May 29, 1790		13
Colleges and Universities	13	37
Farm Products	$ 28,038,000	49
Greenhouse and nursery	7,846,000	30
Dairy products	6,420,000	49
Vegetables	6,313,000	45
Fish	$ 16,744,000	15
Timber Harvested (cubic feet)	2,093,000	47
Minerals	$ 5,982,000	49
Stone	not available	
Sand and gravel	4,605,000	47
Gem stones	not available	
Manufactures*	$1,782,200,000	35
Miscellaneous manufacturing	397,700,000	7
Textile mill products	200,300,000	12
Primary metals industries	181,800,000	21

*See Glossary

STATE BIRD: Hermit thrush
STATE FLOWER: Red clover
STATE TREE: Sugar maple

Vermont

Vermont is the only New England state that does not have a coastline on the Atlantic Ocean. Most of Vermont lies in the highlands of New England. The state's only large lowland area lies along Lake Champlain. This lake forms more than half of Vermont's western boundary.

The highlands. Vermont is nicknamed the "Green Mountain State." It gets this name from a forested mountain range that extends through the state.

East of the Green Mountains, most of the land in Vermont is hilly or gently rolling. The Granite Hills extend from the middle of the state northward to Canada. Several low peaks in the northeastern corner of Vermont are part of the White Mountains, which extend into New Hampshire. Along the Connecticut River is a narrow lowland with fertile soil.

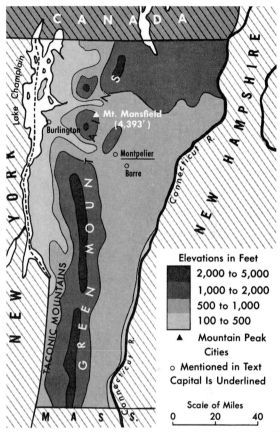

Elevations in Feet

- 2,000 to 5,000
- 1,000 to 2,000
- 500 to 1,000
- 100 to 500
- ▲ Mountain Peak
- Cities
- o Mentioned in Text
- Capital Is Underlined

Scale of Miles
0   20   40

Vermont is the only New England state without a coastline along the Atlantic Ocean. The state's largest lowland borders Lake Champlain.

West of the Green Mountains are both highland and lowland areas. The Taconic Mountains, in the southwestern part of the state, resemble the Green Mountains but are not as high.

The lowlands. North of the Taconics is a broad lowland called the Champlain Valley, which extends all the way into Canada. In the Champlain Valley are the largest stretches of low, level land in Vermont. In summertime, herds of dairy cattle graze on rich, green pastures in the Champlain Valley. Apple orchards and fields of corn and hay spread over much of the countryside.

Facts About Vermont		
	Number or Value	Rank
Area (square miles)	9,609	43
(square kilometers)	24,886	
Population	483,000	48
Capital — Montpelier		
Admission Date:		
March 4, 1791		14
Colleges and Universities	20	32
Farm Products	$263,317,000	43
Dairy products	216,954,000	15
Cattle and calves	19,461,000	41
Poultry and eggs	6,865,000	45
Fish	not available	
Timber Harvested (cubic feet)	42,178,000	35
Minerals	$ 35,453,000	46
Stone	21,630,000	31
Asbestos	not available	2
Sand and gravel	3,588,000	49
Manufactures*	$ 578,900,000	42
Nonelectrical machinery	92,300,000	38
Electrical equipment and		
supplies	84,100,000	35
Printing and publishing	69,300,000	36

*See Glossary

West Virginia

STATE BIRD: Cardinal
STATE FLOWER: Big rhododendron
STATE TREE: Sugar maple

West Virginia lies farther west than any other state in the Northeast. With an average elevation of about 1,500 feet, it is also the highest state in the Northeast. All of West Virginia lies in the Appalachian Highlands region of our country. Two main sections of this region extend through the state. These are the Appalachian Plateau and the Appalachian Ridges and Valleys.

About three fourths of West Virginia lies in the Appalachian Plateau. Rugged mountains, steep-sided hills, and narrow river valleys make up most of this section.

East of the Appalachian Plateau is the Appalachian Ridges and Valleys section of West Virginia. Here, the land is made up of nearly parallel ridges separated by narrow valleys. Spruce Knob, the highest point in the state, is located in this section.

Facts About West Virginia		
	Number or Value	Rank
Area (square miles)	24,181	41
(square kilometers)	62,626	
Population	1,859,000	34
Capital — Charleston		
Admission Date: June 20, 1863		35
Colleges and Universities	25	29
Farm Products	$ 140,632,000	47
Poultry and eggs	34,666,000	32
Dairy products	31,623,000	43
Cattle and calves	26,127,000	40
Fish	$ 5,000	43
Timber Harvested (cubic feet)	129,954,000	22
Minerals	$2,403,177,000	5
Coal	2,218,418,000	2
Natural gas	66,356,000	8
Stone	22,308,000	28
Manufactures*	$2,632,700,000	31
Chemicals and allied products	949,400,000	11
Primary metals industries	532,200,000	12
Stone, glass, and clay products	328,600,000	12

*See Glossary

West Virginia lies entirely within the Appalachian Highlands region of the United States.

Elevations in Feet
2,000 to 5,000
1,000 to 2,000
500 to 1,000
100 to 500

▲ Mountain Peak

Cities
o Mentioned in Text
Capital Is Underlined

Scale of Miles
0   30   60

PICTORIAL STORY OF OUR COUNTRY

Mount Rushmore, in South Dakota, honors four of our presidents.

Our Country

Our country, the United States of America, was established just over two hundred years ago. At that time, the United States was small and weak. It was the home of less than three million people. Most of these people lived on farms or in small villages near the Atlantic coast of North America.

Today the United States is one of the largest and richest countries on earth. It stretches almost three thousand miles, from the Atlantic Ocean to the Pacific. (See the map on pages 60-61.) It also includes the far northern state of Alaska and the island state of Hawaii. Within this huge country are many large, modern cities.

Nearly 220 million people live in the United States today. Each year they produce billions of dollars' worth of goods and services. As a result, Americans live more comfortably than people in most parts of the world. Also, they enjoy a great deal of freedom to live as they please and to take part in their own government.

In the following pages, you will discover how the United States grew from a small, weak country into the powerful nation that it is today. As you read, look for certain ideas or ways of living that have helped to build our nation.

In 1976, the United States was two hundred years old. The picture at the right shows people marching in a parade to celebrate our nation's birthday. Their clothes are like the ones that people wore at the time our country was started. Two hundred years ago, the United States was small and weak. Today it is one of the largest richest countries in the world. Are there certain ideas that helped the United States to grow? If so, what are they? This book will help you answer these questions.

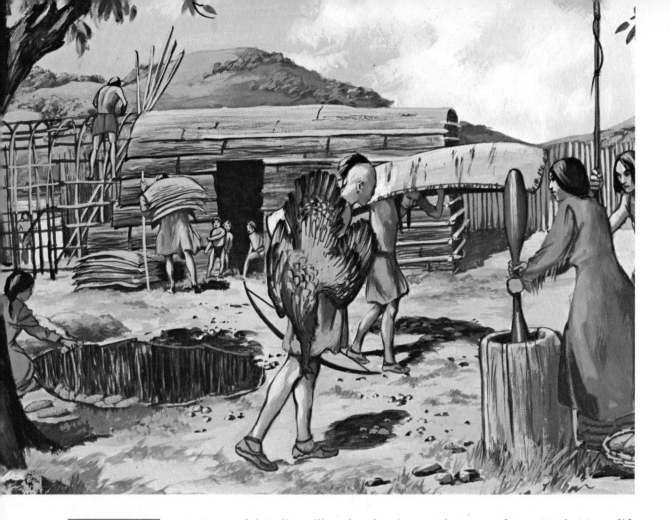

Using
Natural
Resources

An Iroquois* Indian village in what is now the state of New York. Many different groups of Indians lived in North America long ago. They used a number of things they found in the world around them to help them meet their needs. These gifts of nature are called "natural resources." What natural resources are being used by the people in the picture? Look in this book and other books to discover facts that will help you answer this question.

1 People Build Communities in America

■ Who were the first Americans?

People have been living in what is now the United States for many thousands of years. The first Americans were people with brown skin, dark eyes, and straight, black hair.

They were divided into many different groups, or tribes. Most tribes called themselves by names that meant simply "the men" or "the people." Today these early people

*See Glossary

of America are usually known as Indians, or as Native Americans.

The Indians may have come to North America from Asia. No one knows for certain how the Indians first came to North America. But many scientists believe that these people came from the continent* of Asia. There are two main reasons why they think this. First, many Indians look somewhat like the people of Asia. Second, Asia and North America are very close together in the far north. They are separated only by a narrow strip of water called the Bering Strait. (Compare map at right with map of Alaska on page 60.) Long ago, the oceans of the world were not as deep as they are today. A bridge of land may have connected Asia and North America. It would have been possible to travel from one continent to another across this land bridge.

Scientists believe that people began coming to North America at least 25,000 years ago, and possibly more than 100,000 years ago. These people may have been hunting wild animals for food. Or they may have been trying to get away from enemies. As time passed, the Indians settled in many parts of North and South America. (See map at right.)

The Indian tribes of North America were not all alike. They spoke hundreds of different languages, and they had very different ways of life. For example, some tribes got most of their food by hunting animals such as deer and buffalo. Other tribes grew crops such as corn and squash for food. Still others lived mostly on fruit, seeds, and roots they gathered from wild plants.

The Indians are believed to have come from Asia across the Bering Strait. They settled in many parts of North and South America.

ROUTES OF INDIAN SETTLERS

Scale

| 0 | 1000 | 2000 | Miles |

| 0 | 1000 | 2000 | Kilometers |

A European trading ship in the 1500's. People in Europe were eager to trade with countries in eastern Asia. Why? How did the desire for trade cause Europeans to find out about America?

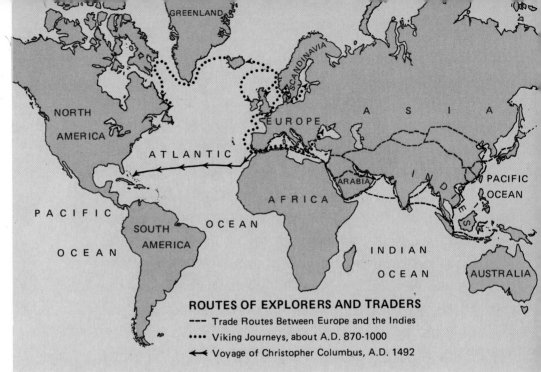

ROUTES OF EXPLORERS AND TRADERS
- - - Trade Routes Between Europe and the Indies
•••• Viking Journeys, about A.D. 870-1000
◄— Voyage of Christopher Columbus, A.D. 1492

■ **How did Europeans learn about America?**

Sailors from Europe began making journeys to faraway lands. Far to the east of America, across the broad Atlantic Ocean, lay the continent of Europe. For thousands of years, people had lived in Europe without knowing anything about the lands on the other side of the ocean. Sailing ships in those days were small and not very safe. Also, sailors did not have any way to find out where they were if they sailed out of sight of land. Many people believed that the ocean was the home of terrible monsters. It is not surprising that only the most daring sailors were willing to sail very far out into the ocean.

Now and then, a ship from Europe may have reached America. For example, it seems certain that bold Viking* sailors landed on the Atlantic coast of North America about one thousand years ago. (See map above.) But news spread slowly in those days, and most Europeans never learned about such journeys.

During the early 1400's, people in Europe began to take more interest in visiting other parts of the world. Better ships and new kinds of tools to help sailors find their way had been developed. As a result, people were able to make longer ocean journeys.

At that time, people in Europe were eager to carry on trade with the lands in eastern Asia known as the Indies. In these lands, it was possible to get spices, silk, and other valuable goods. For years, Asian traders had been bringing these goods by land to ports on the eastern shore of the Mediterranean Sea.* Here, traders from Italy loaded the goods on their ships and carried them to cities in Europe. The prices that Europeans had to pay for these goods were much higher than the prices that the Asian traders had paid for them. Many Europeans wanted to find an ocean route to the Indies so they could buy goods directly from traders there. Then they would no longer have to pay high prices to Italian traders.

Columbus sailed westward and reached America. Some people hoped to find an ocean route to the Indies by sailing east from the southern tip of Africa. But one man had a different plan. He was an Italian sailor named Christopher Columbus. At that time, many Europeans were already saying that the earth was round. Columbus agreed with them. He was sure he could reach Asia by sailing westward across the Atlantic Ocean.

Queen Isabella of Spain agreed to give Columbus the money and ships that he needed for his journey. In August of 1492, Columbus and his crew left Spain in three tiny ships. They sailed for many weeks until they reached a small island off the coast of North America. Columbus thought he had reached the Indies, so he called the people

he found there "Indians." After visiting other islands, he returned to Spain with the news of his exciting discovery.

Before long, other explorers from European countries were sailing westward to see the lands Columbus had found. They soon realized that Columbus had not reached Asia after all. Instead, he had reached a completely new part of the world.

Many people came from Europe to America. In the years that followed the voyage of Columbus, people from several European countries came to America. Some of them were searching for a water route through America to Asia. Others were hoping to find gold and silver or other kinds of treasure. Still others wanted to bring their religion, Christianity, to the Indians.

A Spanish explorer named Francisco Coronado was one of the first Europeans to visit the southwestern part of the United States. He led an army through this area in 1540. Why did Coronado come? What were some of the other reasons why people from Europe came to America?

■ What part did the Spanish play in settling America?

The Spanish built missions and forts in what is now the United States. The first Europeans to settle in America at this time came from Spain. Spanish explorers found rich Indian cities in Mexico and South America. They fought the Indians and took over their lands. In this way, they won a great fortune in gold and silver for Spain.

Hoping to find more riches, other Spaniards journeyed far into North America. They found little gold and silver there. But their journeys made it possible for Spain to claim a large area in what is now the United States.

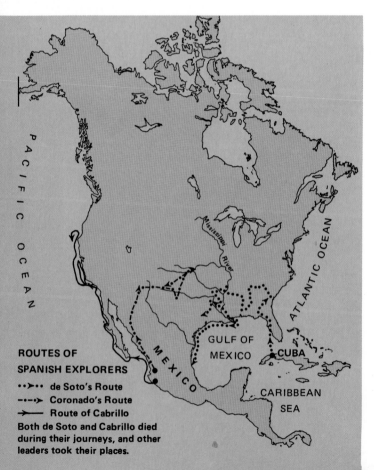

ROUTES OF
SPANISH EXPLORERS
••▷•• de Soto's Route
–•–•▷ Coronado's Route
—▶— Route of Cabrillo
Both de Soto and Cabrillo died during their journeys, and other leaders took their places.

The map at the left shows the routes of three Spaniards who visited different parts of North America in the 1500's. In 1539, Hernando de Soto started on a journey through what is now the southeastern part of our country. He was the first European to see the Mississippi River. In 1540, Francisco Coronado started out from Mexico to look for rich cities that were said to lie farther north. He journeyed for hundreds of miles over deserts and mountains, but he never found the cities he was seeking. Juan Cabrillo was the first European to visit California. He sailed along the Pacific coast in 1542.

Language

See Great Ideas

The mission of **San Xavier** is near Tucson, Arizona. (See map on pages 60-61.) It was built by Spanish missionaries in the 1700's. What is a missionary? If you do not know, look in the Glossary at the back of this book. The missionaries spent much time learning to speak the languages spoken by the Indians. Why was it important for them to do this? If people do not speak the same language, how can they tell their ideas to one another?

As time passed, Spanish settlers began coming here to live. They built missions where the Indians could come to learn about Christianity. (See the picture above.) They also built forts to protect their settlements from being attacked by enemy Indians or by soldiers from other European countries. The first Spanish settlements were established in Florida during the 1500's. Later, other Spanish settlements were started in Texas, New Mexico, Arizona, and California.

Father Jacques Marquette was a French missionary. He and a fur trader named Louis Joliet went much of the way down the Mississippi River in 1673. They were searching for a water route that would lead to Asia. Do you think they found it? Give reasons for your answer.

■ **Which lands were settled by the French, Dutch, and Swedish?**

France claimed a huge amount of land in North America. People from France also visited North America during the 1500's and 1600's. Some sailed along the Atlantic coast. Others traveled up the St. Lawrence River in what is now Canada. (See the map on pages 60-61.) Later, other French explorers made journeys through the Great Lakes* and along the Mississippi River. They claimed a huge amount of land for France. The left-hand map on page 21 shows the French territory in North America.

During the 1600's and 1700's, people from France came to North America to live. Some were traders who bought valuable furs from the Indians in exchange for goods such as cloth, knives, and beads. These furs were sent to Europe, where they could be sold for high prices. Other French people who came to America were soldiers, missionaries, fishers, or farmers.

New Amsterdam was a Dutch settlement along the Hudson River. It later became New York City. What does the picture tell you about New Amsterdam?

The Dutch and Swedish settled near the Atlantic coast. Other European countries also started settlements in North America during the 1600's. Two of these countries were Holland and Sweden. There were Dutch* settlements along the Hudson River in what is now New York State. (See map at right.) The Swedish settled along the Delaware River. But these settlements were small and weak. By 1700, all of them had been taken over by the country of England.

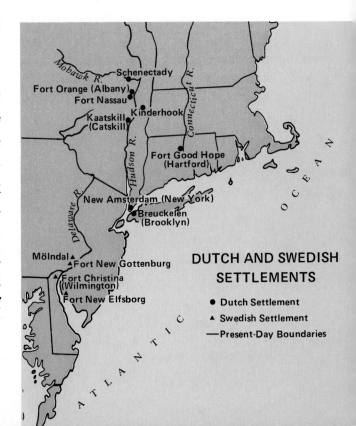

DUTCH AND SWEDISH SETTLEMENTS

- ● Dutch Settlement
- ▲ Swedish Settlement
- — Present-Day Boundaries

■ Why did the English decide to start settlements in America?

The English were slow to settle the lands they claimed. The first explorer from England to visit America was John Cabot. In 1497 he and his men sailed westward across the Atlantic Ocean in search of a water route to the Indies. When they reached the coast of Canada, they claimed the land for the English king.

For many years, the English did not try to settle the lands that Cabot had visited. But as time went on, English leaders became more interested in starting colonies* in America.

From these colonies, the English could buy goods that they could not produce in large enough amounts in England. Among these goods were logs and animal furs. In return, traders in England could sell large amounts of cloth, hardware, and other English goods to the American settlers. At that time, England, France, Holland, and Spain were all rivals of one another. The English decided that if they started colonies along the Atlantic coast, the other European countries would be less likely to claim this land for themselves.

An English settlement was started in Virginia. In 1607, a group of English traders sent about one hundred people to what is now Virginia. There the colonists started a settlement called Jamestown. This was the first successful English settlement in America. At first, life was very hard for the settlers. Many of them died of hunger or sickness. Others were killed by the Indians, who were angry because the settlers often treated them badly. In spite of these troubles, Jamestown kept going. During the years that followed, people from England started many other settlements along the Atlantic coast of North America.

People came to America in search of freedom and a better way of life. Why were so many English people willing to leave their homes and make the long,

Loyalty

See Great Ideas

John Cabot landed on the Atlantic coast of Canada in 1497. Do you think sailors like Cabot could have made successful journeys without the help of loyal followers? Explain your answer. What might have happened if these followers had not been loyal?

dangerous journey to America? For one thing, people who lived in England at that time did not have very much freedom. All English men and women were expected to belong to the Church of England, which was headed by the king. People who belonged to other churches could be put into prison. This was why the Pilgrims* and certain other groups of people decided to move to America. In that faraway land, they would be free to worship as they pleased.

During the 1600's, it was hard to make a good living in England. Most of the farmland was owned by a small number of wealthy families. In earlier times, many English people had been farmers who rented land from these rich landowners. But as time passed, the landowners found they could make more money by

Using Tools

See Great Ideas

Jamestown, Virginia, was the first long-lasting English settlement in America. The picture below shows the settlers building a fort along the banks of the James River. What tools are the people in this picture using? Can you think of some other tools that the settlers might have needed in order to build their fort? Would it have been possible for the European settlers to make homes in the wilderness without using tools? Explain your answer.

raising sheep for wool. They began using their fields as pastures for sheep. Many farmers could not find any land to rent, and it was not easy to get other jobs.

In America, there were large areas of fertile land that had not yet been settled. Farmers could get all the land they wanted free, or at a very low cost. All kinds of workers were needed in America, so anyone who was willing to work hard could be fairly sure of getting a good job. The hope of a better life brought many settlers to America.

■ What was life in the British colonies like?

The colonies grew in population. As the years passed, more and more people made their homes in England's colonies. Settlers came not only from England but also from Ireland, Germany, France, and other European countries. In the meantime, England had joined with the neighboring country of Scotland to form the kingdom of Great Britain.

By 1750 there were thirteen British colonies in North America. (See the map above.) Together these colonies had a population of more than one million. Most of the colonists lived on the Atlantic coast or along

Thirteen British colonies grew up along the Atlantic coast of North America. Which four colonies made up the area known as New England? What were the four Middle Colonies? What were the five Southern Colonies?

rivers that flowed into the ocean. The rest of what is now the United States was mostly a wilderness.

How people in the British colonies made their living. About nine out of every ten colonists in America earned their living by farming. However, there were fewer farmers in New England than in the other colonies. Much of the land in New England was hilly, and the soil was thin and stony. But there were valuable forests in New England, and the

Exchange

See Great Ideas

A street in Philadelphia, the largest city in the British colonies. Philadelphia grew up along the Delaware River. Ships could sail up the river from the Atlantic Ocean to load and unload their goods. As time passed, Philadelphia became an important center for trade. Another word for trade is "exchange." How do you think exchange helped the thirteen colonies to grow?

Atlantic Ocean was rich in fish. Along the coast were many bays where ships could be safe from storms. Boston and other busy cities grew up here. Many people in New England earned their living from the sea. Some of them built ships. Others were sailors, fishers, or traders.

In the Middle Colonies, there were larger areas of level land with rich soil. Farmers here produced large amounts of wheat, beef, and other goods. They sold these goods to people in all of the colonies and also Great Britain. The Middle Colonies were rich in iron ore,* wood, and other resources. Cities like New York and Philadelphia grew up along the Atlantic coast, where there were good harbors for ships.

In the Southern Colonies, the land and climate* were good for farming. Summers were long and hot. There was plenty of rainfall, and the soil in many places was rich. Some of the colonists started large farms called plantations. There they grew crops such as tobacco and indigo.* These crops could be shipped to Europe and sold there for high prices. Much of the work on the plantations was done by black people who had been brought from Africa as slaves.

In colonial days, slavery was carried on in many parts of the world. To get slaves, traders from England and other European countries sailed along the coast of Africa. They gave cloth and other valuable goods to African rulers in exchange for prisoners who had been captured in war. The prisoners were loaded into ships and taken to America. Many died of hunger or sickness along the way. Those who lived were sold to the American settlers. By the late 1700's, about one fifth of all the people in the British colonies were black men and women from Africa.

Discover Our Country's Story

1. Why did the first people who lived in America become known as Indians?
2. Why did people in Europe want to find an all-water route to Asia?
3. How did Christopher Columbus hope to reach Asia? Was he successful? Explain your answer.
4. What parts of the United States were settled by people from Spain?
5. What happened to the Dutch and Swedish settlements in America?
6. Why was Jamestown important in American history?
7. Why did the Pilgrims decide to come to America?
8. Why were there fewer farmers in New England than in the other colonies?
9. Why were the Southern Colonies so well suited to farming?
10. In colonial days, most people did not think it was wrong to own slaves. Why do you suppose they felt this way?

2 The American Communities Form a Nation

■ How did Britain win control of France's lands in North America?

France and Great Britain went to war. At the same time the British colonies were growing larger, France and Great Britain began to quarrel. Both countries claimed an area that lay mostly between the Appalachian Mountains and the Mississippi River. (Compare the left-hand map on page 21 with the map on pages 60-61.) This helped to bring about the French and Indian War,* which began in 1754.

At first, the French seemed to be winning the war. They had good army leaders, and they were helped by several Indian tribes. But there were about twenty times as many people in the British colonies as in the French colonies. Also, Britain had a stronger navy than France. As a result, the British could send more troops and supplies to America.

After years of fighting, the British defeated the French. A treaty* of peace was signed in 1763. Under this treaty, France lost its huge empire in North America. (See right-hand map on page 21.) Britain now ruled over nearly all the land in the eastern part of the continent.

■ Why were the American colonists unhappy under British rule?

A quarrel arose between Great Britain and the colonies. After the French and Indian War, the American colonists began to grow more and more unhappy under British rule. One reason for this was that the colonists were not free to carry on business as they pleased. For example, Britain would not allow the colonists to sell goods directly to foreign countries such as France and Holland. These goods had to be sent to England first. Also, goods that were shipped into and out of the colonies had to be carried in British ships. Some kinds of goods that were made in America could not be sold anywhere except in the colony where they were made. The purpose of all these laws was to help traders and shipowners in Great Britain.

Most people in the colonies strongly disliked the British trade laws. They believed these laws hurt their business and caused them to pay higher prices for goods they bought

*See Glossary

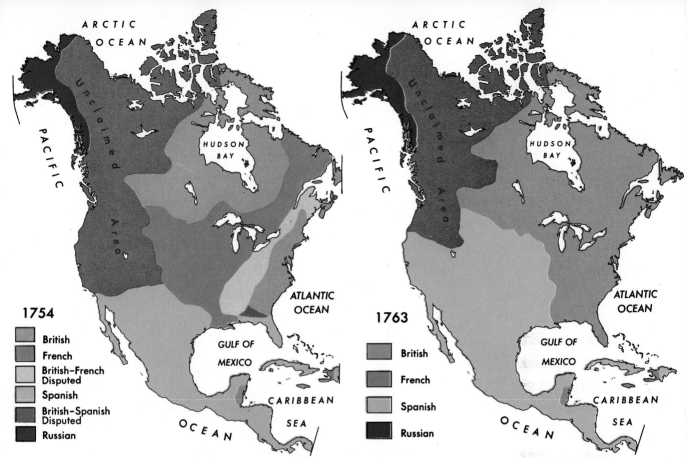

ARCTIC OCEAN

PACIFIC

Unclaimed Area

HUDSON BAY

ATLANTIC OCEAN

1754

- British
- French
- British–French Disputed
- Spanish
- British–Spanish Disputed
- Russian

GULF OF MEXICO

CARIBBEAN SEA

OCEAN

ARCTIC OCEAN

PACIFIC

Unclaimed Area

HUDSON BAY

ATLANTIC OCEAN

1763

- British
- French
- Spanish
- Russian

GULF OF MEXICO

CARIBBEAN SEA

OCEAN

Before and after the French and Indian War. These maps show the lands in North America that belonged to different countries of Europe. The French and Indian War started in 1754. At that time, Great Britain and France both claimed huge amounts of land in North America. At the end of the war, in 1763, France had to give up nearly all of its great empire.

from Britain and other lands. Many colonists broke the laws by trading secretly with foreign countries.

In order to make sure that the trade laws were obeyed, British officers were sent to the colonies to hunt for people who were breaking these laws. The officers were given papers called writs of assistance, which allowed them to search any home or business place in the colonies. The colonists felt that the writs of assistance took away some of their rights as British citizens.

Many colonists had expected that they would be allowed to settle west of the Appalachian Mountains after the French were defeated. But the British were afraid that this would cause trouble with the Indians who lived there. In 1763 the British government sent out an order telling the settlers not to move into the lands west of the Appalachian Mountains.

The colonists became even more unhappy when the British Parliament* passed laws that made them pay certain taxes to Britain. The colonists were not allowed to choose any people to represent them in Parliament, so they felt Parliament had no right to tax them. In the past, the lawmaking body of each colony had decided what taxes people would have to pay. It seemed to the colonists that the British leaders were trying to take away their right to govern themselves.

Americans protested against the British laws. The colonists showed their anger toward Britain in several ways. In some communities, British officers were attacked by groups of citizens. Sometimes British goods were destroyed. For example, colonists who were dressed as Indians dumped a load of tea into the harbor of Boston. This was known as the Boston Tea Party. Many colonists refused to buy any more goods from Great Britain until the laws were changed.

■ How did the colonists gain their independence?

The Revolutionary War began. As time went on, it became clear that the British government was not going to change its ways. Many Americans began to think that stronger measures were needed. In 1774, a number of colonial leaders met in Philadelphia to talk about their troubles with Britain. This meeting was known as the First Continental Congress.* In each colony, groups of citizens began to gather weapons and meet for army drill. In Massachusetts these people were called minutemen, because they could be ready for battle only a few minutes after receiving a warning.

In April of 1775, the British general in Massachusetts sent a group of soldiers from Boston to the nearby villages of Lexington and Concord. The soldiers were ordered to get the weapons and gunpowder that had been stored there by the colonists. Fighting broke out between the British soldiers and a group of minutemen. This was the start of the Revolutionary War.

News of the fighting soon spread from Massachusetts to the other colonies. A short time later, the Second Continental Congress met in Philadelphia. For several years, this Congress led the thirteen colonies in their fight against Britain.

Freedom

See Great Ideas

The picture at the left shows an American lawyer named James Otis speaking in a courtroom against the writs of assistance. (See page 21.) Do you think that the American colonists were used to having very much freedom? Explain. What part do you think the idea of freedom played in the colonists' fight against British rule?

The picture above shows the Second Continental Congress meeting in Philadelphia on July 4, 1776. The Declaration of Independence is being presented to the Congress for its approval.

Colonial leaders signed the Declaration of Independence. When the war began, most of the American colonists still felt a strong loyalty toward Great Britain. But as the fighting went on, many people came to feel that the colonies should break away from Britain and form an independent nation. If the colonies were no longer under British rule, they could govern themselves as they pleased. They could build up new industries and trade freely with all countries. People could settle anywhere without having to ask the British government.

By the summer of 1776, most members of the Second Continental

Why did most people in the Congress believe that the American colonies should break away from Britain? Why did they feel it was important to have a written Declaration of Independence?

Congress were in favor of independence. Thomas Jefferson and several others were asked to prepare a statement that would explain why the colonists wanted to be free of British rule. This statement became known as the Declaration of Independence. It was approved by the Second Continental Congress on July 4, 1776.

Today, we think of July 4 as the "birthday" of our country.

Americans finally won their fight for freedom. Even after the Declaration of Independence was signed, the colonists were not yet free of British rule. The Revolutionary War went on for seven more years. At times, it seemed certain that the

Americans would be defeated. They were fighting a rich and powerful nation. The American soldiers did not have much training. Also, they lacked proper food, clothing, and weapons. Many people in America were not in favor of independence. These people helped the British in a number of ways.

In spite of these troubles, the colonists refused to give up. The American soldiers were fighting to win freedom and to protect their homes, so they showed great loyalty and bravery. The American general, George Washington, was a wise and strong leader. Also, the colonists received much valuable aid from Britain's enemy, France. The French government gave money, weapons, and soldiers to help the Americans.

At Yorktown, Virginia, in 1781, a British army gave itself up to American and French troops led by George Washington. What problems did the American colonists face during the Revolutionary War? Why were they able to overcome these problems and win their freedom from British rule?

In 1781, a British army gave itself up to General Washington at the village of Yorktown, Virginia. Now the British government knew that it had lost the war. A treaty of peace was signed in 1783. In this treaty, Britain agreed that the United States was a fully independent country. The new nation stretched from the Atlantic Ocean to the Mississippi River, and from Canada to Florida. (See the map on page 34.)

■ **What kind of government was established in the new nation?**

The United States did not have a strong national government. When the war ended, the American people faced an important problem. The thirteen states that had won their independence were not really united. Most people had a greater feeling of loyalty to the state in which they lived than they did to the nation.

The national government of the United States was very weak. It could pass laws, but it had no way of making sure that these laws were carried out. Also, it did not have the power to raise the money it needed to carry on its work. Many people were afraid that there would soon be thirteen small, weak countries instead of one large, strong nation.

A new plan of government was written. In 1787, leaders from the different states held a meeting in Philadelphia. They wanted to talk about ways of making the national government stronger. These people decided to write a new plan of government, or constitution,* for the United States.

For almost four months, the American leaders argued about the kind of government that the United States should have. There were many different ideas. Sometimes it seemed that the meeting would never reach

Cooperation

See Great Ideas

The picture at the right shows a crowd of people watching George Washington become the first president of the United States. This happened in New York City in 1789. Do you think cooperation was needed in order to set up a new government for the United States? Could this government have been successful if people had not been willing to work together? Explain.

its goal. But the people at the meeting knew that if they did not cooperate, the United States might fall apart. They agreed to settle their differences.

At last, the leaders in Philadelphia were done with their work. On September 17, 1787, most of them signed their names to the new Constitution of the United States.

The Constitution set up a federal* form of government. Under this plan, the national government would be much stronger than it had been before. For example, it would be able to carry out national laws and settle arguments between states. It would also be able to collect taxes to carry on its work. But the states would still have power to deal with many other kinds of matters.

The national government would be divided into three branches. One branch, Congress, would make the laws. Another branch—headed by the president—would see that the laws were carried out. The third branch would be made up of the Supreme Court* and other national courts.

The Constitution was approved. Before the new plan of government could become law, it had to be accepted by at least nine states. Many people did not want the Constitution. They thought it gave too much power to the national government. Others were in favor of the Constitution, because they thought a strong national government would be able to take care of some of the country's problems.

By the summer of 1788, nine states had approved the Constitution. Now the new government could begin work.

Elections were held to choose a president, a vice-president, and members of Congress. George Washington was elected president. He chose a group of people to help him run the government. This group became known as the Cabinet. Plans were made to build a capital city called Washington in an area along the Potomac River known as the District of Columbia. (Find Washington, D.C., on the map on pages 60-61.)

Discover Our Country's Story
1. Why were the British able to win the French and Indian War?
2. Why did the colonists feel that the British Parliament had no right to tax them?
3. How did the Revolutionary War begin?
4. What caused the British government to decide that it had lost the war in America?
5. Why was a constitution needed for the United States? Is the United States Constitution still being used today? How can you find out?
6. Why were some people against the new Constitution? Why were other people in favor of it? Which side won?

3 The Nation Grows

■ Why did many Americans move west of the Appalachian Mountains?

Pioneers built homes in the wilderness. After the United States became a nation, thousands of settlers moved from the Atlantic coast to the lands west of the Appalachian Mountains. (See map on pages 60-61.) Here they could buy good farmland at a very low cost. Some of the settlers followed trails that led through passes in the mountains. Others went by boat down the Ohio River.

The settlers who built new homes west of the mountains faced many hardships and dangers. Often, thick forests had to be cleared away be-

Rules and Government

See Great Ideas

This picture shows Daniel Boone leading settlers through a pass in the Appalachian Mountains. During the late 1700's, many American families moved west of the mountains to make new homes. Do you think these settlers needed to follow certain rules in order to get along with one another? Do you think they needed some form of government? Explain your answer.

fore the land could be used for farming. The pioneer families had to raise their own food and build their own cabins. They also had to make most of their own furniture and clothing. Sometimes they were attacked by Indians who did not want strangers moving into their hunting grounds. Many settlers died of diseases such as smallpox* and cholera.*

In spite of these troubles, more and more people came to the lands west of the Appalachian Mountains. Towns and cities began to grow up here. As the territories between the Appalachians and the Mississippi River grew in population, they were allowed to enter the Union* as states.

■ How did life in America change during the early 1800's?

Factories were built to make goods needed by Americans. At the time the United States became a nation, most of the goods people used in their homes were made by hand. But a great change was taking place in England. Machines were being made that could do spinning, weaving, and other jobs that people had always done by hand. These machines were too large to be put in people's homes. Instead, large buildings called factories were built. Then workers were hired to come to the factories and run the machines.

Near the end of the 1700's, people in America learned how to make some of the new machines. They built a number of textile* mills, where cotton was spun into thread. These were the first real factories in the United States.

New England was very well suited to manufacturing. In this part of the country, there were wealthy business people

*See Glossary

who had money to spend for building factories. Since there was little good farmland in New England, many people were looking for other ways to earn a living. They could be hired to work in factories. Also, New England had a number of rivers and streams that could supply water-power to run the new machinery.

By the early 1800's, there were many factories in New England. They made clothing, guns, tools, and many other things needed by America's growing population.

Better means of transportation were developed. When the United States was started, it was hard to go from one part of the country to another. Nearly all the roads were narrow, bumpy, and often muddy. People journeyed over these roads on horseback, or in wagons or stagecoaches. Often it was easier to go by boat, but water transportation was very slow. Because it cost so much to ship goods from place to place, there was little trade between different parts of the country.

A railroad train in New Jersey during the 1830's. How is this train different from the ones that are used today? What other kinds of transportation do you see in this picture?

During the early 1800's, great improvements were made in transportation. New roads with hard surfaces were built in many places. Canals were dug to connect waterways such as rivers and lakes. The most important was the Erie Canal in New York State. By using the Erie Canal, people could go by water from the Atlantic coast to the Great Lakes. Large amounts of goods were also carried over this route.

At the same time, people were starting to use a new form of power to run machinery. This was steam power. The first successful steam* engine had been made in the 1760's. Before long, steam engines were being used to run boats and trains. By the middle 1800's, there were hundreds of steamboats on our country's rivers and on the Great Lakes. Railroad lines were being built to connect all the important cities in the United States.

Our country grew rapidly in population. In the early 1800's, the number of people who lived in the United

In the 1800's, trains and steamboats became important means of transportation in the United States. How do you suppose this affected trade between different parts of our country?

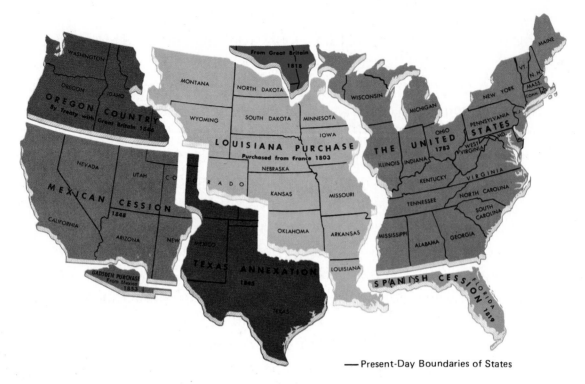

—Present-Day Boundaries of States

How our country grew. The red area on this map shows the size of the United States at the time that our country won its freedom from Great Britain. Later, other pieces of land were added to our country. For example, the United States gained Florida from Spain in 1819.

States grew larger than ever before. More than two million people came here from Ireland, Germany, and other places in Europe. Most of these people were seeking greater freedom or a better way of life. Many of them settled in cities along the Atlantic coast. Others went westward to build new homes on the frontier.

■ How did the United States gain land west of the Mississippi?

The United States bought Louisiana. To the west of the Mississippi River lay a huge piece of land called Louisiana. In 1803, the United States bought this land from France. (See map above.) President Thomas Jefferson sent a group of explorers led by Meriwether Lewis and William Clark to learn more about this new part of our country. Lewis and Clark journeyed all the way across the Louisiana Territory. (See map on page 36.) Then they went westward through the mountains to the Pacific Ocean. They brought back many useful facts about the places they had visited. During the years that followed, thousands of settlers moved into the Louisiana Territory to make their homes.

Texas became part of the Union. In 1821, the people of Mexico won their freedom from Spain. At that time, Mexico took over all the Spanish lands in the western part of North America. (Compare the map below with the maps on page 21.) There were Mexican settlements in Texas, California, and other places. However, these settlements were mostly small and far apart.

During the 1820's, settlers from the United States began moving into Texas. The government of Mexico had told them they could settle there. But as time passed, a quarrel arose between the American settlers and the Mexican government. Even though the settlers had promised to be loyal to Mexico, they still thought of themselves as Americans. In 1835, the settlers revolted. About a year later, they were able to break away from Mexican rule.

The settlers had won their independence from Mexico, but they did not want Texas to remain a separate country. They hoped it would become part of the United States. In 1845, our government annexed* Texas. This made people in Mexico angry. They believed the United

States had been trying all along to take over this area.

The United States gained California and other lands from Mexico. About the same time, American settlers were also moving into California. Like the Texans, these people did not wish to live under Mexican rule. They wanted the United States to take over California too.

In 1846, a war broke out between Mexico and the United States. After about a year of fighting, the United States won this war. Mexico then had to sell California and other lands

THE UNITED STATES AND MEXICO IN 1821

——Present-Day Boundary Between the United States and Mexico

in the Southwest to the United States. (See map on page 34.)

Britain and the United States divided the Oregon Country. Along the Pacific coast was a large piece of land known as the Oregon Country. Both the United States and Great Britain wanted to own it. For a time, it seemed likely that the two countries would go to war over the Oregon Country. But in 1846 they settled their differences by signing a treaty. Under this agreement, the United States got nearly all of the Oregon Country south of a line that stretched from the Rocky Mountains to the Pacific Ocean. Britain took the land north of this line.

■ Why did many people come to the western part of our country?

Pioneers in covered wagons traveled across the West. Years before the United States gained part of the Oregon Country, Americans were coming to this area. In the Oregon Country, there were pleasant valleys where the soil and climate were very good for farming. Many Americans wanted to move to the Oregon Country because they thought they could make a better living there.

Most of the settlers went westward over a route known as the Oregon Trail. (See map on this page.) They carried their belongings in covered wagons that were pulled by oxen or horses. The journey along the two-thousand-mile trail took about six months. It was very hard and dangerous. The settlers had to cross high mountains, wide rivers, and empty deserts. Many people died of sickness or were killed in fights with Indians. But settlers kept on coming.

The search for gold and silver brought many settlers. In 1848, a discovery was made that brought thousands of people to California. An American settler found tiny bits

ROUTES TO THE WEST

- - - - Westbound Route of
Lewis and Clark, 1804-1805
——— Oregon Trail
· · · · · First Railroad Across the West
——— Present-Day Boundaries of States

Pioneers going to the Oregon Country. These people have removed the wheels from their covered wagon and put it on a raft to float down a river. During the 1800's, many people moved to the West to make use of the natural resources there. What were some of these resources?

of gold in a mountain stream near Sacramento. (See map at left.) News of this exciting discovery soon spread to the eastern part of the United States. Before long, thousands of settlers were going to California by ship or by covered wagon in order to hunt for gold. This was known as the "gold rush." The number of people in California grew rapidly. Only two years later, California became a state in the Union.

In the years that followed, large deposits of gold and silver were found in Nevada, Colorado, and other parts of the West. Each discovery brought many miners. Large towns grew up quickly wherever gold and silver were found. Most of these "boomtowns" lasted only a few years, until the gold and silver ran out. But a few mining towns—such as Denver, Colorado—grew into important cities.

Railroads brought many people to the West. For years, people had dreamed of a railroad that would connect the eastern part of the United States with the Pacific coast. In the 1860's, two companies began this difficult task. Workers for one company began laying track westward from Omaha, Nebraska. (See map on page 36.) The other company's workers started east from Sacramento, California. The two railroad lines finally met near Great Salt Lake in Utah in 1869.

As time passed, other railroads were built across the West. Now settlers could travel westward by train instead of making the long, dangerous journey by covered wagon. Soon, people were moving west in growing numbers.

An Indian camp on the Great Plains. Why were the Indians unhappy to see white settlers coming to the West? What changes took place in the Indians' way of life after the settlers came?

The Indians lost their land and their way of life. Many different tribes of Indians lived in the West at the time that white people began coming here. The Indians did not like to have white people settle on their land. Often they had good reasons for being unhappy. For example, in the early 1800's huge herds of buffalo roamed the Great Plains.* The Indians of the plains hunted buffalo to get meat, hides, and other things they needed. But as the years passed, most of the buffalo were killed by white hunters. Then the Indians could no longer find enough buffalo to meet their needs.

In the last half of the 1800's, a number of battles took place between the Indians and United States soldiers. The Indians fought bravely. But they were much fewer in number than the white people, and some of the tribes were not willing to cooperate with each other. Also, the whites had better weapons. At last, the Indians gave up. They had to sell most of their land to the whites and move to places called reservations.*

Farmers came to the Great Plains to make their homes. After railroads were built across the Great Plains, many farmers began to settle in this part of the country. They came because they could get good farmland free or at a very low price. In return for building railroad lines, some companies had been given large amounts of land by the government. They were willing to sell this land cheaply to settlers. Also, the government gave land to people who were willing to farm it for five years.

Life was not easy for the families who settled on the Great Plains. Summers were hot and winters were freezing cold. In most places, the land was covered with thick grass that made it hard to plow the soil. Strong winds or hail sometimes destroyed whole fields of crops. Weeks or months might pass without any rain. Often farmers had to dig deep wells in order to get water. They had to put fences of barbed wire around their fields to keep wandering herds of cattle from eating their crops.

Pioneer farmers on the Great Plains. These people are plowing land so they can plant crops. Why was life very hard for many of the families who settled on the Great Plains?

Some settlers became so unhappy with their hard life that they moved back east. But others refused to give up. Through hard work and courage, they changed the Great Plains into an important farming area.

Discover Our Country's Story

1. What were some problems faced by the settlers who moved west of the Appalachian Mountains?
2. Why was New England a good place for building factories?
3. Why was there little trade at first between different parts of our country?
4. Why was Lewis and Clark's journey important to the United States?
5. Why were the people of Mexico angry when Texas became part of the United States?
6. Why did large numbers of people begin coming to California in 1848?
7. What were "boomtowns"? What happened to most of these towns?
8. How was the building of railroads important to the history of the West?
9. Why did the Indians lose most of the battles they fought against United States soldiers?
10. Why did many farmers come to the Great Plains during the last half of the 1800's?

4   The Union Is Saved

■ How did the United States become a divided country?

The North and the South had different ways of life. In the early 1800's, there were important differences between the northern and southern parts of our country. Hundreds of factories had been built in the North. Many people there lived in cities or large towns. In the South, there were few cities and only a small number of factories. Most people made their living by farming. In some places, there were plantations. On these large farms, cotton was usually the main crop. The owners sold large amounts of cotton to factories in the North and in Europe.

Loyalty

See Great Ideas

Abraham Lincoln was president of the United States at the time that a war broke out between the northern and southern parts of our country. This great struggle became known as the Civil War. Why is Abraham Lincoln remembered today as one of our greatest presidents? How did Lincoln show his loyalty to his country? How did he show his loyalty to certain ideas, such as the idea of freedom for all people? You will need to read more about Lincoln in other books to find the answers to these questions.

Large numbers of slaves worked on plantations in the South. Much of the work on southern farms was done by black people. On page 18, you read how blacks were brought from Africa in colonial days as slaves. These people did not have the freedom to live where they wished or to work at jobs of their own choosing. They had to work all their lives for the white plantation owners.

In colonial days, slavery had been allowed in the North also. But it had never been very profitable there, because farms were much smaller. Also, many people in the North believed that slavery was wrong. By 1800, most states in the North had passed laws saying that people could not own slaves.

Americans disagreed about slavery and other matters. Some people in the North believed that slavery should be ended everywhere in the United States. These people made speeches and wrote books attacking

A slave market in Virginia before the Civil War. White people in the South often said that black people did not mind being slaves. Do you think they were right? Why? Why not? Do you think that human beings everywhere have a deep desire for freedom? Explain.

A Divided Country

The map at the right shows the United States at the time of the Civil War. Slavery was allowed in all the Confederate states. It was not allowed in most states of the Union. These were known as free states. A few states, such as Missouri and Kentucky, allowed slavery but remained loyal to the Union. The western part of Virginia stayed with the Union when the rest of the state joined the Confederacy. It later became the state of West Virginia.

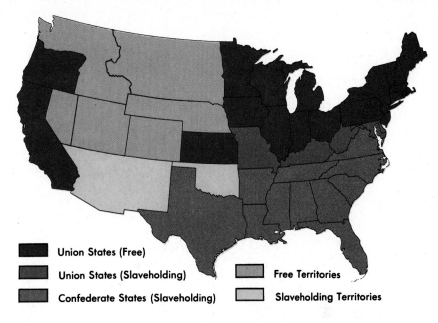

Union States (Free)

Union States (Slaveholding)

Confederate States (Slaveholding)

Free Territories

Slaveholding Territories

slavery. Sometimes they helped black people in the South to escape from their masters. As time passed, more people in the North began to agree with their views.

This movement to do away with slavery made most white people in the South very angry. They were afraid they would not be able to keep up their way of life if they did not have slaves to work for them.

People in the North and the South also disagreed about other matters. One of these was the question of states' rights. Most leaders in the North believed that laws made by the federal government should always be obeyed by the states. On the other hand, many southern leaders believed that states did not have to obey federal laws if they thought these laws were unfair. Some even said that states had the right to leave the Union.

■ How did the Civil War affect our country?

The quarrel between the North and the South led to war. In 1860, Abraham Lincoln became president of the United States. This alarmed many white people in the South, because they thought Lincoln would try to end slavery. Before long, eleven states in the South broke away

The Battle of Mobile Bay was an important navy battle in the Civil War. It took place in 1864 near Mobile, Alabama. (See map on pages 60-61.) Who won the Battle of Mobile Bay? Why was this battle so important? Look in other books to find answers to these questions.

from the Union. They formed a new nation known as the Confederate States of America, or the Confederacy.

In April, 1861, a war broke out between the North and the South. This became known as the Civil War.* It lasted four years and took the lives of more than half a million Americans.

The war ended in victory for the North. For a time, the South appeared to be winning the war. But the North was stronger in several ways. It had more than twice as many people as the South, and much more wealth. There were more factories in the North to make weapons and other things the soldiers needed. In addition, the North had better railroads. The North was aided by thousands of black soldiers who fought for the Union. Also, President Lincoln was a very wise and strong leader.

These advantages helped the North to win the war. In the spring of 1865, the Confederate armies surrendered to the armies of the Union.

Two important results of the Civil War. The victory of the North caused two important things to happen. First, the eleven Confederate states were brought back into the Union. Second, slavery was ended in all parts of the United States.

*See Glossary

Discover Our Country's Story
1. What were some important differences between the North and the South during the early 1800's?
2. Why did slavery come to an end in the North?
3. How did people in the North and the South disagree on the question of states' rights?
4. Why were many white people in the South alarmed when Abraham Lincoln became president?
5. Why was the North able to win the Civil War?

5   Our Country Becomes a World Leader

■ How did the United States become a great manufacturing nation?

The Civil War helped industry to grow. During the Civil War, industry grew rapidly in the United States. The American soldiers needed large amounts of such things as clothing, food, and weapons. To help meet these needs, new factories were started. And many older factories made more goods than ever before.

After the war, industry grew even faster. There were now more people in the United States, so there were more customers for the goods that factories made. Also, the new railroads made it possible to ship goods quickly and cheaply from one place to another. Because of this, factories could sell their goods to people in all parts of the country.

Inventors discovered new ways of making goods. Another reason why industry grew so rapidly was that people found new ways to make use of our country's rich natural resources. For example, there were large deposits of coal and iron ore in the United States. Coal and iron ore could be used in making steel. Although steel was a very useful metal, it had always been slow and costly to produce. But in the 1850's,

Using
Natural
Resources

See Great Ideas

The picture at right shows a group of ironworkers in New York State. During the last half of the 1800's, Americans discovered new ways of using certain natural resources to meet their needs. What were some of these resources? How did the new discoveries affect the growth of industry in the United States?

people found a way to make large amounts of steel rapidly and cheaply. Soon many steel plants were built in the United States. The steel was used by other factories in making many different kinds of goods.

People were also discovering new ways of using natural resources to produce heat, light, and power. One of these resources was a dark, oily liquid that came out of the ground in certain places. This was called petroleum. For a long time, people thought petroleum was worthless. But then they found that it could be made into kerosene* and other valuable products. Kerosene became widely used as a fuel in lamps and stoves.

People in America were also learning about a new form of power called electricity. In 1879, Thomas Edison made the first successful electric light. Edison and other inventors also developed machines that could make large amounts of electricity.

*See Glossary

Using Tools

See Great Ideas

The picture above shows Henry Ford and his wife, Clara Bryant Ford, in a workshop behind their home in Detroit, Michigan. The year was 1896, and Henry Ford was just finishing work on his first automobile. Ford was not the first person ever to build an automobile, but he was the first to make cars that were cheap enough for most people to buy. Can you explain how he did this?

Soon electricity was being used to run many kinds of machinery.

About the same time, people were discovering new ways of sending messages from place to place. Alexander Graham Bell invented the first telephone in 1876. Radio was another new form of communication.* It was developed in the early 1900's.

Because of new inventions, transportation was also improved. The first automobiles were built in the late 1800's by people in Europe and the United States. In 1903, two brothers from Ohio named Wilbur and Orville Wright built the first successful airplane.

Factory owners discovered better ways of making goods. As the years passed, factory owners in the United States found new and better ways of making goods. One of the most important of these was the assembly-line method. It was developed mostly by an auto maker named Henry Ford. The frame of an automobile was put on a large belt that moved slowly past a line of workers. Each worker added a different part to the frame until the car was finished.

The assembly-line method made it possible to build large numbers of cars at a price most people could pay. It worked so well that factories began to use it in making many different kinds of goods.

All of these new discoveries helped industry to grow rapidly in the United States. By the early 1900's, our country was producing more factory goods than any other country.

■ **How did great cities grow up in the United States?**

People moved from farms to cities. Before the Civil War, only one out of every five Americans lived in a city or large town. But in the years that followed, great changes took place in people's way of living. Farmers began to use new machines and better ways of farming. These made it possible for one farmer to raise enough food for many people. At the same time, more workers than ever before were needed in factories, stores, and offices. Thousands of people moved from farms to cities to get jobs. As more and more newcomers arrived, the cities grew rapidly. For example, Chicago was more than twenty times as large in 1910 as it was in 1860. By 1910 nearly half of all Americans lived in cities or large towns.

Immigrants* came from many lands. Many of the people who settled in the growing cities were immigrants from other lands. Between 1865 and 1915, more than twenty-six million people came to the United States to live. Most of them were from European countries such as Germany, Italy, Sweden, and Poland. Some also came from Mexico, Canada, and other countries in North and South America. A much smaller

*See Glossary

Division of Labor

See Great Ideas

The picture above shows a famous street called the Bowery in New York City during the 1890's. In the years that followed the Civil War, American cities grew rapidly. What were some of the reasons for this? Was there *more* division of labor in the cities than in the country? Or was there *less*? How do you think this affected the number of people who wanted to move from the farms to the cities? Look for "Great Ideas" on the Contents page to find information that will help answer these questions.

number of people came from China, Japan, and other countries in Asia.

Most of these people came to America because they had heard it was a "land of opportunity." In the lands where they were born, they had found it hard to earn a good living. They hoped it would be easier to find good jobs in America. Some people came to America because they wanted more freedom than they could have in their own countries.

Life was not easy for most of the immigrants at first. These people were often very poor. Because most of them did not have any special training, they could not get good jobs. Many could not speak English when they arrived. Often they found it hard to give up their old ways of

doing things and learn a new way of life. Some of them were treated unkindly by other people in America. This was partly because they seemed strange and "different." Also, many Americans were afraid the newcomers would take their jobs away from them by working for less money.

As time passed, life became easier for most of the immigrants. The children and many of the older people went to school. There they learned the English language and American ways. As they gained more education, they were able to get better jobs. Many of our country's leaders during the last one hundred years have been immigrants or sons and daughters of immigrants.

■ How did the United States become
involved in world problems?

Americans began to take more interest in other countries. During the 1700's and 1800's, most Americans paid little attention to what was happening in other parts of the world. Wide oceans separated America from Europe, Asia, and Africa. Transportation and communication were still quite slow. Americans were interested mostly in developing the resources of their own huge country.

As time passed, an important change began to take place. The United States was now becoming one of the richest and strongest countries in the world. It was carrying on more and more trade with other nations. Many Americans felt the United States should play a more important part in the world.

A chance to do this came in 1898, when the United States went to war against Spain. At that time, Spain ruled the island of Cuba in the West Indies. American soldiers were sent to Cuba to help the people of that island win their independence from Spain. After a few months of fighting, the Americans defeated the Spanish. Spain had to give Cuba its freedom. The United States became owner of two Spanish possessions. These were the island of Puerto Rico, in the West Indies, and the Philippine Islands, off the coast of Asia. About the same time, the United States took over the Hawaiian Islands.

The United States entered a war in Europe. In 1914, a terrible war broke out between two groups of countries in Europe. On one side were the Central Powers, which included Germany and Austria-Hungary. On the other side were Britain, France, Russia, and several other countries. They were called the Allies. The great struggle between the Allies and the Central Powers became known as World War I.

At first, the United States tried to stay out of the war in Europe. But German submarines began to attack Allied ships in the Atlantic Ocean. A number of Americans on these ships were killed. The Germans also did other things that made the American people angry. In 1917 the United States joined the war on the side of the Allies. American soldiers were sent to Europe to fight. In the fall of 1918, the Central Powers finally gave up.

Another war took the lives of many Americans. For a few years, there was peace in most parts of the world. But in 1933 a group of people called the Nazis* took over the government in Germany. Their leader, Adolf Hitler, wanted to conquer other countries and make Germany the most powerful nation in Europe. The leaders of Italy and Japan also decided to go to war to gain more lands. Together, these three countries became known as the Axis. They were opposed by Britain, France, the Soviet Union, and other countries. In 1939, Germany attacked the neighboring country of Poland. This was the start of World War II.

Again, people in the United States hoped to stay out of war. But in 1941, Japanese airplanes made a surprise attack on a large group of American warships docked at Pearl Harbor in

the Hawaiian Islands. This attack brought our country into the war against the Axis. Millions of Americans were sent to fight in many parts of the world.

By working together, the United States and its allies were able to defeat the Axis. First Italy and then Germany surrendered to the Allied armies. In the meantime, scientists who were working for the United States government built a powerful new weapon called the atomic bomb. In August, 1945, atomic bombs destroyed two Japanese cities. Partly because of this, Japan gave up the war a short time later.

The United Nations was formed to work for world peace. By the end of World War II, many people had come to believe that there must never again be a world war. Atomic bombs and other weapons had become too powerful. If these new weapons were ever used in another war, they might destroy all life on earth.

An American battleship on fire after the Japanese attack at Pearl Harbor in 1941. Where is Pearl Harbor? Why was the attack at Pearl Harbor so important in American history?

Cooperation

See Great Ideas

The picture above shows people from different countries at a meeting of the United Nations in New York City. What is the United Nations? Why was the United Nations formed? Do you think it is important for countries to cooperate with one another in order to solve their problems? Give facts to explain your answer. What sometimes happens when countries do not cooperate?

In 1945, most countries of the world joined together in forming a new organization to work for world peace. This was the United Nations. Today about 150 countries are members of the United Nations, which meets in New York City. The United Nations tries to settle disagreements that might lead to war. It also tries to help the poorer countries of the world provide a better way of life for their people.

Communism spread to many parts of the world. After World War II ended, the United States was faced with a new problem. For almost thirty years, the Soviet Union had been ruled by a group of people who were known as Communists.* The Communists believed that industry, trade, and most other activities in a country should be run by the government. They wanted people all over the world to follow the Communist way of life.

For a time, it seemed to many Americans that the Communists might reach their goal. Communist governments came to power in several countries of eastern Europe, such as Poland and Hungary. In 1949 the huge country of China also fell under Communist rule.

Most people in the United States were strongly against communism. They were afraid it could take away their freedom. The United States made agreements with a number of friendly countries in Europe and Asia. These countries promised to help each other in case of a Communist attack.

The struggle between the Communist countries and the non-Communist countries became known as the Cold War. Both sides made their armies larger. They also developed new weapons and war equipment, such as hydrogen* bombs and guided* missiles. Sometimes real fighting broke out between the two sides. For example, there was a war between Communist and non-Communist forces in the small Asian country of Korea. This war lasted from 1950 to 1953. Another war took place in the Asian country of Vietnam from 1957 to 1975. About half a million American soldiers were killed or wounded in these two wars.

In the last few years, the Communist and non-Communist countries have grown a little more friendly toward one another. Some people believe that the Cold War is mostly over. Other people think that the Cold War will last as long as the Communist and non-Communist countries have such different ways of life.

Discover Our Country's Story

1. How did the Civil War help American industry to grow? Why did industry keep on growing after the war was over?
2. What important changes took place in transportation and communication during the late 1800's and early 1900's?
3. Why did many people from Europe come to America after 1865?
4. Why did many immigrants have a hard time when they first came to America?
5. Why did most Americans take little interest in other countries during the 1700's and 1800's?
6. What were some things that happened because of the Spanish-American War?
7. Why did the United States take part in World War I? Why did it take part in World War II?
8. What was the Cold War, and how did it come about?

6 Years of Amazing Change

■ **How have science and industry changed American life?**

In the last thirty years, great changes have taken place in our country. Today our way of life is very different from what it was in the past.

Changes brought about by science. Some of these changes have been brought about by science. For example, scientists have learned how to use the energy* stored in atoms.* This energy can be used to make powerful weapons. It can be used to produce electricity. Also, rockets have been built to carry people far from the earth. American astronauts* have already landed on the moon. Someday they may be able to make even longer trips in space.

Changes caused by industry. Important changes have also been taking place in industry. Many new machines have been invented. Some of these machines do not need people to guide them. They can run by themselves. The use of

*See Glossary

A giant rocket takes off from the earth for a flight into space. Do you think space flights will be important to Americans in years to come? Explain.

machines like these is called automation. Other new machines can do the hardest math problems in a few seconds. These machines are called computers.

The new machines have helped industry to grow. By using them, workers can produce more goods than ever before. (See the charts below.) This is why most Americans have a comfortable way of life. They can afford to buy many kinds of goods. For example, most American families own cars and television sets. This is not true in many other countries. There, only a few rich families can buy such things.

Pollution is a serious problem. The growth of our industry has brought many good things to people in the United States. But it has also led to some major problems. One of these is pollution.*

Air pollution is caused in several ways. People burn fuels such as coal and oil to heat their buildings. They also burn these fuels to produce electricity. Sometimes rubbish is burned to get rid of it. The smoke from all these fires goes into the air. There

Great changes have taken place in our country in the last thirty years. Some of these changes are shown on the charts below. The chart at left shows the number of people in the United States. Our population has grown from about 152 million in 1950 to almost 220 million today. The middle chart shows the value of all goods and services produced in our country. As you can see, production has grown very rapidly since 1950. The chart at right shows the average family income in the United States. The average family income grew from about $3,300 in 1950 to about $13,700 in 1975. It is still growing rapidly today.

Our Changing Nation

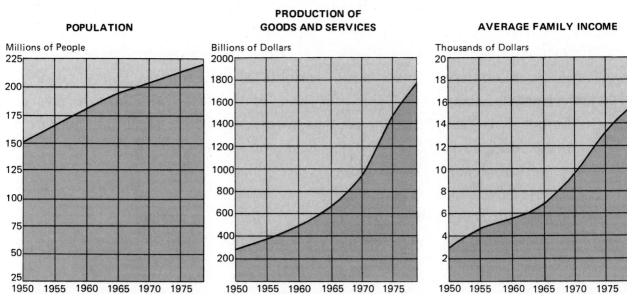

POPULATION — Millions of People

PRODUCTION OF GOODS AND SERVICES — Billions of Dollars

AVERAGE FAMILY INCOME — Thousands of Dollars

it mixes with fumes from cars, trucks, buses, and airplanes.

Water can become polluted also. This happens when cities and factories dump their waste materials into rivers and lakes.

Today many Americans are worried about pollution. Scientists have found that people can become very sick from breathing polluted air. Polluted water is not safe for drinking, bathing, and other uses. Our country's leaders are seeking ways to stop pollution. They want to make our air and water clean again.

The need to use resources carefully. The growth of industry has led to another problem. Each year, American factories use huge amounts of natural resources. Today some of these resources are starting to run out. For example, we no longer produce enough oil, or petroleum,* to meet our needs. So we must buy large amounts of oil from other countries. If these countries ever stopped selling us oil, we would be in serious trouble.

In the future, we will have to use our resources more carefully to keep from running out. We must also find new ways of getting the things we need. For instance, sunlight is a source of energy that will never be used up. Some people are now using sunlight to heat their houses. Someday it may also be possible to use sunlight in producing electric power.

■ How has the concern for human needs changed American life?

Basic needs of people. All people on earth are alike in certain ways. They all have needs they must meet in order to live happy, useful lives. These are called basic human needs. (See "Needs of People" in Table of Contents.) For example, every person needs food, clothing, and shelter. Every person needs goals to work for. Every person needs a chance to think and learn. And every person needs some kind of faith. Today, Americans are trying to make sure that all our citizens have a chance to meet their basic human needs.

Some people did not have equal rights and freedoms. Thirty years ago, many Americans did not have an equal chance to meet their needs. Among these people were:

. . . blacks

. . . Jews*

. . . American Indians

. . . people whose ancestors* came

from certain countries, such as Mexico, Puerto Rico, China, and Japan.

These people lacked a number of the rights and freedoms that other Americans enjoyed. For example, in some places black children could not go to the same schools as white children. Some hotels and resorts would not admit Jews as guests. Mexican-Americans were sometimes

Freedom

See Great Ideas

The picture above shows a civil rights march in Boston, Massachusetts, during the 1960's. What do we mean by "civil rights"? Why did some Americans feel they needed to hold marches for civil rights? Did the civil rights movement succeed in reaching its goals? Give facts to back up your answer. Are there still any people in our country today who do not enjoy the same rights and freedoms as other Americans? If so, who are they?

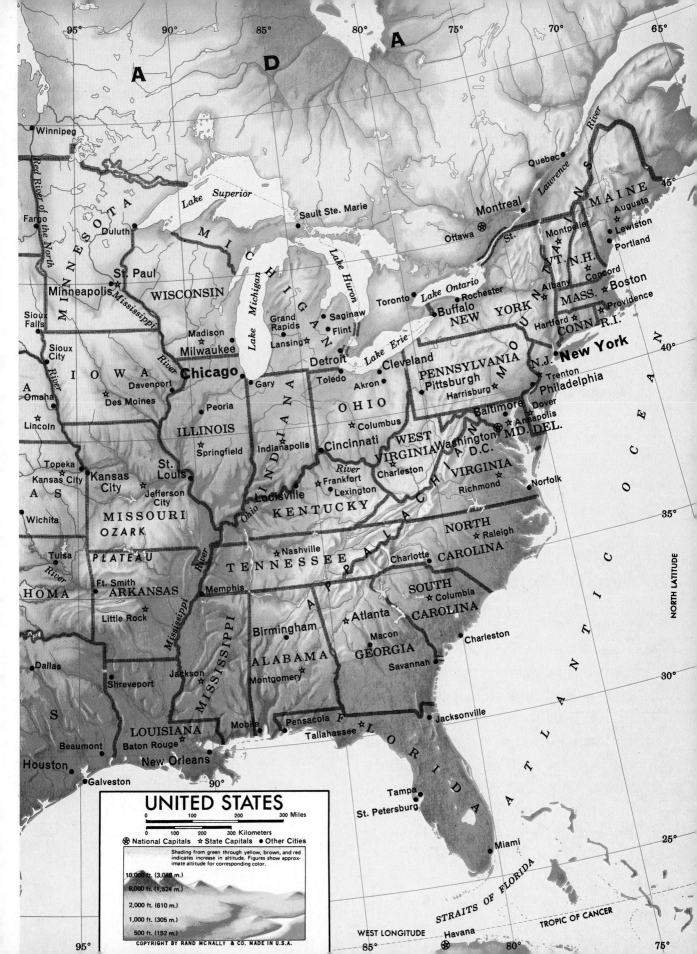

refused jobs that other Americans could get easily. Some people would not sell houses or rent apartments to Indian families.

Women, too, were often treated unfairly in our country. For example, some companies would not hire women for certain jobs. If they did hire women, they would often pay them less money than men. This was true even if the women did exactly the same kind of work.

People work for equal rights and freedoms. During the 1950's, an important change took place. Some of the people who had been treated unfairly began to demand equal rights. They held marches and public meetings to call attention to what they wanted. Soon they were joined by other Americans who supported their fight for freedom. This became known as the civil* rights movement.

As time passed, the civil rights movement began to reach its goals. Our federal and state governments passed laws to protect the rights of minority* groups. Today it is against the law to treat a person unfairly just because that person belongs to a certain group. Women and minority groups now enjoy more rights than ever before in our history.

Today some people cannot meet their needs. Even today, however, many Americans find it hard to meet their needs. For example, millions of people cannot find steady jobs. Sometimes this is because they are too old, or their health is poor. They may not have the education or the skills needed to get a well-paying job. Sometimes there are simply not enough jobs for all the people who need them.

Usually, people who lack steady jobs do not have much money. They cannot afford to buy the proper kinds of food, clothing, and shelter. Many of them live in run-down areas called slums. When they become ill, they cannot afford medical care. Sometimes their illnesses keep them from holding full-time jobs.

Business and government are helping. Many things are being done to help Americans who have trouble meeting their needs. For instance, our government runs training programs for workers without jobs. Here, people learn skills they can use in industry. Business companies also carry on programs of this kind. Many cities have built apartment buildings where people can live without paying very much money. Our government provides money for people who are too old or too ill to hold steady jobs.

Government programs have helped many Americans to meet their needs. But these programs often cost a lot of money. Also, many people are needed to carry them out. Today, more than sixteen million Americans work for the government. Our national government spends more than thirteen times as much money each year as it did in 1948. Most of this money comes from taxes that our citizens must pay to the government.

Doing our part as citizens. In the years to come, many more exciting

Rules
and
Government

See Great Ideas

The picture below shows a woman scientist at work. In the past, women could work only at certain kinds of jobs. Today, all kinds of jobs are open to women. How did laws help to bring about this change? Sometimes people think that laws take away part of their freedom. But can laws also protect a person's freedom? If so, how?

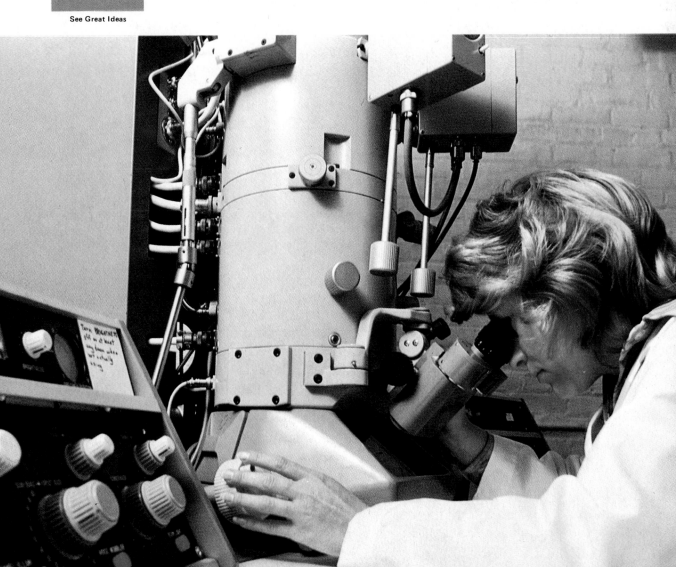

Education

See Great Ideas

Working on a classroom project. In our country today, most young people have a chance to get a good education. Nearly all children attend grade school and high school. Many students also go on to college. Do you think education is one of the great ideas that have built our nation? What would happen if most of our citizens did not have a good education? Would our government be able to do its job well? Give reasons for your answers.

changes will take place in our country. Will these changes be good or bad? The answer is largely up to us. We must all do our part as citizens. We must continue to live by the great ideas that built our nation— ideas such as freedom, loyalty, and cooperation. In this way, we can make our country even better and stronger than it is today.

Discover Our Country's Story

1. What important changes have taken place in the United States during the last thirty years? How have these changes affected your family?
2. Why is pollution a serious problem today? What are some examples of pollution in your own community?
3. What is being done today to help people who have trouble meeting their needs?
4. In what ways do you think the United States will change in the years ahead?

Index

Explanation of abbreviations used in this Index: *p* — picture   *m* — map

---

PRONUNCIATION KEY: hat, āge, cãre, fär; let, ēqual, tèrm; it, īce; hot, ōpen, ôrder; oil, out; cup, pùt, rüle, ūse; child; long; thin; ᴛнen; zh, measure; ə represents a in about, e in taken, i in pencil, o in lemon, u in circus.

Acknowledgments

Grateful acknowledgment is made to the following for permission to use the illustrations found in this book:

American Heritage: Pages 8-9, painting by Frederic Remington
Anheuser-Busch, Inc.: Pages 12-13, courtesy of August A. Busch, Jr.
Cincinnati Art Museum: Pages 38-39, bequest of Mrs. W. D. Julian
Confederation Life Collection: Pages 14-15
Ford Archives: Page 48, painting by Norman Rockwell
Francis G. Mayer, Art Color Slides, New York City: Pages 42-43, painting by Eyre Crowe
Grant Heilman: Pages 10-11 by Alan Pitcairn
H. Armstrong Roberts: Pages 1, 2-3, 52-53, and 63
Herb Orth, LIFE Magazine, © Time Inc.: Pages 22-23
Ken Heyman: Page 64
Kennedy Galleries, New York: Pages 32-33
Metropolitan Museum of Art: Pages 46-47, painting by John Ferguson Weir, gift of Lyman G. Bloomingdale, 1901
Museum of the City of New York: Pages 50-51
NASA: Page 56
New York Public Library: Page 13; pages 18-19, engraving by William Birch and Son
Phillip Gendreau: Page 41
The Fideler Company: Pages 4, 6-7, 28-29, 30-31, and 40
Thomas Williams: Page 16
United Nations: Page 54
United States Department of Commerce, Bureau of Public Roads: Page 37
Van Cleve Photography: Page 59 by David Kelley
Wadsworth Atheneum, Hartford, Conn.: Pages 44-45
Yale University Art Gallery: Pages 24-25 and 26-27, paintings by John Trumbull

Grateful acknowledgment is made to Scott, Foresman and Company for the pronunciation system used in this book, which is taken from the Thorndike-Barnhart Dictionary Series. Grateful acknowledgment is made to Rand McNally & Company for cartographic data on pages 60-61 and for permission to use the globes in this book.

SKILLS MANUAL

CONTENTS

Thinking

One of the main reasons you are attending school is to learn how to think clearly. Your social studies class is one of the best places in which to grow in the use of your thinking skills. Here you will learn more about using the thinking skills that will help you understand yourself, your country, and your world.

There are seven different kinds of thinking skills. As you use all seven, you will become more successful in school and in life. You will be able to understand yourself and your world much better. You will be a happier and more useful citizen as well.

Seven kinds of thinking

1. **Remembering** is the simplest kind of thinking. Everything you can remember is called your store of knowledge.

    Example: Remembering facts, such as the names of state capitals.

2. **Translation** is changing information from one form into another.

    Example: Reading a map and putting into words the information you find there.

3. **Interpretation** is discovering how things relate to each other, or how things are connected.

    Example: Comparing two pictures to decide in what ways they are alike or in what ways they are different.

4. **Application** is using your knowledge and skills to solve a new problem.

    Example: Using social studies skills to prepare a written report.

5. **Analysis** is the kind of thinking you use when you try to find out how something is organized, or put together. When you

1

use this kind of thinking, you separate complicated information into its basic parts. Then you can see how they were put together and how they are related to each other.

Example: Separating main ideas from supporting facts.

6. **Synthesis** is putting ideas together in a form that not only has meaning but is also new and original.

Examples: Painting a picture; or writing something original, which might be a paragraph or an entire poem, story, or play.

7. **Evaluation** is the highest level of thinking. It is judging whether or not something meets a given standard.

Example: Deciding which of several different sources of information is the most reliable; or judging the success of a class discussion.

Solving Problems

The social studies will be more worthwhile to you if you learn to think and work as a scientist does. Scientists use a special way of studying called the problem-solving method. During the 1900's, the use of this method has helped people gain much scientific knowledge. In fact, we have gained more scientific knowledge during the 1900's than people had discovered earlier throughout the history of human beings on this planet.

The problem-solving method is more interesting than simply reading a textbook and memorizing answers for a test. By using this method, you can make your own discoveries. Using the problem-solving method will also help you learn how to think clearly. It will involve you in using

all of the seven different kinds of thinking skills. To use this method in learning about our country, you will need to follow these steps.

1. **Choose an important, interesting problem** that you would like to solve. (A sample problem to solve is given on the opposite page.) Write the problem down so that you will have clearly in mind what it is you want to find out. If there are small problems that need to be solved in order to solve your big problem, list them, too.

2. **Think about all possible solutions** to your problem. List the ones that seem most likely to be true. These possible solutions are called "educated guesses," or hypotheses. You will try to solve your problem by finding facts to support or to disprove your hypotheses.

Sometimes you may wish to do some general background reading before you make your hypotheses. For example, if you were going to solve the sample problem on the opposite page, you might want first to read about the land features of the Northeast. Then, make your hypotheses based on what you have discovered.

3. **Test your hypotheses** by doing research. This book provides you with four major sources of information. These are the pictures, the text, the maps, and the Glossary. To find the information you need, you may use the Table of Contents and the Index. The suggestions on pages 4-7 will help you find and evaluate other sources of information.

As you do research, make notes of all the information that will either support your hypotheses or disprove them. You may discover that information from one source does not agree with information from another. If this should happen, check still further. Try to decide which facts are correct.

4. Summarize what you have learned. Your summary should be a short statement of the main points you have discovered. Have you been able to support one or more of your hypotheses with facts? Have you been able to prove that one or more of your hypotheses is not correct? What new facts have you learned? Do you need to do more research?

You may want to write a report about the problem. To help other people share the ideas you have come to understand, you may decide to include maps, pictures, or your own drawings with your report. You will find helpful suggestions for writing a good report on pages 7 and 8.

A sample problem to solve

As you study our country, you may wish to try to solve problems about our country as a whole. Or, you may wish to study one major region. The following sample problem to solve is about the Northeast as a region.

Mountains and rolling hills make up much of the Northeast. Very little of this part of our country is low and level. How do the land features of the Northeast affect the lives of the people? In forming hypotheses to solve this problem, you will need to think about how the land features of the Northeast affect the following:

a. where the cities grew up
b. industry
c. farming

The suggestions on the next two pages will help you find the information you need for solving this problem.

Learning Social Studies Skills

What is a skill?

A skill is something that you have learned to do well. To learn some skills, such as swimming or playing baseball, you must train the muscles of your arms and legs. To learn others, such as typing, you must train your fingers. Still other skills call for you to train your mind. For instance, reading with understanding is a skill that calls for much mental training. The skills that you use in the social studies are largely mental skills.

Why are skills important?

Mastering different skills will help you to have a happier and more satisfying life. You will be healthier and enjoy your free time more if you develop skills needed to take part in different sports. By developing art and music skills, you will be able to share your feelings more fully. It is even more important for you to develop your mental skills. These skills are the tools that you will use in getting and using the knowledge you need to live successfully in today's world.

Developing a skill

If you were to ask fine athletes or musicians how they gained their skills, they would probably say, "Through practice."

To develop mental skills, you must practice also. Remember, however, that a person cannot become a good ballplayer if he or she keeps throwing the ball in the wrong way. A person cannot become a fine musician by practicing the wrong notes. The same thing is true of mental skills. To master them, you must practice them correctly.

The following pages have suggestions about how to perform correctly several important skills needed in the social studies. For example, to succeed in the social studies you must know how to find the information you need. You need to know how to prepare reports and how to work with others on group projects. Study these skills carefully, and use them.

How To Find Information You Need

Each day of your life you seek information. Sometimes you want to know certain facts just because you are curious. Most of the time, however, you want information for some certain reason. If you enjoy baseball, for instance, you may want to know how to figure batting averages. If you collect stamps, you need to know how to find out what countries they come from. As a student in today's world, you need information for many reasons. As an adult, you will need even more knowledge in order to live successfully in tomorrow's world.

You may wonder how you can possibly learn all the facts you are going to need during your lifetime. The answer is that you can't. Therefore, knowing how to find information when you need it is very important to you. Following are suggestions for finding good sources of information and for using these sources to find the facts that you need.

Written Sources of Information

Books

You may be able to find the information you need in books that you have at home or in your classroom. To see if a textbook or other nonfiction* book has the information you need, look at the table of contents and the index.

Sometimes, you will need to go to your school or neighborhood library to find books that have the information you want. To make the best use of a library, you should learn to use the card catalog. This is a file that contains information about the books in the library. Each nonfiction book has at least three cards, filed in alphabetical order. One is for the title, one is for the author, and one is for the subject of the book. Each card gives the book's special number. This number will help you to find the book. All the nonfiction books in the

library are arranged on the shelves in numerical order. If you cannot find a book that you want, the librarian will help you.

Reference volumes

You will find much useful information in certain books known as reference volumes. Among these are dictionaries, encyclopedias, atlases, and other special books. Some companies publish a book each year with facts and figures and general information about the events of the year before. Such books are generally called yearbooks, annuals, or almanacs.

Newspapers and magazines

These are important sources of up-to-date information. Sometimes you will want to look for information in papers or magazines that you do not have at home. You can almost always find the ones you want at the library.

The *Readers' Guide to Periodical Literature* is kept for use in most libraries. It will direct you to magazine articles about the subject you are interested in. This is a series of volumes that list articles by title, author, and subject. In the front of each volume is an explanation of the abbreviations used to indicate the different magazines and their dates.

Booklets, pamphlets, and bulletins

You can get many materials of this kind from local and state governments, as well as from our federal government. Chambers of commerce, travel bureaus, trade organizations, private companies, and embassies of other countries publish materials that have a wealth of information.

Many booklets and bulletins give correct information. Remember, however, that some of them were written to promote certain goods or ideas. Information from such sources should be checked carefully.

*See Glossary

Reading for Information

The following suggestions will help you to save time and work when you are looking for information in books and other written materials.

The table of contents and the index

The table of contents appears at the beginning of the book and generally is a list of the chapters in the book. By looking at this list, you can almost always tell if the book has the kind of information you need.

The index is a more detailed list of the things that are talked about in the book. It will help you find the pages on which specific facts are talked about. In most books, the index is at the back. Encyclopedias often place the index in a separate volume.

At the beginning of an index, you will generally find an explanation that makes it easier to use. For instance, the beginning of the Index for this book tells you that *p* means picture and *m* means map.

The topics, or entries, in the index are arranged in alphabetical order. To find all the information you need, you may have to look under more than one entry. For example, to find out what pages of a social studies book have information about cities, you would look up the entry for cities. You could also see if cities are listed by their own names.

Skim the written material

Before you begin reading a chapter or a page, skim it to see if it has the information you need. In this way you will not waste time reading something that is of little or no value to you. When you skim, you look mainly for topic headings, topic sentences, and key words. Imagine you are looking for the answer to the question: "What are the people in the West doing to conserve their forest resources?" In a book about the West or about the United States, you might look for a topic heading that mentions forest resources. When you find this heading, you might look for the key words, "conserving forests."

Read carefully

When you think you have found the page that has the information you are looking for, read it carefully. Does this page tell you exactly what you want to know? If not, you will need to look further.

Other Ways of Getting Information

Direct experience

What you see or live through for yourself may be a good source of information if you have watched carefully and remembered accurately. Firsthand information can often be obtained by visiting places in your community or nearby, such as museums, factories, or government offices.

Radio and television

Use the listings in your local newspaper to find programs about the subjects in which you are interested.

Movies, filmstrips, recordings, and slides

Materials on many different subjects are available. You can get them from schools, libraries, museums, and private companies.

Resource people

Sometimes, you will be able to get information by talking with a person who has special knowledge. Once in a while, you may wish to invite someone to speak to your class and answer questions.

Evaluating Information

During your lifetime, you will constantly need to evaluate what you see, hear, and read. Information is not true or worthwhile simply because it is presented on television or is written in a book, magazine, or newspaper. The following suggestions will help you in evaluating information.

Primary and secondary sources of information

A primary source of information is a firsthand record. For instance, a photograph taken of something while it is happening is a primary source. So is the report you write about a field trip you take. Original documents, such as the Constitution of the United States, are primary sources also.

A secondary source is a secondhand report. If you write a report about what someone else told you he or she saw, your report will be a secondary source of information. Another example of a secondary source is a history book.

Advanced scholars like to use primary sources whenever possible. However, these sources are often difficult to obtain. Most students in elementary and high school use secondary sources. You should always be aware that you are using secondhand information when you use a secondary source.

Who said it and when was it said?

The next step in evaluating information is to ask, "Who said it?" Was she a person with special training in the subject about which she wrote? Was he a newsman who is known for careful reporting of the facts?

Another question you should ask is "When was it said?" Changes take place rapidly in our world, and the information you are using may be out of date. For instance, suppose you are looking for information about a country. If you use an encyclopedia that is five years old, much of the information you find will not be correct.

Is it mostly fact or opinion?

The next step in evaluating information is to decide if it is based on facts or if it consists mostly of unsupported opinions. You can do this best if you know about these three kinds of statements:

1. Statements of fact that can be checked. For example, "Voters in the United States choose their representatives by secret ballot" is a statement of fact that can be checked by finding out how voting is carried on in different parts of our country.

2. Inferences, or conclusions that are based on facts. The statement "The people of the United States live in a democracy" is an inference. This inference is based on the fact that the citizens choose their representatives by secret ballot, and on other facts that can be proved. It is important to remember that inferences can be false or only partly true, even though they are based on facts.

3. Value judgments, or opinions. The statement "It is always wrong for a country to go to war" is a value judgment. Since a value judgment is an opinion, you need to look at it very carefully. On what facts and inferences is it based? What facts and conclusions do you think form the basis of the opinion, "It is always wrong for a country to go to war"? Do you agree or disagree with these conclusions? Trustworthy writers or reporters are careful to let their readers know which statements are their own opinions. They also try to base their opinions as much as possible on facts that can be proved.

Why was it said?

The next step in evaluating information is to find out the purpose for which it was prepared. Many books and articles are prepared in an honest effort to give you accurate information. Scientists writing about new scientific discoveries will generally try to report their findings as accurately as possible. They will be careful to distinguish between things they have actually seen and conclusions they have drawn from their observations.

Some information, however, is prepared mostly to persuade people to believe or act a certain way. Information of this kind is called propaganda.

Some propaganda is used to promote causes that are generally thought to be good. A picture that shows Smokey the Bear and the words "Only you can prevent forest fires" is an example of this kind of propaganda.

Propaganda is also used to make people support causes they would not agree with if they knew more about them. This kind of propaganda may be made up of information that is true, partly true, or false. Even when it is true, however, the information may be presented in such a way as to mislead you.

Propaganda generally appeals to people's feelings rather than to their thinking ability. For this reason, you should learn to recognize information that is propaganda. Then you can think about it calmly and clearly, and evaluate it intelligently.

Making Reports

There are many times when you need to share information or ideas with others. Sometimes you will need to do this in writing. Other times you will need to do it by speaking. One of the best ways to develop your writing and speaking skills is by making written and oral reports. The success of your report will depend on how well you have organized your material. It will also depend on your skill in presenting it. Here are some guidelines that will help you in preparing a good report.

Decide upon a goal

Have your goal clearly in mind. Are you mostly interested in sharing information? Do you want to give your own ideas on a subject? Or are you trying to persuade other people to agree with you?

Find the information you need

Be sure to use more than one source. If you are not sure how to find information about your subject, read the suggestions on pages 4 and 5.

Take good notes

To remember what you have read, you must take notes. Before you begin taking notes, however, you will need to make a list of the questions you want your report to answer. As you do research, write down the facts that answer these questions. You may find some interesting and important facts that do not answer any of your questions. If you feel that they might be useful in your report, write them down, too. Your notes should be short and in your own words except when you want to use quotations. When you use an exact quotation, be sure to put quotation marks around it.

You will be able to make the best use of your notes if you write them on file cards. Use a separate card for each statement or group of statements that answers one of your questions. To remember where your information came from, write on each card the title, author, and date of the source. When you have finished taking notes, group the cards according to the questions they answer.

Make an outline

After you have reviewed your notes, make an outline. This is a general plan that shows the order and the relationship of the ideas you want to include in your report. The first step in making an outline is to pick out the main ideas. These will be the main headings in your outline. (See sample outline below.) Next, list under each of these headings the ideas and facts that support or explain it. These related ideas are called subheadings. As you arrange your information, ask yourself the following questions.

a. Is there one main idea I must put first because everything else depends on this idea?
b. Have I arranged my facts in such a way as to show relationships among them?

c. Are there some ideas that will be clearer if they come after other ideas have been explained?

d. Have I included enough facts so that I can end my outline with a summary statement or a logical conclusion?

When you have finished your first outline, you may find that some parts of it are too short. If so, you may wish to do more research. When you feel that you have enough information, make your final outline. Remember that this outline will serve as a guide for your finished report.

Example of an outline

The author of this Skills Manual prepared the following outline before writing "Making Reports."

I. Introduction
II. Deciding upon a goal
III. Finding information
IV. Taking notes
   A. List main ideas to be researched
   B. Write on file cards facts that support or explain these ideas
   C. Group cards according to main ideas
V. Making an outline
   A. Purpose of an outline
   B. Guidelines for arranging information
   C. Sample outline of this section
VI. Preparing a written report
VII. Presenting an oral report

Special guidelines for a written report

Using your outline as a guide, write your report. The following suggestions will help you to make your report interesting and clear.

Create word pictures that your readers can see in their minds. Before you begin, imagine that you are going to make a movie of the subject you plan to write about. What scenes would you like to show? Next, think of the words that will bring these same pictures into your readers' minds.

Group your sentences into good paragraphs. It is generally best to begin a paragraph with a topic sentence that says to the reader, "This is what you will learn about in this paragraph." The other sentences in the paragraph should help to support or explain the topic sentence.

A sample paragraph. Below is a sample paragraph from a textbook about the northeastern part of our country. The topic sentence has been underlined. Notice how clear it is and how well the other sentences support it. Also notice how many pictures the paragraph puts in your mind.

One of the most interesting sights in the Erie-Ontario Lowland is beautiful Niagara Falls. These falls are located on the Niagara River, which forms part of the border between the United States and Canada. The Niagara River flows northward from Lake Erie to Lake Ontario. About halfway between these two lakes, the river plunges over a steep cliff, forming Niagara Falls. Each year, thousands of tourists come to see these famous falls. Waterpower from the falls is used to produce electricity for factories and homes in both the United States and Canada.

Other guidelines. There are two other things to remember in writing a good report. First, use the dictionary to find the spelling of words you are not sure about. Second, make a list of the sources of information you used. Put this list at the beginning or end of your report. This list is called a bibliography.

Special guidelines for an oral report

When you are going to give a report orally, you will also want to arrange your information in a logical order by making an outline. Prepare notes to guide you during your talk. These notes should be complete enough to help you remember all the points you want to make. You may even write out certain parts of your report that you would rather read.

When you present your report, speak directly to your audience. Pronounce your words correctly and clearly. Remember to speak slowly enough for your listeners to follow what you are saying. Use a tone of voice that will hold their interest. Stand up straight, but try not to be too stiff. Remember, the only way to improve your speaking skills is to practice them correctly.

Holding a Group Discussion

One of the important ways in which you learn is by exchanging ideas with other people. You do this often in everyday conversation. You are likely to learn more, however, when you take part in the special kind of group conversation that we call a discussion. A discussion is more orderly than a conversation. It generally has a definite, serious purpose. This purpose may be the sharing of information or the solving of a problem. In order to reach its goal, the discussion group must arrive at a conclusion or make a decision of some kind.

The guidelines below will help you to have a successful discussion.

Be prepared

Think about the subject to be discussed ahead of time. Prepare for the discussion by reading and taking notes. You may also want to make an outline of the ideas you want to share with the group.

Take part

Take part in the discussion. Express your ideas clearly and in as few words as possible. Be sure that the statements you make and the questions you ask deal with the subject being talked about.

Listen and think

Listen thoughtfully to others. Encourage all of the members of the discussion group to express their ideas. Do not make up your mind about a question or a problem until all of the facts have been given.

Be courteous

When you speak, address the whole group. Ask and answer questions politely. When you do not agree with someone, give your reasons in a friendly way.

Working With Others

In school and throughout life, you will find that there are many things that can be done better by a group than by one person working alone. Some of these projects would take too long to finish if they were done by one person. Others have different parts that can be done best by people with different talents.

Before your group begins a project, you should decide several matters. First, decide exactly what goal you are trying to reach. Second, decide what part of the project each person should do. Third, decide when the project is to be finished.

Do your part

Remember that the success of your project depends on every member of the group. Be willing to do your share of the work and to accept your share of the responsibility.

Follow the rules

Help the group decide on reasonable rules. Then follow them. When a difference of opinion cannot be settled by discussion, make a decision by majority* vote.

Share your ideas

Be willing to share your ideas with the group. When you present an idea for discussion, be prepared to see it criticized or even rejected. At the same time, have the courage to stand up for an idea or a belief that is really important to you.

Be friendly, thoughtful, helpful, cheerful

Try to express your opinions seriously and sincerely without hurting others or losing their respect. Listen politely to the ideas of others.

Learn from your mistakes

Look for ways in which you can be a better group member the next time you work with others on a project.

Building Your Vocabulary

When you do research in many different kinds of reading materials, you are likely to find several words you have never seen before. If you skip over these words, you may not fully understand what you are reading. The following suggestions will help you to discover the meanings of new words and build your vocabulary.

1. See how the word is used in the sentence. When you come to a new word, don't stop reading. Read on beyond the new word to see if you can discover any hints as to what its meaning might be. Trying to figure out the meaning of a word from the way it is used may not give you the exact definition. However, it will give you a general idea of what the word means.

2. Sound out the word. Break the word up into syllables, and try to pronounce it. When you say the word aloud, you may find that you know it after all but have simply never seen it in print.

3. Look in the dictionary. When you think you have figured out what a word means and how it is pronounced, look it up in the dictionary. First, check the pronunciation. Have you pronounced it correctly? Then, check the meaning of the word. Remember, most words have more than one meaning. Did you decide on the right definition?

4. Make a list of the new words you learn. In your own words, write a definition of each word you place on your list. Review this list from time to time.

Learning Map Skills

The earth is a sphere

Our earth is round like a ball. We call anything with this shape a sphere. The earth is, of course, a very large sphere. Its diameter* is about 8,000 miles (12,874 kilometers*). Its circumference* is about 25,000 miles (40,233 kilometers). The earth is not quite a perfect sphere. It is somewhat flat at the North and South poles.

Globes and maps

The globe in your classroom is also a sphere. It is a small-size copy of the earth. The surface of the globe shows the shapes of the areas of land on the earth. It also shows the shapes of the different bodies of water. By looking at the globe, you can see exactly where the continents,* islands, and oceans are. Globes are made with the North Pole at the top. But they are often tipped to show the way the earth is tipped. Maps are flat drawings. They may show part or all of the earth's surface.

Scale

Globes and maps give information about distance. When you use them, you need to know what distance on the earth is represented by a given distance on the globe or map. This relationship is called the scale. The scale of a globe or map may be shown in several different ways.

On most maps, the scale is shown by a small drawing. For example:

Scale	0	200	400 Miles
	0	322	644 Kilometers

Sometimes, the scale is shown in this way: 1 inch = 400 miles (644 kilometers).

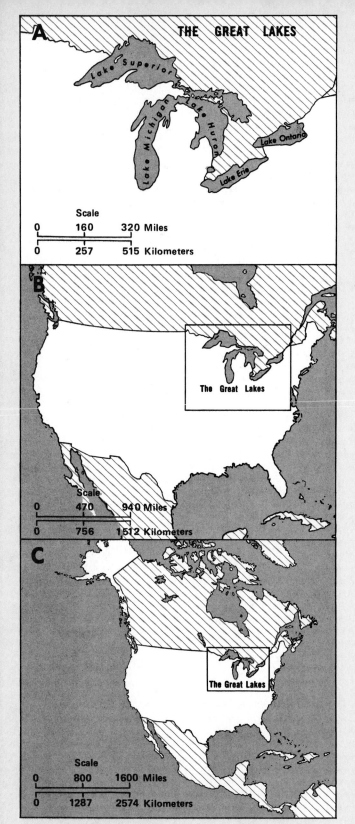

Scale
0   160   320 Miles
0   257   515 Kilometers

Scale
0   470   940 Miles
0   756   1512 Kilometers

The Great Lakes

Scale
0   800   1600 Miles
0   1287   2574 Kilometers

The Great Lakes

The Great Lakes area is a different size on each of the three maps above. This is because one inch on each of these maps represents a different distance on the earth.

Finding places on the earth

Map makers, travelers, and other interested people have always wanted to know just where certain places are. Over the years, a very accurate way of giving such information has been worked out. This system is used all over the world.

In order to work out a means of finding anything, you need starting points and a measuring unit. The North and South poles and the equator are the starting points for the system we use to find places on the earth. The measuring unit for our system is called the degree (°).

Parallels show latitude

When we want to find a place on the earth, we first find out how far it is north or south of the equator. This distance measured in degrees is called north or south latitude. The equator stands for zero latitude. The North Pole is located at 90 degrees north latitude. The South Pole is at 90 degrees south latitude.

All points on the earth that have the same latitude are the same distance from the equator. A line connecting such points is called a parallel. This is because it is parallel to the equator. (See globe D on the next page.)

Meridians show longitude

After we know the latitude of a place, we need to know its location in an east-west direction. This is called its longitude. The lines that show longitude are called meridians. They are drawn so as to connect the North and South poles (See globe E on the next page.) Longitude is measured from the meridian that passes through Greenwich, England. This line of zero longitude is called the prime meridian. Distance east or west of this meridian measured in degrees is called east or west longitude. The meridian of 180 degrees west longitude is the same as the one of 180 degrees east longitude. This is because 180 degrees is exactly halfway around the world.

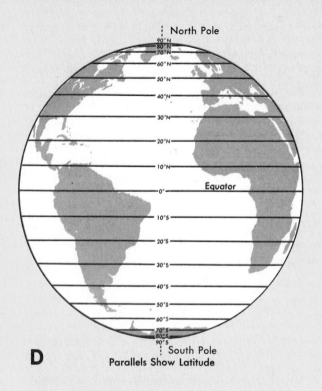

D
Parallels Show Latitude

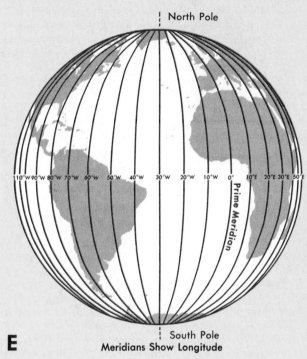

E
Meridians Show Longitude

Finding places on a globe

The location of a certain place might be given to you like this: 30° N 90° W. This means that this place is located 30 degrees north of the equator, and 90 degrees west of the prime meridian. See if you can find this place on the globe in your classroom. It is helpful to remember that parallels and meridians are drawn every ten or fifteen degrees on most globes.

The round earth on a flat map

An important fact about a sphere is that you cannot flatten out its surface perfectly. To prove this, you might do the following. Cut an orange in half. Scrape away the fruit. You will not be able to press either piece of orange peel flat without crushing it. If you cut one piece in half, however, you can press these smaller pieces nearly flat. Next, cut one of these pieces of peel into three smaller pieces, shaped like those in drawing F on the opposite page. You will be able to press these pieces quite flat.

A map like the one shown in drawing F can be made by cutting the surface of a globe into twelve pieces shaped like the smallest pieces of your orange peel. Such a map would be accurate. However, an "orange-peel" map is not easy to use, because the continents and oceans are cut apart.

A flat map can never show the earth's surface as truthfully as a globe can. On globes, shape, size, distance, and direction are all accurate. A single flat map of the world cannot be drawn to show all four of these things correctly. But flat maps can be made that show some of these things accurately. The different ways of drawing maps of the world to show different things correctly are called map projections.

The Mercator projection

Drawing G, on the opposite page, shows a world map called a Mercator projection. When you compare this map with a globe, you can see that continents, islands, and oceans have almost the right shape. On this kind of map, however, North America seems larger than Africa. This is not true. On Mercator maps, lands far from the equator appear larger than they are.

Because they show true directions, Mercator maps are very useful to sailors and fliers. For instance, the city of Lisbon, Portugal, lies almost exactly east of Baltimore, Maryland. A Mercator map shows that a ship could reach Lisbon by sailing from Baltimore straight east across the Atlantic Ocean. A plane could also reach Lisbon by flying straight east from Baltimore.

The shortest route

Strangely enough, the best way to reach Lisbon from Baltimore is not by going straight east. There is a shorter route. In order to understand why this is so, you might like to do the following.

On your classroom globe, find Lisbon and Baltimore. Both cities lie just south of the 40th parallel. Take a piece of string and connect the two cities. Let the string follow the true east-west direction of the 40th parallel. Now, draw the string tight. Notice that it passes far to the north of the 40th parallel. The path of the tightened string is the shortest route between Baltimore and Lisbon. The shortest route between any two points on the earth is called the great* circle route.

A Round Globe on a Flat Surface

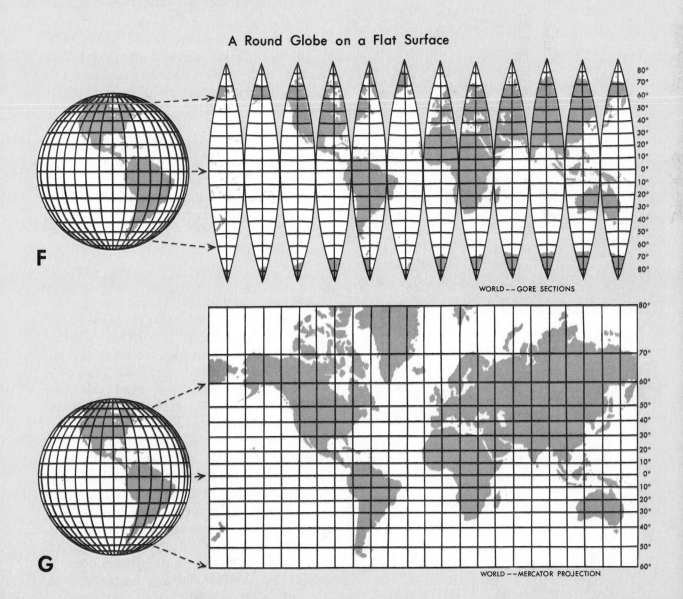

F

WORLD – – GORE SECTIONS

G

WORLD – – MERCATOR PROJECTION

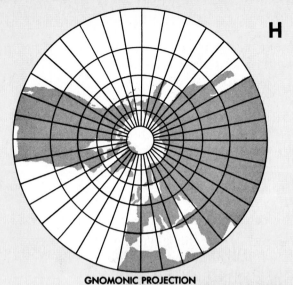

H

GNOMONIC PROJECTION

The gnomonic (nō mon´ik) **projection**

Using a globe and a piece of string is not a very handy or accurate way of finding great circle routes. Instead, sailors and fliers use a special kind of map called the gnomonic projection. (See drawing H, at left.) On this kind of map, the great circle route between any two places can be found simply by drawing a straight line between them.

Special-Purpose Maps

Maps that show part of the earth

For some uses, we would rather have maps that do not show the whole surface of the earth. A map of a very small part of the earth can be drawn more accurately than a map of a large area. It can also include more details.

Drawing I, on this page, shows a photograph and a map of the same small part of the earth. The drawings on the map that show the shape and location of things on the earth are called symbols. The small drawing that shows directions is called a compass* rose.

Maps for special purposes

Maps can show the location of many different kinds of things. For instance, a map can show what minerals are found in certain places, or what crops are grown. A small chart that lists the symbols and their meanings is usually included on a map. This is called the key.

Symbols on some geography maps stand for the amounts of things in different places. For instance, map J, at left, gives information about the number of people in the southwestern part of the United States. The key tells the meaning of the symbols. In this case the symbols are dots and circles.

On different maps, the same symbol may stand for different things and amounts.

Scale

0   120 Feet

0   37 Meters

N W E S

I

J

Denver

Shading Shows Approximate
Population of Urban Areas

15,000,000
10,000,000
5,000,000
2,500,000
1,000,000
500,000
250,000
50,000

ONE DOT EQUALS 10,000 PERSONS

Scale

0   200   400 Mi.

0   322   644 Km.

1 inch = 400 Mi. (644 Km.)

14

Each dot on map J stands for 10,000 persons. On other maps, a dot might represent 5,000 sheep or 1,000 bushels of wheat.

There are other ways of giving information about quantity. Different designs or patterns may be used on a rainfall map to show the areas that receive different amounts of rain each year.

Relief Maps

The roughness of the earth's surface

From a plane, you can see that the earth's surface is rough. You can see mountains and valleys, hills and plains. For some uses, globes and maps that show these things are needed. They are called relief globes and maps.

Since globes are three-dimensional* copies of the earth, you may wonder why most globes do not show the roughness of the earth's surface. The reason for this is that the highest mountain on the earth is not very large when it is compared with the earth's diameter. Even a very large globe would be smooth nearly everywhere.

In order to make a relief globe or map, you must use a different scale for the height of the land. You might start with a large flat map. One inch on your flat map may stand for a distance of 100 miles (161 kilometers) on the earth. Now you are going to make a small copy of a mountain on your map. On the earth, this mountain is two miles (3.2 kilometers) high. If you let one inch stand for this height on the earth, your mountain should rise one inch above the flat surface of your map. Other mountains and hills should be copied on this same scale.

By photographing relief globes and maps, flat maps can be made that show the earth much as it looks from an airplane. Map K, at right above, is a photograph of a relief map. Map L is a photograph of a relief globe.

Topographic maps

Another kind of map that shows the roughness of the earth's surface is called a topographic, or contour, map. On this kind of map, lines are drawn to show different heights of the earth's surface. These are

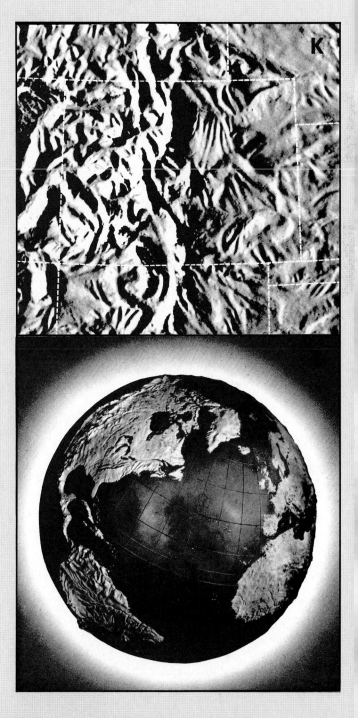

15

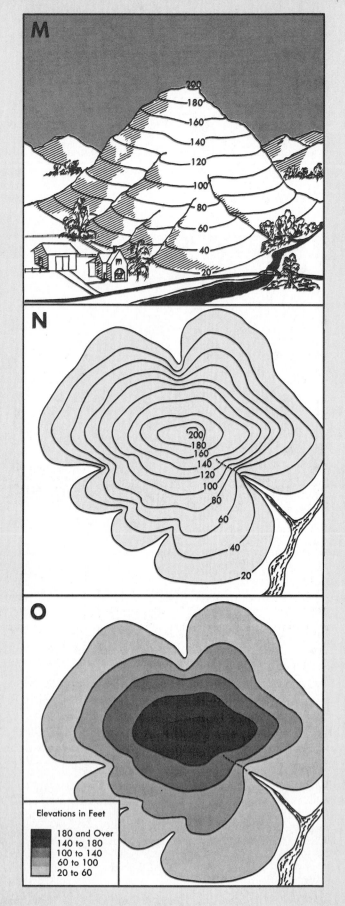

called contour lines. The maps on this page help to explain how topographic maps are made.

Map M is a drawing of a hill. Around the bottom of the hill is our first contour line. This line connects all the points at the base of the hill that are exactly twenty feet above sea level. Higher up the hill, another contour line is drawn. It connects all the points that are exactly forty feet above sea level. A line is also drawn at a height of sixty feet. Other lines are drawn every twenty feet until the top of the hill is reached. Since the hill is shaped somewhat like a cone, each contour line is shorter than the one just below it.

Map N shows how the contour lines in the drawing of the hill M can be used to make a topographic map. This map gives us a great deal of information about the hill. Since each line is labeled with the height it stands for, you can tell how high the different parts of the hill are. It is important to remember that land does not really rise in layers, as you might think when you look at a topographic map. Wherever the contour lines are far apart, you can be sure that the land slopes gently. Where they are close together, the slope is steep. With practice, you can picture the land in your mind as you look at such a map. Topographic maps are especially useful to people who design such things as roads and buildings.

On a topographic map, the spaces between the contour lines may be filled in with different shades of a color. If a different shade of brown were used for each different height of land shown in map N, there would be ten shades. It would be very hard for you to tell these different shades of brown apart. Therefore, on map O, at left, black and four shades of brown were used to show differences in height of forty feet. The key shows the height of the land represented by the different shades. On some topographic maps, different colors are used to stand for different heights.

Needs of People

All people on earth must meet certain needs in order to be healthy and happy. Scientists who study human beings tell us that these basic needs are the same for everyone. It does not matter if you are rich or poor . . . tall or short . . . fat or thin . . . dark-skinned or light-skinned. You have the same basic needs as everyone else.

There are three kinds of basic needs. These are: physical needs, social needs, and the need for faith.

Physical Needs

Some basic needs are so important that people will die or become seriously ill if they fail to meet them. These are called physical needs. They include the need for each of the following:

1. air
2. water
3. food
4. protection from heat and cold
5. sleep and rest
6. exercise

Although all people share these needs, they do not all meet them in the same way. How do you meet your physical needs?

Social Needs

People also have social needs. They must meet these needs in order to have a happy and useful life. Social needs include:

An outdoor concert in Louisville, Kentucky. All people on earth have certain basic needs. Some of these are called social needs. For example, feeling that you belong to a group is a social need. Do you think the members of this orchestra have a feeling of belonging to a group? Why do you think this? What are some other basic needs that all people share?

1. Belonging to a group. All people need to feel they belong to a group of people who respect them and whom they respect. Belonging to a family is one of the main ways people meet this need. What can the members of a family do to show that they love and respect each other? How do the members of your family help one another?

Having friends also helps people meet their need for belonging to a group. What groups of friends do you have? Why are these people your friends? Do you suppose young people in other countries enjoy doing the same kinds of things with their friends as you enjoy doing with your friends? Why? Why not?

2. Goals. To be happy, every person needs goals to work for. What goals do you have? How can working toward these goals help you have a happy life? What kinds of goals do you think other young people in our country have?

3. A chance to think and learn. All people need a chance to develop and use their abilities. They need opportunities to find out about things that make them curious. What would you like to learn? How can you learn these things? How can developing your abilities help you have a happy life?

4. A feeling of accomplishment. You share with every other person the need for a feeling of accomplishment. All people need to feel that their lives are successful in some way. What gives you a feeling of accomplishment? Can you imagine what life would be like if you never had this feeling?

The Need for Faith

In addition to physical and social needs, all people also have a need for faith. You need to believe that life is precious and that the future is something to look forward to. You may have different kinds of faith, including the following:

1. Faith in yourself. In order to feel secure, you must have faith in your own abilities. You must feel that you will be able to do some useful work in the world and that you will be generally happy. You must believe that you can work toward solving whatever problems life brings to you. How do you think you can build faith in yourself?

2. Faith in other people. You also need to feel that you can count on other people to do their part and to help you when you need help. What people do you have faith in? What do you think life would be like without this kind of faith?

3. Faith in nature's laws. Another kind of faith that helps people face the future with confidence is faith in nature's laws. The more we learn about our universe, the more certain we feel that we can depend on nature. How would you feel if you couldn't have faith in nature's laws?

4. Religious faith. Throughout history, almost all human beings have had some kind of religious faith. Religion can help people understand themselves and the world they live in. It can bring them joy, and it can give them confidence in times of trouble. Religion can also help people live together happily. For example, most religions teach people to be honest and to love and help their neighbors.

Meeting Needs in Communities

No person can meet his or her needs alone. Only by living and working with others can a person have a happy, satisfying life. For this reason, people everywhere on earth have always lived in communities.

Over the years, people have followed certain ideas or ways of living that help them to live together in communities. We call these the "great ideas." In other parts of this book, you can discover how the great ideas have helped people in the United States to meet their basic needs.

Great Ideas
That Built Our Nation

People have been living in America for thousands of years. During this time, they have always met their needs in communities. No one can meet his or her needs all alone. Only by living and working with other people can a person have a happy, satisfying life.

In order to make community life successful, people have developed certain ways of living. We call these the "great ideas." Let us examine ten great ideas that have been important in our country's history.

cooperation   using tools
loyalty   division of labor
freedom   exchange
rules and government language
using natural resources education

What great ideas do you think are illustrated by the pictures on this page?
1. Cutting timber in a western forest.
2. The city of Los Angeles, California.
3. A factory worker in Rhode Island.

Exploring the moon. The astronaut is driving a lunar roving vehicle on the moon. At left is the lunar module that brought him to the moon from a spacecraft circling high overhead.

Cooperation

A Great Idea

Working together is called cooperation. This is one of the great ideas that helped build our nation. For example, the early settlers in America needed to cooperate. They worked together to provide the food they needed. In what other ways do you think the early settlers cooperated with one another?

How is cooperation important to communities today? What are some important jobs that require cooperation? What are some other examples of cooperation in the community where you live? Do you think our country could have sent astronauts to the moon if people had not worked together on the space program? Explain.

Loyalty

A Great Idea

People discovered long ago that in order to live together successfully in a community, they had to be loyal to each other. People were willing to do unpleasant or difficult tasks simply because they felt a strong sense of loyalty to their community. Members of families had to be loyal to each other in order to have a happy family life.

In every truly successful community on the earth today, people are usually loyal to each other. They are loyal to their community, their country, and their leaders. Do you think the astronaut shown on page 20 is loyal to our country? What are some things you can do to show that you are loyal to our country? Do you think that the leaders of a community should be loyal to the people? Why do you think this?

The people in successful communities are also loyal to their ideas and beliefs. Most people in our country, for example, are loyal to the principles of democracy, and to the ideas of freedom, justice, and equality. In addition, they are loyal to their religious faith.

Boy scouts looking at a statue of Abraham Lincoln. Lincoln was president of our country during the Civil War.* Why do you think Lincoln is honored today? Is it partly because of his loyalty to certain principles, such as the idea of freedom for all people? Explain your answer.

Do you think boy scouts need to be loyal to certain persons and ideas? Is loyalty important to organizations such as the Boy Scouts of America? Why? Why not?

*See Glossary

Freedom

A Great Idea

The idea of freedom has been important to Americans since the early days of our country's history. Many of the settlers who came to America from Europe during the 1600's and 1700's were seeking more freedom than they had in their homelands.

By the middle of the 1700's, there were thirteen British colonies along the Atlantic coast of North America. During the 1760's and early 1770's, Britain began to take away some of the freedoms the colonists had enjoyed. On July 4, 1776, representatives of the thirteen colonies approved the Declaration of Independence. In this famous document, the colonists declared

Minutemen fighting British troops at Concord, Massachusetts. Minutemen were American colonists who fought to gain freedom from British rule during the Revolutionary War. They were called minutemen because they could be ready for battle in only a few minutes. Why did the colonists want to be free from British rule? You may wish to do research to discover answers to this question.

The White House, the home of our country's president. In the United States, all citizens are free to take part in electing the president and other government leaders.

their freedom from British rule. They set up a new nation called the United States of America.

At the time our country was founded, there were many people here who did not enjoy all the same rights and freedoms as other Americans. For example, most black people lived in slavery. They were forced to work all their lives for white masters. The Civil War* finally led to the ending of slavery throughout the United States.

For a long time after the founding of our country the freedom of women was limited in certain ways. For instance, women could not vote in elections or testify as witnesses in a court of law. A married woman had no right to any property of her own. Any wages that she earned became the property of her husband.

Gradually women began to gain more rights and freedoms. One state after another passed laws giving married women the right to own property. The Nineteenth Amendment to the Constitution, which became law in 1920, guaranteed to women throughout the United States the right to vote.

Today most Americans enjoy a large amount of freedom. For example, they are free to live where they please and to work at jobs of their own choosing. They can express their ideas freely without fear of punishment. They are also free to worship God in their own way, or not to worship at all if they so desire.

Are there any people in the United States today who do not enjoy as much freedom as other Americans? Who are they? What is being done to help these people gain more freedom?

Rules and Government

A Great Idea

People in every community need to follow rules in order to live together successfully. Why is this true? What kinds of rules do people in your own community follow? How do these rules make life safer and more pleasant for everyone? What would it be like to live in a community that had no rules?

In every community, there must be a person or a group of persons to make the rules and see that they are carried out. In other words, all communities need some form of government. Who makes the rules in your local community? Who enforces the rules that these people make?

Although every successful community has some form of government, not all governments are alike. The United States is a democracy. This means that its citizens have a share in governing themselves. Do you think it is important for people to take part in their own government? Why do you think this?

A committee meeting in California. These men and women are all members of the California legislature, which makes the laws for that state. Do you think laws are necessary? Why? Why not?

Pouring melted steel into molds in a Pennsylvania steel plant. Many important products are made from steel. Do research to discover what mineral resources are used in making steel.

Using Natural Resources

A Great Idea

The picture above shows a farmer growing crops in an irrigated* field in the West. In growing crops, farmers use certain natural resources. By "natural resources" we mean any gifts of nature that people use to meet their needs. Some important natural resources are listed below. Which of these do you think farmers use?

air	water	wild animals
soil	sunshine	wild plants
	minerals	

Over the years, people in various parts of the world learned how to make greater use of the earth's resources. The world's first farmers began to use soil, sunshine, and rain to grow crops. They also began to raise animals for food. Later, people began to use different metals for making tools and weapons.

Today, we use hundreds of natural resources in meeting our needs. Stone and trees are just as important to us as they were to earlier people. We use these materials both in building and manufacturing. Farmers today use sunshine, soil, and water, just as early people did. Minerals such as coal and iron ore are among our most valuable resources. What are some natural resources that are used by people in your community?

A lumber mill in Florida. Lumber is one of the many valuable products we get from forests.

People have always depended on the earth's resources to help them in meeting their needs for food, clothing, and shelter. Early people hunted wild animals for food and for skins to make clothing. They added to the food supply by gathering the fruits, seeds, and roots of wild plants. These early people lived in caves or built shelters from tree branches, mud, or animal skins. They used wood, stones, bones, and shells to make tools and weapons. Compared to people who lived later, however, the people of early times made very little use of the natural resources in the world around them.

Using Tools
A Great Idea

A tool is anything that people use to help them do work. Some tools, such as hammers and shovels, are very simple. Other tools are large or complicated. Tools that have a number of moving parts are called machines. What kinds of tools do you have in your home? How do these tools help the members of your family to meet their needs?

The early settlers who came to our country brought with them several important kinds of tools. Among these were guns and axes. With their rifles, the settlers killed wild animals to get meat for food and skins for making clothing. They also used guns

A huge scoop used for mining phosphate* rock. This scoop is pulled across the phosphate rock deposit to gather up large amounts of the mineral. Then a giant crane lifts the filled scoop and empties it into a bin. Do you think it would be possible to produce large amounts of minerals without the use of tools such as these? Explain.

Cutting down trees in colonial days. The early settlers in America used axes to clear the land so they could grow crops. They used the logs for building cabins.

to protect themselves from unfriendly Indians. With their axes, they chopped down trees in the forests so they could use the cleared land for growing crops. Axes were also used to cut logs for building cabins.

Today people in our country use many kinds of modern machines to produce the goods they need. Many of these machines are very complicated and are run by electricity. Do you think that people who use modern machines can have more goods to enjoy than people who use only a few simple tools? Why do you think this?

A worker in a textile factory in Hawaii. In a factory, the work is divided among people who do different jobs. This is known as division of labor.

Division of Labor

A Great Idea

In every community, not all the people do exactly the same kind of work. Instead, they work at different jobs. For example, some people earn their living by farming. Others work in factories or offices. Dividing up the work of a community among people who do different jobs is known as division of labor. By using division of labor, people are able to obtain more goods and services than they could if they tried to meet all of their needs by themselves. Why do you suppose this is so?

Division of labor also makes it possible for each person to work at the job he or she can do best. For example, this textile worker (see picture above) is very skillful at his job. He also enjoys it very much. He probably would not like to do some other kind of work that did not require the skills he has learned. On the other hand, the people who produce the food, appliances, and other things he buys might not enjoy the kind of work he does.

Division of labor also helps people produce many useful things that one person working alone could not produce. Do you think it would ever be possible for one person to make and use all of the many tools needed to manufacture such things as automobiles and refrigerators?

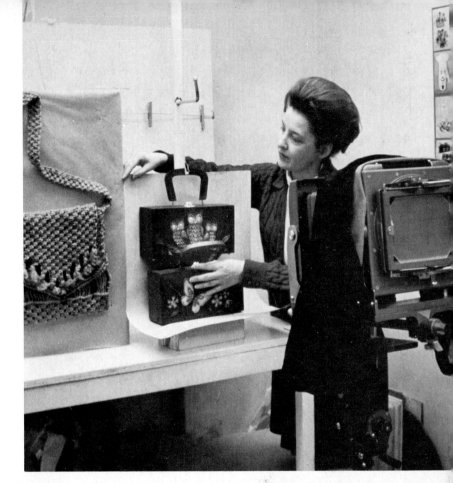

This photographer is preparing to take a picture of some handbags for a magazine advertisement.

The people shown below are members of a hospital operating team. Like the photographer, they provide a service instead of helping to make a product. Other people who perform services are teachers, lawyers, telephone operators, and police officers.

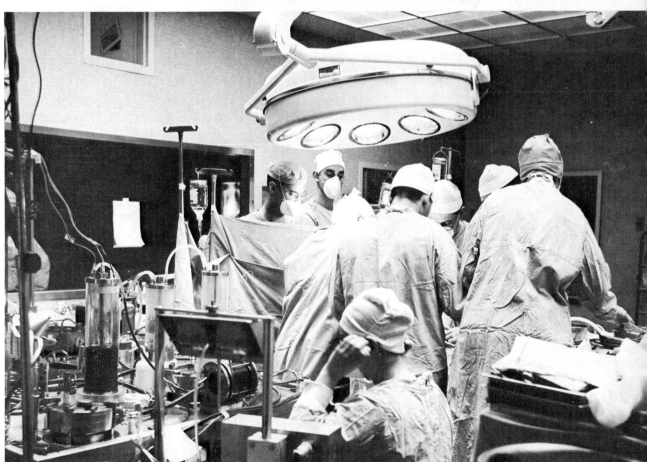

Shopping for food. What will this woman give the store in exchange for the things she needs? Do you think it would be possible for her to get these things without using the idea of exchange?

Exchange

A Great Idea

When people use division of labor, they need to exchange goods and services with each other. In this way, they can get goods and services they do not produce themselves. What would it be like to live in a community where people did not use the great idea of exchange? Explain.

In early times, people often traded goods and services directly with each other. Today most people work at jobs where they earn money. They use this money to buy the goods and services they need. Do you think money makes it easier to carry on exchange? Give reasons for your answer.

Language

A Great Idea

Throughout history, people have felt the need to communicate with each other. In order to work together, people need to share their ideas and feelings. Early people communicated in several ways. For example, they smiled, frowned, made gestures with their hands, and drew pictures. Their most important way of communicating, however, was by speaking. Scientists who have studied the beginnings of language believe that all human beings—even those who lived in earliest times—have had some form of spoken language.

Human beings did not develop written language until about five thousand years ago. Writing made it possible for people to store information so that it could be used at a later time. Writing also enabled people to communicate over long distances. Today, almost every language in the world can be written as well as spoken.

Every day, you use language to communicate with others. You talk with your family and your friends. On school days, you talk with your teachers and the other members of your class. You write notes and letters. You write out much of your schoolwork. Do you think it is important to use spoken language in such a way as to communicate clearly with other people? Why do you think this? Do you think it is important to be able to put your thoughts and feelings into writing? Explain.

People in New York City's Chinatown. What does this picture tell you about language in our country?

Education

A Great Idea

In every community, the older people pass on their ideas and skills to the younger people. This is one kind of education. Do you think it would be possible to have a successful community without education? Why? Why not?

In early times, parents taught their children most of the things they needed to know. Today, most American children get a large part of their education in school. Do you think education is important for every person? Why do you think as you do?

High school students in a science class. In most parts of the world, young people receive much of their education in school. Do you think education is important for everyone? Why? Why not?

Word List
(Glossary)

Complete Pronunciation Key

The pronunciation of the word is shown just after the word, in this way: **Iroquois** (ir′ ə kwoi). The letters and signs used are pronounced as in the words below. The mark ′ is placed after a syllable with a primary or strong accent, as in the example above. The mark ′ after a syllable shows a secondary or lighter accent, as in **electronic** (i lek′ tron′ ik).

a	hat, cap	j	jam, enjoy	u	cup, butter
ā	age, face	k	kind, seek	u̇	full, put
ã	care, air	l	land, coal	ü	rule, move
ä	father, far	m	me, am	ū	use, music
		n	no, in		
b	bad, rob	ng	long, bring		
ch	child, much			v	very, save
d	did, red	o	hot, rock	w	will, woman
		ō	open, go	y	young, yet
		ô	order, all	z	zero, breeze
e	let, best	oi	oil, voice	zh	measure, seizure
ē	equal, see	ou	house, out		
ėr	term, learn				
		p	paper, cup	ə	represents:
f	fat, if	r	run, try	a	in about
g	go, bag	s	say, yes	e	in taken
h	he, how	sh	she, rush	i	in pencil
		t	tell, it	o	in lemon
i	it, pin	th	thin, both	u	in circus
ī	ice, five	ŦH	then, smooth		

abstract. Refers to a painting or a sculpture that does not look like a person or an object. Instead, the work of art represents the artist's ideas or feelings about a subject.

Aleutian (ə lü′ shən) **Islands.** A long chain of islands that are part of Alaska. The Aleutians extend southwestward into the Pacific Ocean.

Aleuts (al′ ē üts). A group of people who live on the Aleutian Islands and in other parts of Alaska. Their language and customs are similar to those of the Eskimos. Many Aleuts earn their living by fishing, raising sheep, or hunting fur seals. See **Aleutian Islands.**

alewife. A fish of the herring family. It is found along the Atlantic coast and in the Great Lakes. Alewives are sometimes used for food. They are also made into products such as oil and fertilizer.

alfalfa. A plant with cloverlike leaves. Hay made from alfalfa is used as food for farm animals.

altitude. Height above the level of the sea. For example, a mountain that rises 10,000 feet (3,050 meters) above sea level has an altitude of 10,000 feet.

ammonia (ə mōn′ yə). A colorless gas with a sharp smell. The ammonia used for cleaning around the house is really ammonia dissolved in water. Ammonia is an important chemical used in industry. It is used in making products such as fertilizers and explosives.

ancestors. People from whom one is descended. They include your grandparents, great-grandparents, and others farther back in your family.

anchovy (an′ chō vē). A very small fish, used mainly in sauces and relishes.

annex. To make one territory part of another.

Appalachian (ap/ə lā/chən) **Plateau.** The westernmost section of the Appalachian Highlands region. See **plateau.**

aqueduct (ak/ wə dukt). A canal, tunnel, or large pipe for carrying water. An aqueduct usually carries the water from a river or a lake to the place where it is to be used.

Arab. Refers to a group of people who live mainly in northern Africa and Southwest Asia. Arabs speak the Arabic language. Most of them follow the religion of Islam. See **Islam.**

architecture. The art of designing buildings.

astronaut. A pilot or a crew member of a space-craft.

atomic energy. Energy that is stored in atoms. See **atoms.**

atoms. Pieces of matter too small to be seen except with a special microscope. When atoms are split or combined in certain ways, great amounts of energy are released. This energy can be used for many purposes, including the production of electricity.

automation. The use of machinery that needs only a few, if any, people to run it.

bale. A large bundle of material that is squeezed together and tied with rope, wire, or straps.

basic chemicals. Common chemicals that are produced in large amounts for use in industry. Ammonia and certain strong acids are examples of basic chemicals. See **chemicals.**

basin. An area of land that is largely surrounded by higher land. Also, the total area of land that is drained by a river and its branches.

bauxite (bôk/ sīt). An ore that is the chief source of aluminum. See **ore.**

bearings. Objects such as metal balls and rollers that enable one part of a machine or a mechanical device to slide smoothly over or around another part. Ball bearings are used in roller-skate wheels, for example.

bill. A suggested law to be voted on by a legislature. See **legislature.**

bituminous (bə tü/ mə nəs) **coal.** Another name for high-grade soft coal. This is the most plentiful and important type of coal.

blackout. A period of time during which electricity is cut off from an area.

blast furnace. A furnace in which iron is made from iron ore. It is called a blast furnace because a strong blast of air is blown into the bottom of the furnace.

bluegrass. Any one of about 200 kinds of grass with bluish green stems and blue flowers. The best known is Kentucky bluegrass, a useful lawn and pasture grass.

boll (bōl). The seed pod of a plant such as cotton. The white fibers found in cotton bolls are used to make cotton cloth.

borates. A group of certain chemicals that are somewhat like salt. Several borates are found in nature as minerals. A common borate is called borax. It is used for softening water and for cleaning. See **chemicals.**

breakwater. A wall built in the water to protect a harbor or a beach from waves. Breakwaters are usually built of stone and concrete.

British Parliament. See **parliament.**

Buddhism (bùd/ iz əm). A religion founded in India about 2,500 years ago. It teaches that selfishness is the cause of all sorrow, and that brotherly love among all people is the way to happiness.

butte (būt). A flat-topped hill that rises steeply from the land around it. A butte is somewhat like a mesa, but smaller. See **mesa.**

cancer. A serious disease marked by a harmful growth or growths in the body.

Cancer, Tropic of. See **Tropic of Cancer.**

candidate. A person who seeks a job or an office, such as president. Each candidate in an election hopes to get the most votes.

canyon. A valley with high, steep sides.

capital. A city that serves as the center of government for a country or a state. In economics, "capital" refers to wealth that is used to produce more wealth. Money, factory buildings, and machines are important forms of capital.

capitol. A building in which lawmakers meet. When spelled with a capital "C," this word means the building in Washington, D.C., where the United States Congress meets. See **United States Congress.**

Capricorn, Tropic of. See **Tropic of Capricorn.**

carbon. A common substance found in nature in many different forms. A diamond is pure carbon. So is graphite, the black writing material in your pencil. Anthracite, a high-quality coal, is almost entirely carbon. Carbon is found in all living things, in many kinds of rock, and in petroleum.

cash crops. Crops that farmers raise to be sold, rather than to be used by themselves and their families.

Celsius (sel′sē əs). Refers to a scale for measuring temperature. On the Celsius scale, which is part of the metric system, 0° represents the freezing point of water and 100° represents the boiling point. To change degrees Celsius to degrees on the Fahrenheit scale, multiply by 1.8 and add 32. See **metric system** and **Fahrenheit**.

centimeter (sen′tə mē′tər). A unit in the metric system for measuring length. It is equal to about .39 inch. See **metric system**.

cession. The giving up of territory by one country to another.

chemicals. Substances that are made when two or more substances act upon one another. Examples are salt, soda, ammonia, and aspirin.

chemist. A person who studies, tests, or makes chemicals. A chemist usually works in a laboratory. See **chemicals**.

cholera. A disease caused by polluted food or water. Early settlers who traveled west often had to use whatever food or water they could find. Many became sick or died.

Christianity. A religion that is followed by more people than any other religion in the world. It is based on the teachings of Jesus Christ, who lived nearly two thousand years ago. There are three main branches of Christianity. These are the Roman Catholic Church, the Eastern Orthodox churches, and the Protestant churches.

circumference (sər kum′ fər əns). The distance around something, such as a circle or a ball.

citrus fruit. Any of several kinds of fruit. Oranges, grapefruit, lemons, and limes are some of the common citrus fruits.

civil rights. The rights and freedoms that belong to a person as a member of a community, a state, or a country. There are many different civil rights. Among them are the right to speak freely and to attend the church of one's choice. Others are the right to own property, the right to a fair trial, and the right to get a job or a place to live without discrimination. (See **discrimination**.) Sometimes the right to vote is also thought of as a civil right.

Civil War, 1861-1865. A war between the northern and southern parts of our country. The northern states were called the Union. The southern states were called the Confederacy. The Union won the Civil War.

climate. The average weather conditions of a given place over a period of many years.

coke. A fuel made by roasting coal in special ovens from which the air has been shut out.

coking coal. Coal that is good for making coke. See **coke**.

colonial. Refers to a certain period of time in the history of the United States. The colonial period began when the first European colonies were started in America. It lasted until the thirteen British colonies became the United States.

colony. A settlement outside the country that controls it. In American history, usually means any one of thirteen colonies along the Atlantic coast. These colonies were started by people from England in the 1600's and 1700's. Later, the thirteen colonies became the United States.

commercial (kə mėr′ shəl). Having to do with business or trade.

communicate. To share ideas and feelings with other people. Speaking and writing are two of the most important ways of communicating.

communication. Sharing ideas and feelings with other people. Speaking is the main way in which we communicate with people who are near enough to hear us. Writing helps us communicate with people who are not close by. Other means of communicating over a distance include such things as the telegraph, radio, and television.

Communist. Refers to certain countries in which the government controls industry, farming, trade, education, and most other activities. The word Communist also refers to political parties and to people who favor such a system of government control.

compass rose. A small drawing put on a map to show directions. Here are three examples of compass roses:

PRONUNCIATION KEY: hat, āge, cāre, fär; let, ēqual, tėrm; it, īce; hot, ōpen, ôrder; oil, out; cup, pùt, rüle, ūse; child; long; thin; ᴛʜen; zh, measure; ə represents a in about, e in taken, i in pencil, o in lemon, u in circus. For the complete key, see page 35.

37

complicated. Made up of a number of different parts.

composer. A person who writes music.

computer. A machine that stores information and uses this information to solve difficult problems.

concrete. A hard, strong material that is used for such things as buildings and roads. Concrete is made by mixing cement, sand, gravel, and water. This mixture becomes hard as it dries.

conservation. Saving or protecting something so it will not be wasted. For example, forests and soil need to be conserved.

conserve. To protect or keep safe.

constitution. A set of rules telling how a country or a state is supposed to be governed. When this word is written with a capital "C," it usually means the Constitution of the United States. Our Constitution was adopted in 1788. It has been in use ever since.

conterminous (kən tėr′mə nəs) **United States.** The forty-eight states of the United States that are enclosed by an unbroken boundary. The word conterminous means "having the same boundary."

continent. One of the six largest land areas on the earth. These are Eurasia, Africa, North America, South America, Australia, and Antarctica. Some people think of Eurasia as two continents—Europe and Asia.

Continental Congress. A meeting of leaders from the colonies in America that later joined together to form the United States. There were two Continental Congresses. The First Continental Congress met in 1774 to discuss the quarrel between the colonies and Great Britain. The Second Continental Congress met in 1775, soon after the Revolutionary War began. On July 4, 1776, it approved the Declaration of Independence. For several years after this, the Second Continental Congress served as the government of the United States.

conveyor belt. A moving belt, usually made of canvas, rubber, or metal, that carries things from one place to another.

cowhand. A person who takes care of cattle.

crop rotation. A way of farming in which different crops are raised on the same land in different years.

crude oil. Petroleum as it comes from the ground.

cultivate. To break up the soil around the roots of growing plants, mainly for the purpose of killing weeds. Also, to prepare and use land for growing crops.

Declaration of Independence. A public statement made by leaders of the American colonies on July 4, 1776. This statement said that the colonies were independent, or free, of Great Britain.

Delmarva Peninsula. A peninsula along the Atlantic coast of the United States. It is about 180 miles (290 kilometers) long and 70 miles (113 kilometers) across at its widest part. Most of the state of Delaware and parts of Maryland and Virginia lie on this peninsula.

democracy. A country in which people govern themselves. The people choose their leaders and make decisions by majority vote. See **majority.**

density of population. The average number of people per square mile, square kilometer, or some other unit of area, in a given place. Density of population may be found by dividing the total number of people in an area by the number of square miles or other units of the area.

depressed area. An area where many of the people are unable to find jobs.

descent. Birth or ancestry. For example, we might say that a certain person born in the United States is of French descent. This means that some or all of that person's ancestors were born in France.

diameter (dī am′ə tər). A straight line that joins opposite sides and passes through the center of something, such as a circle or a ball. Also, the length of such a straight line.

diesel (dē′ zəl) **engine.** A kind of engine often used in trucks and trains. Instead of gasoline, it burns a petroleum product called diesel oil.

discrimination. Keeping rights and freedoms from people because they belong to certain groups. Usually, people are discriminated against because they belong to minority groups. (See **minority group.**) Although women are not a minority group, they have also suffered from discrimination.

District of Columbia. A piece of land set apart as the home of the federal government of the United States. The District of Columbia lies in the eastern part of our country, between Maryland and Virginia. It is not part of any state. Washington, our national capital city, covers the entire area of the District of Columbia.

drift mine. A type of mine in which a tunnel is dug into the side of a hill.

drought (drout). A long period of dry weather.

dry farming. A way of farming used in areas where there is little water. Dry farmers in these areas raise crops that need little moisture. They leave part of their land idle, or fallow, each year. This lets the soil store up moisture.

Dutch. People from the Netherlands. (See **Netherlands.**) Also, the language spoken by these people.

Eastern Orthodox (ôr′ thə doks). Refers to one of the three main branches of Christianity. (See **Christianity.**) Most of the churches that belong to this branch are in western Asia and eastern Europe. Eastern Orthodox also refers to the members of these churches.

ecology (ē kol′ ə jē). Refers to the relationships living things (plants, animals, and human beings) have to each other and to their environment. Also, the study of these relationships. See **environment.**

electric power. Electricity.

electric power plant. A plant that uses machines called generators to produce electricity. The generators are run by other machines called turbines, which are usually powered by steam. Turbines may also be powered by the force of falling water.

electron. The smallest possible amount of electricity.

electronic (i lek ′tron′ik). Refers to certain kinds of electrical devices, such as vacuum tubes and transistors. Also refers to products that use such devices. Radios, television sets, and computers are examples of electronic products.

electron microscope. A microscope is a special tool used by scientists for making very tiny things look larger. An electron microscope is different from a regular microscope in that it uses a beam of electrons instead of light to show the shape of an object. See **electron.**

energy. Power, or force, that can be used to do work. In earliest times, people used only their own muscles to do work. Since then, they have learned to use many other sources of energy. Some of these are wind, flowing water, and fuels such as coal, oil, and natural gas.

engineer. A person who plans or builds such things as machinery, bridges, and roads.

engineering. The kind of work that engineers do. See **engineer.**

environment (en vī′ rən mənt). Everything that surrounds living things and influences their growth and development. The environment of a person includes such things as air, sunlight, water, land, plants, animals, and other people.

equator (i kwā′ tər). An imaginary line around the earth, dividing it into a northern half and a southern half.

equinox (ē′ kwə noks). Either of two times of the year when the sun shines directly on the equator. They take place about March 21 and September 22. At these two times, day and night are each twelve hours long everywhere on the earth.

Erie Canal. A canal in New York State. It connected the Hudson River, near the city of Albany, with the port city of Buffalo, on Lake Erie. It was finished in 1825. In the early 1900's, the Erie Canal became part of a larger system of canals called the New York State Barge Canal.

erosion. The wearing away of the earth's surface by the forces of nature. These forces include falling rain, running water, ice, wind, and waves. Erosion may be helpful to people, as when soil is formed from rock. Or it may be harmful, as when rich soil is washed away.

Eskimos. Certain people who live in the far northern parts of North America and eastern Asia. The Eskimos in Alaska include two groups. These are the Inuit and the Yupiit. Many Eskimos earn their living by hunting and fishing. Others have jobs in factories and offices.

essay. A piece of writing that usually tells what the writer thinks about a subject.

etcher. An artist who uses acid to make a design or a picture on a metal plate. The plate is then inked and used to print copies of the design or picture.

Eurasia (yu̇ rā′ zhə). The largest continent on the earth. It is sometimes thought of as two separate continents—Europe and Asia. See **continent.**

evaporate (i vap′ ə rāt). To change from a liquid to a gas or vapor. For example, when the water on a wet sidewalk disappears, it is said to evaporate. The water changes into a gas called water vapor, which mixes with the air.

explosives. Substances that can be exploded. For example, the gunpowder used in firecrackers is an explosive.

PRONUNCIATION KEY: **h**at, **ā**ge, **c**ãre, **f**är; **l**et, **ē**qual, **t**ėrm; **it**, **ī**ce; **h**ot, **ō**pen, **ô**rder; **oil**, **ou̇**t; **cup**, **pu̇**t, **rü**le, **ū**se; **child**; **long**; **thin**; **ᴛ**Hen; **zh**, measure; **ə** represents **a** in about, **e** in taken, **i** in pencil, **o** in lemon, **u** in circus. For the complete key, see page 35.

export (ek spôrt′). To send goods from one country or region to another, especially for the purpose of selling them. These goods are called exports (eks′pôrts).

fallow. Farmland on which no crop is being grown is said to be fallow.

Fahrenheit (far′ ən hīt). Refers to a scale for measuring temperature in which the freezing point of water is represented by 32° and the boiling point by 212°. See **Celsius**.

federal. A system of government in which the constitution gives great powers to the central government to govern the country, yet leaves control of local affairs to the states. The national government, as separate from the governments of the states, is called the federal government.

feedlot. A place where cattle are kept while being fattened for market.

fertile. Good for producing crops.

fertilizer. A substance that farmers add to their soil. The fertilizer helps the soil produce more and better crops.

fiber. A thread or a threadlike part.

fiction. Novels, short stories, and other writings that tell about people and happenings that are not real.

Filipino (fil′ ə pē′ nō). Refers to people from the Philippines or people whose ancestors were from the Philippines. See **ancestors**.

First Continental Congress. See **Continental Congress**.

fission. The splitting or breaking apart of atoms in a way that releases large amounts of energy. See **atoms**.

fossil. The remains or traces of a plant or an animal that lived long ago. For example, an animal bone that has turned into rock is called a fossil. The fossil fuels—coal, oil, and natural gas—were formed from the remains of plants and animals that lived millions of years ago. Over the years, the forces of nature changed these remains into the fuels we take from the earth today. Sometimes you can actually see the pattern of a fern in a piece of coal.

foundry. A place where melted metal is poured into hollow forms called molds. When the metal cools, it hardens into the desired shape. Then the mold is removed.

freeway. A broad highway that is designed to carry heavy traffic at high speeds. Freeways have no traffic lights or crossroads.

French and Indian War, 1754-1763. A war in North America. In this war, Great Britain and its American colonies defeated the French. Indians fought on both sides. As a result of the war, Great Britain took over most of the land that the French had claimed in North America.

frontier (frun tir′). An area that lies between settled lands and the wilderness.

fusion. The combining of atoms in a way that releases large amounts of energy. See **atoms**.

generator. A machine used to make electricity. In electric power plants, the generators are usually run by other machines called turbines. The turbines are run by the force of steam or of falling water.

Georgian (jôr′ jən) **style.** A style of building much used in Britain and its colonies in the 1700's and early 1800's. A house built in the Georgian style was usually very impressive. It had a central doorway, often with tall columns. On each side of the doorway were the same number of windows.

gin (jin). A machine that separates cotton fibers from seeds and other materials. The fibers are pulled through holes that are too small to let the seeds and other materials through.

glacier (glā′ shər). A mass of ice that moves slowly down a slope or valley.

Great Britain. A large island that lies off the western coast of Europe. It includes three parts—England, Scotland, and Wales. Long ago, these were three countries with different rulers. Wales was joined to England during the 1500's. Then, in 1707, England and Wales were united with Scotland to form the kingdom of Great Britain. The ruler of Great Britain also ruled the British colonies in America. Later, the northern part of Ireland became part of the kingdom of Great Britain. Today, the official name for this country is "The United Kingdom of Great Britain and Northern Ireland."

great circle. Any imaginary circle around the earth that divides its surface exactly in half. The equator, for example, is a great circle. The shortest route between any two points on the earth always lies on the great circle that passes through them.

Great Lakes. Five huge lakes in the central part of North America. These are Lakes Superior, Michigan, Huron, Erie, and Ontario.

Great Lakes-St. Lawrence Waterway. A great inland waterway that includes the St. Lawrence

River, the five Great Lakes, and several smaller connecting waterways. The system of canals, dams, and locks on the St. Lawrence between Lake Ontario and the city of Montreal, Canada, is known as the St. Lawrence Seaway. See **lock**.

Great Plains. A part of our country that is made up of broad, level plains. It lies east of the Rocky Mountains and extends from Canada to Mexico.

Great Valley. A long chain of valleys in the eastern part of the United States. The Great Valley forms a large part of the Appalachian Ridges and Valleys section of the Appalachian Highlands.

gristmill. A mill for grinding grain.

groundwater. Water that soaks into the ground and collects in layers of soil and rock. This is the water that supplies wells and springs.

growing season. The period of time when crops can be grown outdoors without danger of being killed by frost.

guided missile. A kind of rocket that can be used to carry bombs to enemy countries during a war. Some guided missiles are directed by radio signals sent from the ground. Others are guided by an electronic device inside the missile. See **electronic**.

hardwood. Refers to trees that have broad leaves, rather than needles. Oaks and maples are examples of hardwood trees.

hectare (hek′ tär). A unit in the metric system for measuring area. It is equal to about 2.47 acres. See **metric system**.

Huguenots (hū′ gə nots). The name given to the Protestants in France during the 1500's and 1600's. The Huguenots were often made to suffer by French Roman Catholics. Thousands of Huguenots were put in prison or killed. Many fled to other countries. See **Protestant** and **Roman Catholic**.

humid (hū′ mid). Refers to air that contains a large amount of moisture.

hydrochloric acid. A strong, colorless acid. It is widely used in industry for cleaning metals. It is also used in dyeing and in food processing.

hydroelectric (hī′ drō i lek′ trik). Refers to hydroelectricity. See **hydroelectricity**.

hydroelectricity (hī′ drō i lek′ tris′ ə tē). Electricity produced from waterpower.

hydrogen bomb. A very powerful bomb. In this kind of bomb, atoms are combined in a way that releases large amounts of energy. See **atoms**.

hypotheses (hī poth′ə sēz). Possible answers or solutions to a problem. Sometimes hypotheses are called "educated guesses." A hypothesis may turn out to be wrong. But it helps us find the right answer.

illustrate. To explain or to show more clearly with diagrams, maps, or pictures.

immigrant. A person who moves into a country or region with the purpose of making a new home there.

immigration. Moving into a country or region with the purpose of making one's home there. Also, the movement of immigrants into a country or region.

import. To bring goods into a country or region from another country or region, especially for the purpose of selling them. These goods are called imports.

income. The money a person or a business makes during a given period of time. For example, a person's yearly income might include wages for a job plus profits from a business. See **profit**.

indigo (in′ də gō). A plant from which a deep-blue dye is made. Also, the name of the dye.

insurance. A means of protection that provides money in case of illness, accident, or some other event.

Intracoastal (in′ trə kōs′ təl) **Waterway.** A protected water route used by boats along the Atlantic and Gulf coasts of our country. It includes rivers, bays, and canals.

invest. To use money for the purpose of making more money.

iron ore. A rocklike mineral that contains enough iron to make it worth mining.

Iroquois (ir′ ə kwoi). A group of Indian tribes that once lived mostly in what is now lower Canada and central New York State.

irrigate. To supply dry land with water. Ditches, canals, pipelines, and sprinklers are common means used to irrigate farmlands.

irrigated truck farm. A vegetable farm to which water is supplied by such means as ditches, canals, pipelines, and sprinklers. See **truck farm**.

PRONUNCIATION KEY: hat, āge, cãre, fär; let, ēqual, tėrm; it, īce; hot, ōpen, ôrder; oil, out; cup, pùt, rüle, ūse; child; long; thin; ŦHen; zh, measure; ə represents a in about, e in taken, i in pencil, o in lemon, u in circus. For the complete key, see page 35.

irrigation. The act or practice of irrigating. See **irrigate.**

Islam (is′ ləm). One of the world's major religions. Islam was founded by an Arabian prophet named Mohammed, who was born in A.D. 570. According to this faith, there is only one God, called Allah, and Mohammed is his prophet. Followers of Islam are called Moslems, or Muslims.

Jew. A member of a group of people held together for more than three thousand years by their history and their religious faith. The history of the Jews began in southwestern Asia, probably about 1900 B.C. The Jewish faith, called Judaism, is one of the world's major religions. See **Judaism.**

Judaism (jü′ dā iz əm). One of the world's major religions. It is based on the teachings of the Old Testament, and on the Talmud, which is an interpretation of these teachings. Followers of Judaism are called Jews. The main beliefs of Judaism are that there is only one God, that God is good, and that God wants people to follow his laws. Two other major religions, Christianity and Islam, grew out of Judaism.

jury. A group of persons who serve in a court of law. The jury studies the facts and decides whether or not the person charged with a crime is guilty.

kaolin (kā′ ə lin). A fine, white clay used to make chinaware.

kerosene. An oily liquid that is usually made from petroleum. One hundred years ago, many people used kerosene as a fuel in lamps and stoves. Today, kerosene is used mainly as a fuel in jet airplanes.

Korean War, 1950-1953. A war between North Korea and South Korea, two countries in eastern Asia. The United Nations sent soldiers to help South Korea. Many of these soldiers were Americans. See **United Nations.**

kilometer (kə lom′ ə tər). A unit in the metric system for measuring length. It is equal to about .62 mile. See **metric system.**

labor union. A group of workers who have joined together to deal with their employers on such matters as higher wages and better working conditions.

Latino. A person who was born in Latin America or whose ancestors were Latin Americans. Latin America includes all of North and South America south of the United States. For example, people from Mexico, Cuba, and Puerto Rico are Latinos.

latitude. Distance north or south of the equator, measured in units called degrees.

legal. Refers to anything that is allowed by law. Also refers to anything having to do with the law or courts of law.

legislature. A group of persons who have the power to make laws for a state or a country.

Lent. A special period observed by many Christian churches before Easter. People often give up certain foods or say extra prayers during this time.

levees. High, wide walls made of earth or concrete. They are built along rivers or lakes to prevent flooding.

lignite. A low-grade coal that is about half carbon and half water. (See **carbon.**) When lignite is burned, it gives off less heat than coal that contains more carbon.

lint. The long fibers obtained from the cotton plant.

livestock. Farm animals such as cattle, hogs, sheep, horses, and chickens.

lock. A section of a canal or river that is used to raise or lower ships from one water level to another. Gates at each end permit ships to enter or leave the lock. When a ship is in the lock, the gates are closed. The water level in the lock is raised or lowered to the level of the part of the canal or river toward which the ship is going. Then the gates in front of the ship are opened, and the ship passes out of the lock.

majority (mə jôr′ ə tē). Usually, any number over half. The term "majority vote" refers to a way in which groups of people make decisions. In this system, important questions are decided and people are elected to office by the largest number of votes.

Manhattan. One of the five boroughs into which New York City is divided. The Borough of Manhattan consists mainly of an island, also called Manhattan, that lies at the mouth of the Hudson River. It also includes several very small islands nearby.

manufactures (man′ yə fak′ chərz). This word usually means goods that are produced in factories. Sometimes, fact tables show dollar figures for manufactures. These figures represent the value added to goods or raw materials by factories in a certain area. The value added is figured out in an interesting way. From the amount of money received from the sale of goods, the cost of the materials needed to make them is subtracted. The amount of money left is the value added by the factories.

Mediterranean (med ′ə tə rā ′nē ən) **Sea.** An inland sea about 2,330 miles (3,749 kilometers) long. It lies south of Europe, west of Asia, and north of Africa.

menhaden (men hā′ dən). A fish found along the Atlantic and Gulf coasts of the United States. Menhaden are chiefly used to make fertilizer, cattle feed, and oil.

mesa (mā′sə). A small plateau that rises steeply from the land around it. (See **plateau**.) A mesa has a flat top. Mesa is a Spanish word that means table.

mesquite (mes kēt′). A spiny, low-growing tree with long roots. It grows in the southwestern part of the United States and in other dry lands. Parts of the mesquite plant are eaten by cattle.

meter. In the metric system, the basic unit for measuring length. It is equal to 39.37 inches. See **metric system**.

metric system. A system of measurement used in many countries throughout the world, especially in science. In this system, the meter is the basic unit of length.

metropolitan (met ′rə pol ′ə tən) **area.** A thickly populated area that includes at least one large central city. Besides the central city, a metropolitan area usually includes several smaller towns and settled sections.

Midwest. A part of the United States. The Midwest includes the states of Illinois, Indiana, Iowa, Michigan, Minnesota, Missouri, Ohio, and Wisconsin.

mineral. Any of certain substances found in the earth. Diamonds and coal are examples of minerals.

minority (mə nôr′ə tē) **group.** A group of people who differ in race, religion, or national origin from the people who make up the largest group in a country or a region.

missile. A weapon, such as a bomb or rocket, that travels through the air without a pilot. Missiles may be guided by radio signals from the ground. They may also be guided by an electronic device within the missile. See **electronic**.

missionary. A person who is sent out by a religious group to persuade other people to follow the same religion.

mohair. The long, silky hair of the Angora goat. Also, yarn or cloth made of mohair.

mold. A hollow container in which something can be shaped. For example, liquid Jello is poured into a mold. After it has become solid, it may be turned out in the shape of the mold.

monuments. Objects or structures, such as buildings, put up to keep people or events from being forgotten.

mural. A picture, usually very large, that is painted on a wall.

national origin. Generally refers to the country where a person was born, or where one's parents or grandparents were born.

natural resources. Useful things found in nature, such as soil, water, trees, and minerals. See **mineral**.

Nazi (nät′sē). Refers to a political party in Germany called the National Socialists. This undemocratic party controlled the country from 1933 to 1945. Adolf Hitler was leader of the National Socialists and dictator of Germany. Under his leadership, Germany tried to gain control of much of the world. See **World War II**.

Netherlands. A small country in northwestern Europe. The Netherlands is often known as Holland, although this name really refers only to part of the country.

newsprint. An inexpensive, coarse paper made mostly from wood pulp. It is mainly used for newspapers.

Nobel Prize. Any one of several prizes given each year for important work in such fields as science, writing, and world peace.

nonfiction. Writing that deals with real people and events.

nonmetallic minerals. Minerals that do not provide metals. (See **mineral**.) Examples of nonmetallic minerals are sulfur and limestone.

novel. A long story, usually telling about people who did not really live and events that did not really happen.

novelist. A person who writes long stories, called novels. Usually, the people in a novel did not really live, and the events did not really take place.

nuclear (nü′ klē ər). Refers to the production or use of atomic energy. See **atomic energy**.

PRONUNCIATION KEY: hat, āge, cãre, fär; let, ēqual, tėrm; it, īce; hot, ōpen, ôrder; oil, out; cup, pút, rüle, ūse; child; long; thin; ℋHen; zh, measure; ə represents a in about, e in taken, i in pencil, o in lemon, u in circus. For the complete key, see page 35.

Old State House. A building in Boston where the government leaders of the Massachusetts Bay Colony met. Later, the Old State House served as the first capitol for the state of Massachusetts. (See **capitol.**) This building is now used as a museum.

ore. Rock or other material that contains enough metal to make it worth mining.

Oregon Trail. The main route taken by the pioneers who traveled westward in the mid-1800's to settle in what is now the state of Oregon. This trail went from Independence, Missouri, to the Willamette Valley in Oregon.

oxygen (ok′sə jən). A colorless, odorless, tasteless gas. It makes up about one fifth of the air we breathe. Combined with other substances, oxygen is found in all plants and animals. It is also found in water and in many kinds of rock.

parliament (pär′lə mənt). In some countries, a group of people who make the laws. In many ways a parliament is like the Congress of the United States. When "parliament" is spelled with a capital "P," it usually means the parliament of Great Britain.

pasteurize (pas′chə rīz). To heat a liquid such as milk to a high temperature and then cool it rapidly. This process kills harmful germs.

patchwork. Pieces of cloth of different colors and shapes, which have been sewed together. Also, anything that looks like patchwork.

patchwork quilt. A warm covering for a bed. The top is made from patches of cloth, of different colors and shapes. These have been sewed together.

peninsula (pən in′sə lə). An area of land that is almost surrounded by water. It is connected to a larger area of land.

petrochemicals (pet′rō kem′ə kəlz). Chemicals obtained from petroleum or natural gas. Petrochemicals are used in making hundreds of products, such as paint, fertilizer, and synthetic rubber. See **chemicals.**

petroleum. Also called oil. A thick oily liquid that comes from the earth. Petroleum may be dark brown or greenish black in color. Gasoline and many other useful things are made from petroleum.

phosphate rock. A kind of rock that contains chemicals needed by plants. It is ground up and used in making fertilizer. See **chemicals.**

Piedmont (pēd′mont) **Plateau.** A section of the Appalachian Highlands that extends from New York into Alabama. Most of the land in the Piedmont is gently rolling or hilly.

Pilgrims. A group of English colonists who came to America in 1620. The Pilgrims had left England because they had not been allowed to worship God as they pleased. They started a colony called Plymouth in what is now Massachusetts.

planet. The earth or any one of the other heavenly bodies that move around the sun. The nine main planets are Mercury, Venus, Earth, Mars, Jupiter, Saturn, Uranus, Neptune, and Pluto.

plateau (pla tō′). A large, generally level area of high land.

plywood. A material made by gluing together thin sheets of wood.

polio. A short form of the word poliomyelitis. This is a serious disease that causes fever and weakness of the muscles. Some people die from polio and some become lame.

pollute. To make something dirty or impure.

pollution. Making something dirty. For example, air or water may become polluted.

population. The total number of people living in any particular place. See **density of population.**

potash. See **potassium salts.**

potassium salts. A group of certain chemicals, many of which are found in nature as minerals. Most of them are commonly referred to as potash. Potassium salts are used in making fertilizer, medicine, photographic supplies, and many other products. See **chemicals.**

prairie. A large area of level or rolling land covered with grass. A prairie usually has no trees.

prejudice. An opinion that is formed without knowing all the facts. The dislike for a person just because he or she belongs to a different group is a common kind of prejudice.

process. A method or way of doing something, or the steps taken to get a thing done. Also, to treat foods or other substances in some special way to make them more useful. For example, corn is said to be processed when it is canned or made into cornflakes.

produce (prə düs′). To make or to raise. For example, factories produce manufactured goods. Farms produce crops and livestock.

profit. The money earned by a business. It is the amount of money taken in, minus the money spent in running the business.

Protestant. Refers to one of the three main branches of Christianity. Also, a member of any one of the many different Protestant groups, such as the Methodists, Baptists, or Presbyterians. See **Christianity.**

prune. To cut off dead or useless parts of a tree, bush, or other plant. Usually, a plant is pruned to give it a better shape or to aid its growth.

Puerto Rico (pwer′ tō rē′ kō). An island about 1,000 miles (1,609 kilometers) southeast of Florida. The United States has had control of Puerto Rico since 1898. Today, this island governs itself with the help of the United States.

Puget-Willamette (pū′ jit wə lam′ ət) **Lowland.** A long valley in the western part of Oregon and Washington. It is about 350 miles (563 kilometers) long and 50 miles (80 kilometers) wide.

Pulitzer (pū′ lit sər) **Prize.** Any one of several prizes given each year in the United States for good work in such fields as newspaper writing, literature, music, and cartooning. The prizes are named for Joseph Pulitzer (1847-1911), a newspaper editor and publisher. Pulitzer left a large amount of money for these prizes.

pulp. A soft, damp material usually made from wood or rags. It is used in making paper.

purify. To make pure or clean.

pyrites (pī rī′tēz). Various minerals that include sulfur combined with metals such as iron, copper, and nickel. Both copper and nickel may be produced by smelting ores that contain pyrites, but it is not practical to obtain iron in this way. (See **smelting.**) A gas formed during the smelting process is used to make sulfuric acid, which is an important industrial chemical. The gas is also used in refrigeration.

quarry (kwôr′ē). An open pit in the earth from which stone is taken for use in building.

rain shadow. An area is said to lie in a rain shadow if mountains shelter it from moist winds. When moist winds rise to go over mountains, they are cooled and lose moisture in the form of rain or snow. By the time they have crossed the mountains, they are drier. As the winds move down to the lower land on the other side of the mountains, they become warmer. This causes them to take up moisture instead of losing it. Thus the land in the rain shadow is drier than the land on the other side of the mountains.

raw materials. Substances that can be manufactured into useful products. For example, iron ore is the main raw material needed for making iron and steel. Many manufacturing plants use steel as a raw material for making machinery and other metal products.

raw sugar. A form of sugar obtained from the juice squeezed from sugarcane. It is yellowish brown in color because the sugar crystals are covered with a thin film of molasses. Raw sugar is refined to produce the white sugar sold in stores.

recession (ri sesh′ən). A time when business activity slows down and many people are put out of work.

refinery. A place where useful products are made from something found in nature. For example, petroleum is made into gasoline, kerosene, and other useful products in a refinery.

research. A careful search for facts or truth about a subject.

reservation. An area of land owned by the government and set aside for some special use. Especially, an area set aside for use by Indians.

reservoir. A lake that stores large amounts of water until it is needed. The water may be used in homes, in manufacturing, or for farming. A reservoir may be a natural lake. Or it may be a lake formed by a dam on a river.

responsibility. Duty. Something that a person ought to do because it is the right thing to do, such as obeying the law.

retail (rē′tāl). Refers to stores that sell goods directly to the people who will use the products. Grocery stores and department stores are examples of retail stores.

Revolutionary War, 1775-1783. A war between Great Britain and thirteen British colonies in America. The colonies won the war and became states in a new country. This was the United States.

rickets. A disease of children in which the bones are not straight. It is caused by a lack of sunlight or a lack of vitamin D in the diet.

Roman Catholic. Refers to a church that is one of the three main branches of Christianity. Also refers to members of this church. See **Christianity.**

rosin. A hard, brittle substance that is made, along with turpentine, from the sap of living pine trees or from dead pinewood. Rosin is used in products such as paint, varnish, and soap.

PRONUNCIATION KEY: hat, āge, cãre, fär; let, ēqual, tėrm; it, īce; hot, ōpen, ôrder; oil, out; cup, pṳt, rüle, ūse; child; long; thin; ₮Hen; zh, measure; ə represents a in about, e in taken, i in pencil, o in lemon, u in circus. For the complete key, see page 35.

sagebrush. A low, bushy plant with grayish green leaves. Sagebrush grows in the western part of the United States. It is sometimes used for fuel. It is also used as winter feed for sheep and cattle.

Scandinavia. A large area in northern Europe that includes the countries of Norway, Sweden, and Denmark.

scientist. An expert in some branch of science. A scientist makes an orderly study of natural laws and facts about nature.

scrap. Metal that is thrown away. Steel scrap is often used to replace part of the iron ore needed to make steel. Each ton of steel scrap used saves two tons of iron ore.

sculptor. An artist who makes figures or statues, usually of marble, wood, metal, or some other hard material.

sculptures. Works of art that are three-dimensional. (See **three-dimensional.**) For example, a statue made of marble, wood, or some other hard material.

sea level. The level of the surface of the sea. All surfaces on land are measured according to their distance above or below sea level.

Second Continental Congress. See **Continental Congress.**

segregation (seg′ rə gā′ shən.) In the United States, the separation of black people from white people, either by law or by custom. Under segregation, blacks generally attend separate schools, eat in separate restaurants, and sit in separate sections of buses. In many cases, they also live in separate sections of cities.

shale. A kind of rock that was probably formed from clay.

silage (sī′lij). Chopped green cornstalks or other plants that have been stored in a silo. A silo is an airtight building, usually shaped like a cylinder. Silage is used to feed cattle or other livestock.

slag. The waste material that is produced when ore is smelted to obtain metal. See **smelt.**

slate. A dark-colored rock, usually bluish gray, that splits easily into thin layers. Slate is used to make shingles, blackboards, and other items.

slum. A crowded, run-down part of a city or town. Most of the people who live in slums are very poor.

smallpox. A serious disease from which many people once died.

smelt. To separate the metal from the other materials in ore by melting the ore in a special furnace.

smelter. A place where smelting is done. Also, a furnace in which ore is smelted. See **smelt.**

smelting. The process by which metal is obtained from ore.

social scientist. A person who is skilled in any of the social sciences. These are sciences that deal with people. They include history, geography, and economics.

solar system. Our sun and the planets and smaller heavenly bodies that revolve around it.

solstice (sol′ stis). Either of two times of the year when the direct rays of the sun are farthest from the equator. This occurs about June 21 and about December 22.

South. A region of the United States, which includes Alabama, Arkansas, Florida, Georgia, Kentucky, Louisiana, Mississippi, North Carolina, South Carolina, Tennessee, and Virginia. "South" also refers to the states that opposed the Union in the Civil War. See **Civil War.**

Soviet Union. Short name for the Union of Soviet Socialist Republics, or U.S.S.R. Also called Russia. This country is located in Eurasia. See **Eurasia.**

State Supreme Court. In most states, the highest court of law.

standard of living. The way of living in a community or a country that people think of as necessary for a happy, satisfying life. In a country with a high standard of living, many different goods and services are thought of as necessary for most of the people. In a country with a low standard of living, many of these same things are enjoyed by only a few very wealthy people.

steam engine. An engine that is run by steam. To produce the steam, water is heated by burning a fuel such as coal or oil. Steam engines are often used to run trains and ships. They are also used in power plants to produce electricity.

stock. The total capital of a corporation. (See **capital.**) The stock of a company is usually divided into small portions called shares. A person may buy one or more of these shares. He or she then owns part of the business.

strike. The stopping of work by a group of workers. The purpose of a strike is usually to force a business to pay higher wages or provide better working conditions.

strip-mining. A way of digging up minerals that are deposited in flat strips near the surface of the earth. To reach these deposits, the layers of soil and rock that lie on top of the minerals must be removed.

suburb. An outer part of a city, or a smaller community near a city.

sulfuric (sul fyur′ ik) **acid.** A heavy, colorless, oily liquid. It is used in refining petroleum and in making fertilizers, chemicals, steel, and plastics.

Supreme Court. The most important court of law in the United States. It meets in the nation's capital, Washington, D.C. The Supreme Court has nine judges, who are called justices. Their job is to make sure that our country is being governed according to the rules in the Constitution. See **constitution.**

suspension bridge. A bridge hung from thick wire ropes called cables. The cables are fastened to high towers on each side of the water or gap to be bridged.

synthetic (sin thet′ ik). Refers to certain substances such as plastics and nylon, developed to replace similar natural materials.

terminus. The end of a transportation route.

textile. Cloth, or the thread used to make cloth.

three-dimensional (də men′ shə nəl). Refers to anything that has height, length, and width.

thresh. To separate the grain from the husks and stems of the plant.

tinplate. Thin sheets of steel that have been coated with tin.

tobacco. A plant that is used mainly for making products such as cigars and cigarettes. In recent years, scientists have discovered that the use of tobacco products is harmful. They have reported that smoking helps to cause cancer, heart trouble, and other serious diseases.

treaty. An agreement, usually in writing, between two or more nations.

Tropic of Cancer. An imaginary line around the earth, about 1,600 miles (2,574 kilometers) north of the equator.

Tropic of Capricorn. An imaginary line around the earth, about 1,600 miles (2,574 kilometers) south of the equator.

tropics. The part of the earth that lies between the Tropic of Cancer and the Tropic of Capricorn. The weather in the tropics is generally hot all year round. See **Tropic of Cancer** and **Tropic of Capricorn.**

truck farm. A farm on which vegetables are raised to be sold. One meaning of the word "truck" is to trade things. Formerly vegetables often were traded for other products.

try. To bring a person before a judge or jury in a court of law. The judge or jury decides whether or not the person is guilty of breaking a law.

turbine. An engine commonly run by the force of water or steam striking against blades. Turbines are used to run electric generators. See **generator.**

turpentine. An oily liquid prepared from the sap of living pine trees or from dead pinewood. It is often used for thinning paints and varnishes.

Union. The United States of America. During the Civil War, the northern states were called the Union. See **Civil War.**

United Nations. An organization of countries from all over the world. It was started in 1945 to work for world peace. About 150 countries now belong to the United Nations.

United States Congress. The lawmaking, or legislative, branch of the United States government. It is made up of the Senate and the House of Representatives.

United States Supreme Court. See **Supreme Court.**

Upper Peninsula. The northern part of the state of Michigan. It lies mainly between Lake Superior and Lake Michigan.

uranium (yu rā′ nē əm). A very heavy, silver-white metal. It is important as the source of certain materials used to produce atomic energy. See **atomic energy.**

urban. Having to do with cities or large towns.

victim. A person who is harmed by something or someone.

Vikings. People who lived along the seacoast in Scandinavia about one thousand years ago. (See **Scandinavia.**) The Vikings were fine sailors and fierce warriors. They often invaded other countries in northern Europe. Some of them settled on the islands of Iceland and Greenland.

volcano. An opening in the earth's crust through which melted rock, called lava, and other materials are forced to the surface. These materials often build up to form a hill or mountain, also called a volcano.

weather. The condition of the air or atmosphere at a given time and place. A description of weather includes such things as wind, sunshine, temperature, and moisture. The average weather conditions of a particular place

---

PRONUNCIATION KEY: hat, āge, cãre, fär; let, ēqual, tėrm; it, īce; hot, ōpen, ôrder; oil, out; cup, pùt, rüle, ūse; child; long; thin; ₮Hen; zh, measure; ə represents a in about, e in taken, i in pencil, o in lemon, u in circus. For the complete key, see page 35.

47

over a long period of time make up its climate.

West Indies. A large group of islands in the Atlantic Ocean. They lie between the United States and South America. The West Indies got their name because Columbus thought he had reached lands in eastern Asia called the Indies.

wholesale. Having to do with selling large amounts of goods to businesses for resale. For example, a wholesale hardware company might buy a large amount of hammers from the manufacturer. The wholesale company would then sell the hammers to hardware stores throughout our country. These hardware stores, which sell the hammers to the people who are going to use them, are called retail stores. See **retail.**

wood pulp. See **pulp.**

World War I, 1914-1918. A war that was fought in many parts of the world. On one side were the Central Powers. These were Germany, Austria-Hungary, Turkey, and Bulgaria. They were defeated by the Allies.

These included Great Britain, France, Russia, Japan, the United States, and other countries.

World War II, 1939-1945. A war that was fought in many parts of the world. On one side were the Allies, which included the United States, Great Britain, the Soviet Union, France, and many other countries. On the other side were the Axis Powers, which included Germany, Italy, and Japan. The Allies defeated the Axis Powers.

X-ray. A ray that can go through substances that light cannot go through. X-rays can be used to photograph such things as broken bones inside the body.

yucca (yuk′ə). Any of several plants of the lily family that grow in warm, dry areas. Some yucca plants are short but others are as tall as trees. The leaves of the yucca are usually stiff, narrow, and pointed. Yucca flowers are white.

Acknowledgments

Grateful acknowledgment is made to the following for permission to use the illustrations found in the Thinking Aids section of this book:

A. Devaney, Inc.: Page 26
Alpha Photo Associates, Inc.: Pages 21 and 27
Camera Hawaii: Page 30
De Wys, Inc.: Page 23
Field Enterprises: Pages 22-23, painting by Frederick Coffey Yohn
Grant Heilman: Page 34
H. Armstrong Roberts: Pages 31 (lower) and 33
Kaiser Steel Corporation: Page 19 (lower left)
Louisville Chamber of Commerce: Page 17
Magnum Photos, Inc.: Page 31 (upper)

NASA: Page 20
Shostal Associates, Inc.: Page 19 (upper left and lower right)
Sirlin Studios: Pages 24-25
Texasgulf: Pages 28-29
The Fideler Company: Page 29 by Adrian Beerhorst
United States Department of Agriculture, Soil Conservation Service: Pages 26-27
United States Department of Interior, Bureau of Reclamation: Page 32

Grateful acknowledgment is made to Scott, Foresman and Company for the pronunciation system used in this book, which is taken from the Thorndike-Barnhart Dictionary Series. Grateful acknowledgment is made to the following for permission to use cartographic data in this book: Creative Arts: Bottom map on page 15; Base maps courtesy of the Nystrom Raised Relief Map Company, Chicago 60618: Top map on page 15; United States Department of Commerce, Bureau of the Census: Bottom map on page 14.